bad machinery

THE CASE OF THE GOOD BOY

AN ONI PRESS PUBLICATION

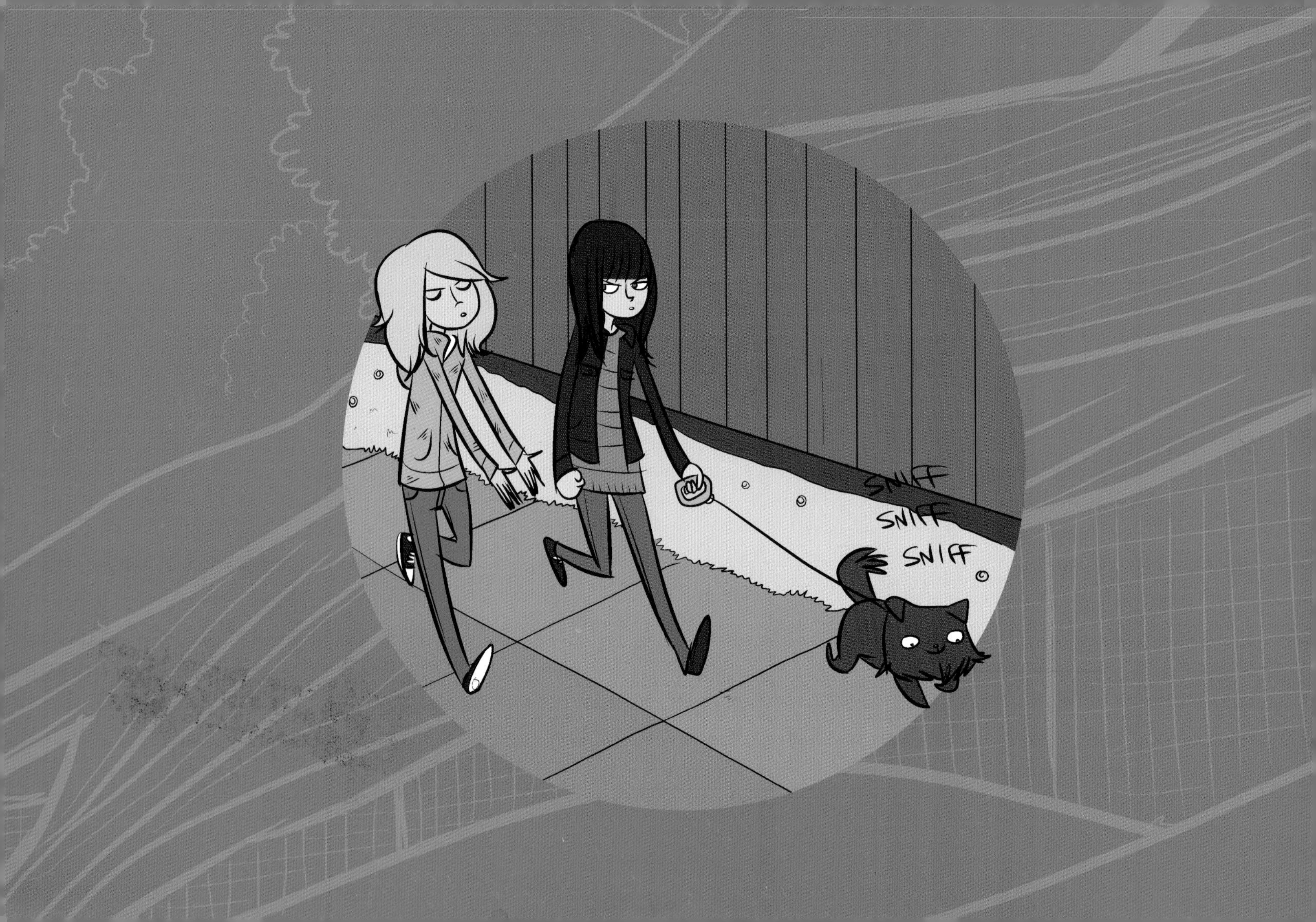
SNIFF
SNIFF
SNIFF

bad machinery

THE CASE OF THE GOOD BOY

by
John Allison

Original edition edited by
James Lucas Jones & Jill Beaton

Pocket edition edited by
Ari Yarwood

Designed by
Hilary Thompson

PUBLISHED BY ONI PRESS INC.
publisher, **Joe Nozemack**
editor in chief, **James Lucas Jones**
sales manager, **David Dissanayake**
publicity coordinator, **Rachel Reed**
director of design & production, **Troy Look**
graphic designer, **Hilary Thompson**
digital prepress technician, **Angie Dobson**
managing editor, **Ari Yarwood**
senior editor, **Charlie Chu**
editor, **Robin Herrera**
administrative assistant, **Alissa Sallah**
director of logistics, **Brad Rooks**
logistics associate, **Jung Lee**

onipress.com
facebook.com/onipress
twitter.com/onipress
onipress.tumblr.com
instagram.com/onipress
badmachinery.com

FIRST EDITION: FEBRUARY 2014
POCKET EDITION: AUGUST 2017

ISBN 978-1-62010-421-7
EISBN 978-1-62010-115-5

PRINTED IN CHINA.

LIBRARY OF CONGRESS CONTROL NUMBER: 2017901451

1 2 3 4 5 6 7 8 9 10

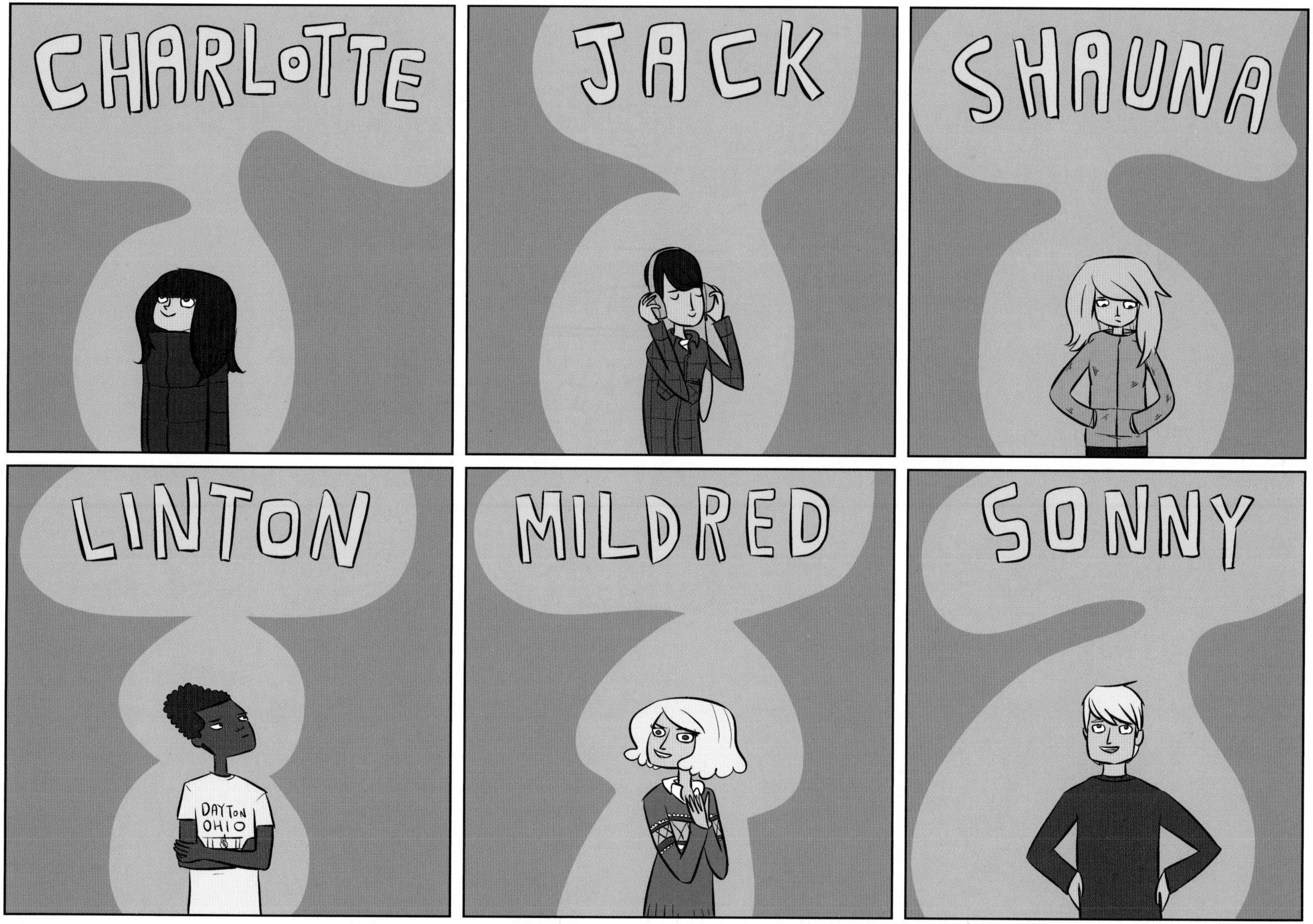
CHARLOTTE
JACK
SHAUNA
LINTON
DAYTON
OHIO
MILDRED
SONNY

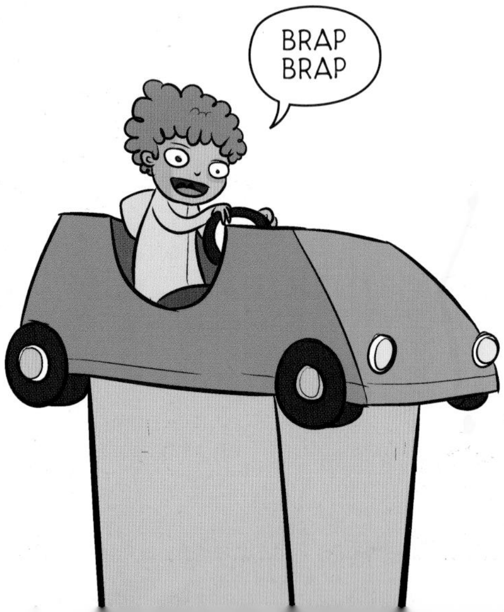
BRAP
BRAP

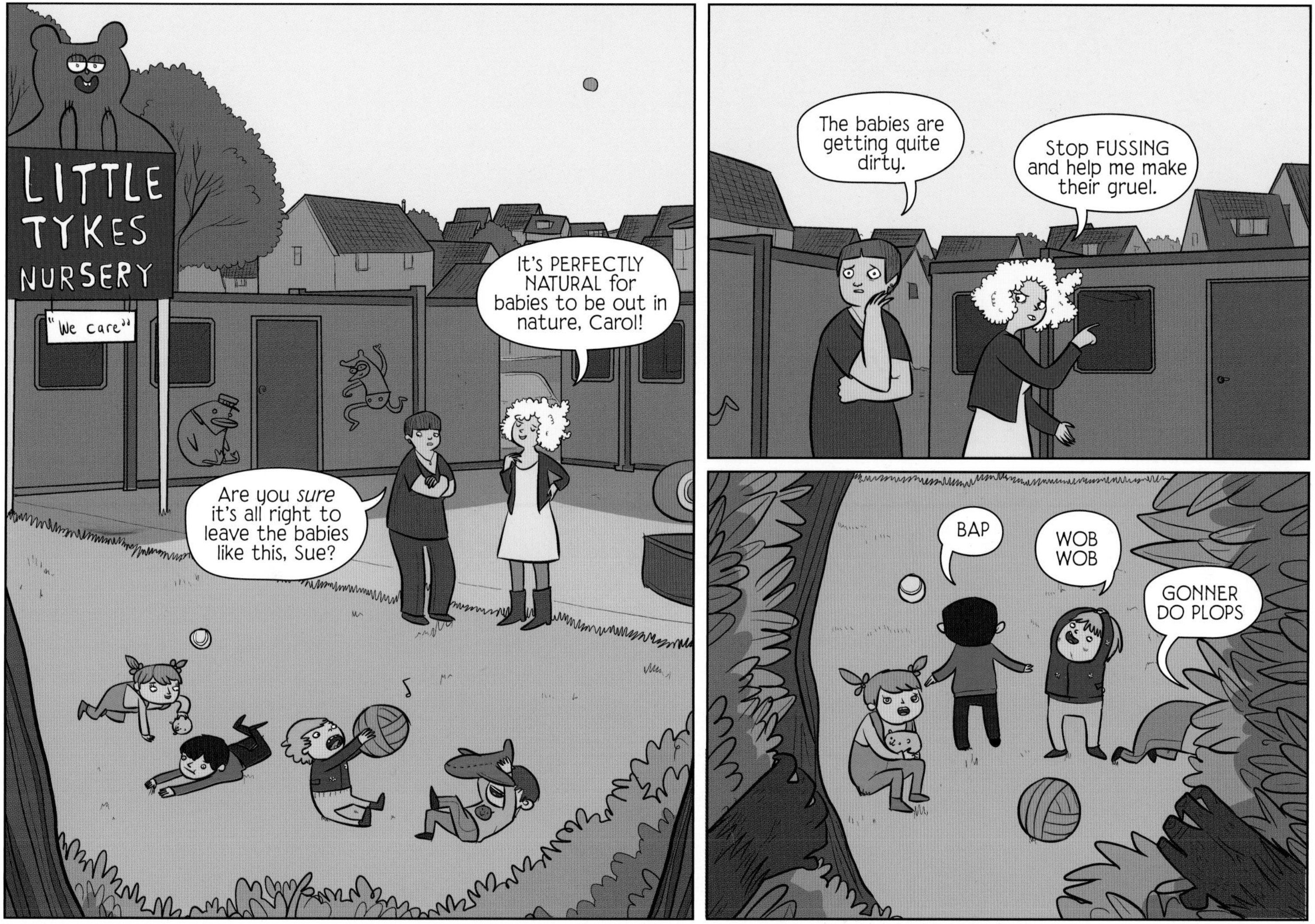
LITTLE TYKES NURSERY
"We care"
Are you *sure* it's all right to leave the babies like this, Sue?
It's PERFECTLY NATURAL for babies to be out in nature, Carol!
The babies are getting quite dirty.
Stop FUSSING and help me make their gruel.
BAP
WOB WOB
GONNER DO PLOPS

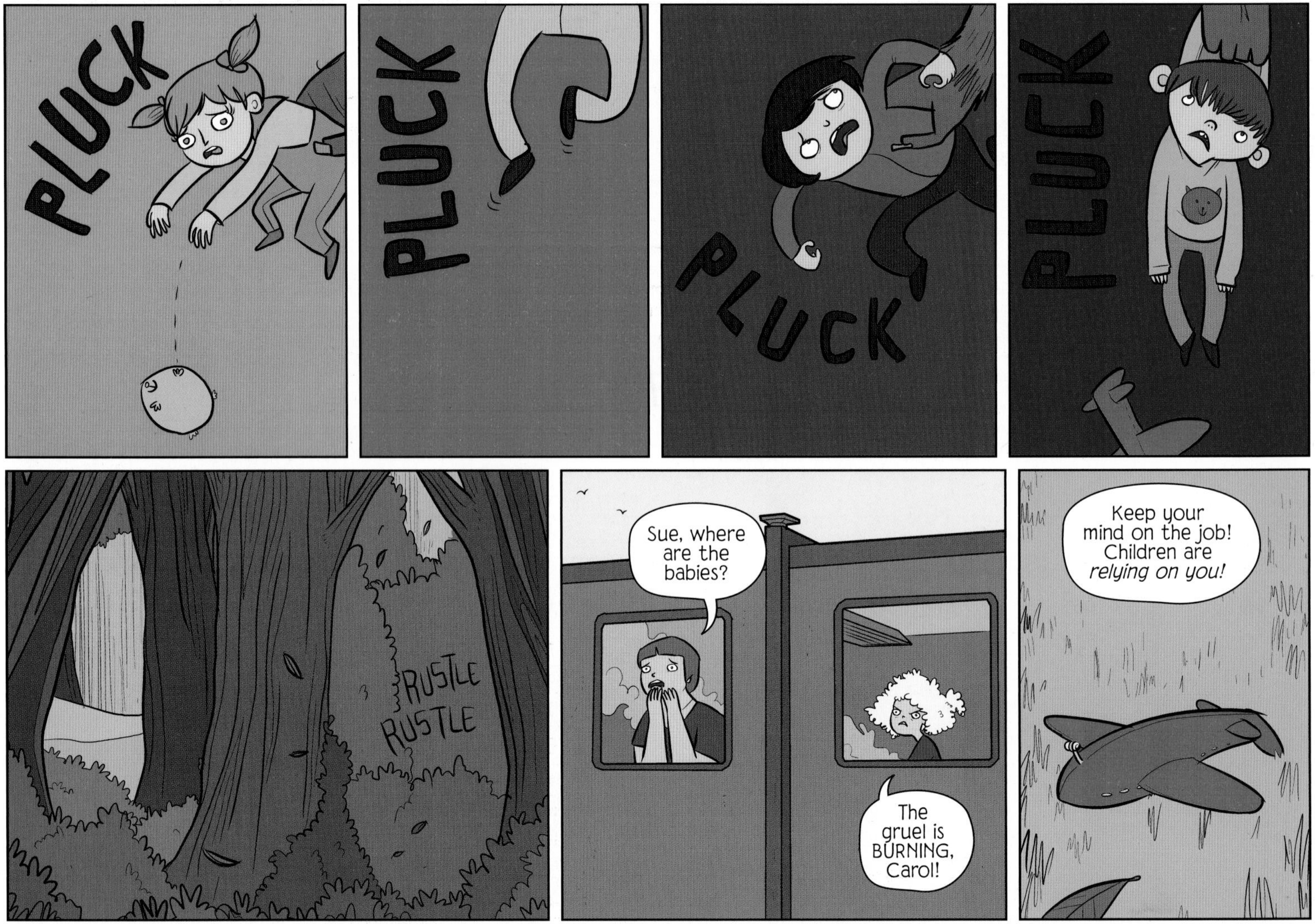
PLUCK
PLUCK
PLUCK
PLUCK
RUSTLE
RUSTLE
Sue, where are the babies?
The gruel is BURNING, Carol!
Keep your mind on the job! Children are *relying on you!*

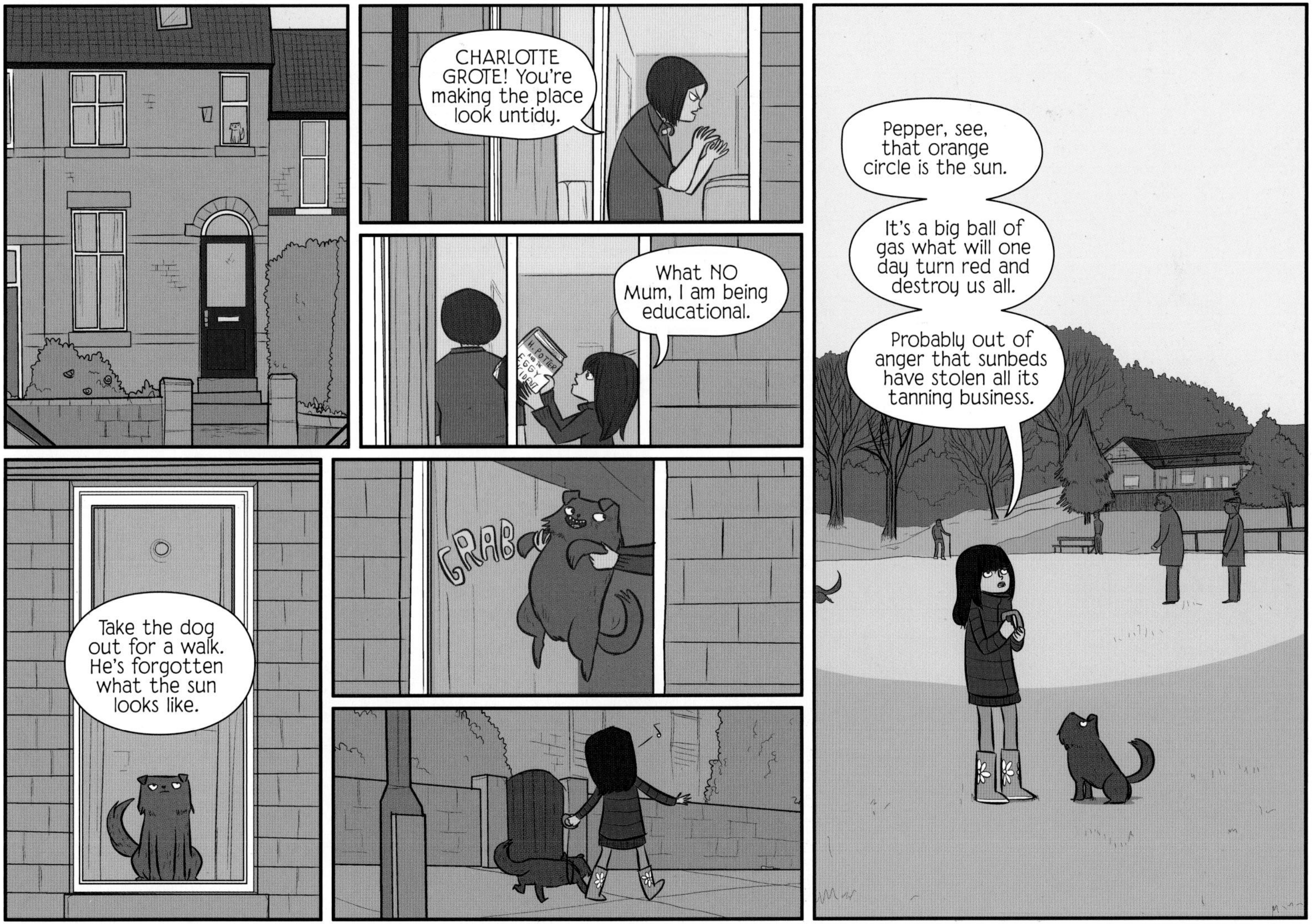

CHARLOTTE GROTE! You're making the place look untidy.
What NO Mum, I am being educational.
Take the dog out for a walk. He's forgotten what the sun looks like.
GRAB
Pepper, see, that orange circle is the sun.
It's a big ball of gas what will one day turn red and destroy us all.
Probably out of anger that sunbeds have stolen all its tanning business.

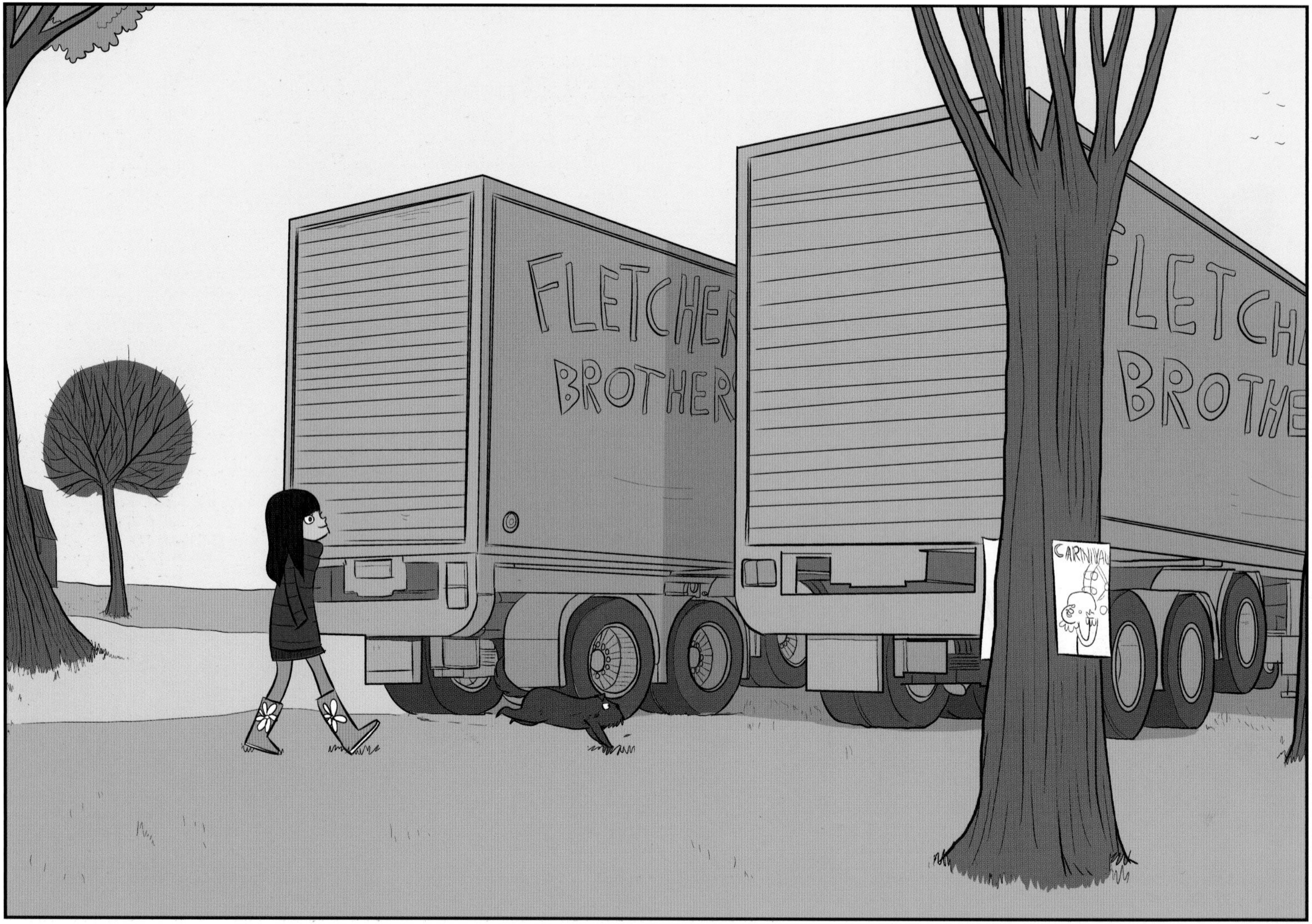
FLETCHER
BROTHER
FLETCH
BROTHE
CARNIVAL

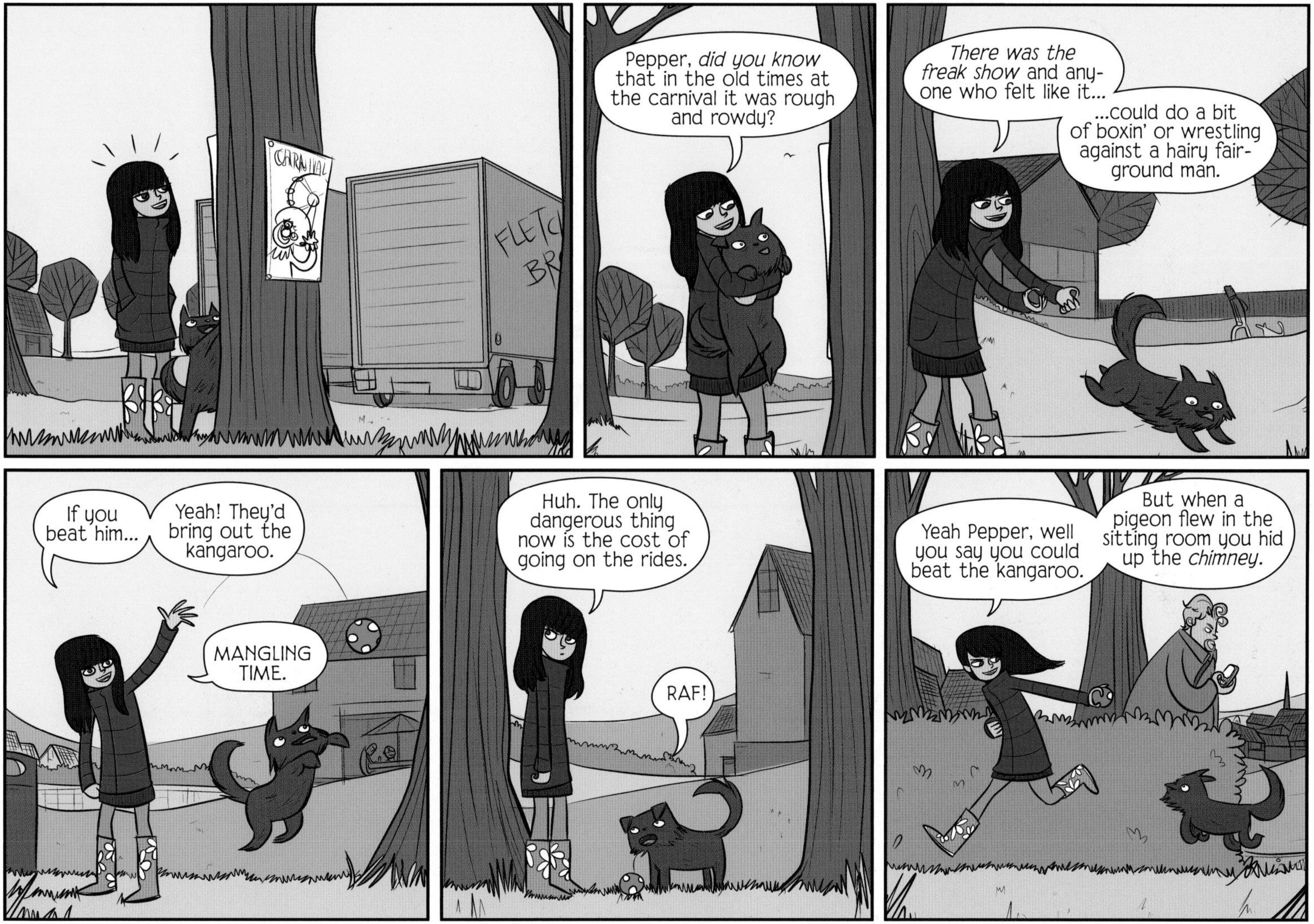
CARNIVAL
Pepper, *did you know* that in the old times at the carnival it was rough and rowdy?
There was the freak show and any-one who felt like it...
...could do a bit of boxin' or wrestling against a hairy fair-ground man.
If you beat him...
Yeah! They'd bring out the kangaroo.
MANGLING TIME.
Huh. The only dangerous thing now is the cost of going on the rides.
RAF!
Yeah Pepper, well you say you could beat the kangaroo.
But when a pigeon flew in the sitting room you hid up the *chimney*.

FIGHT!

ARCH-DUKE
GRR-DINAND

LADY
PROBLEMS

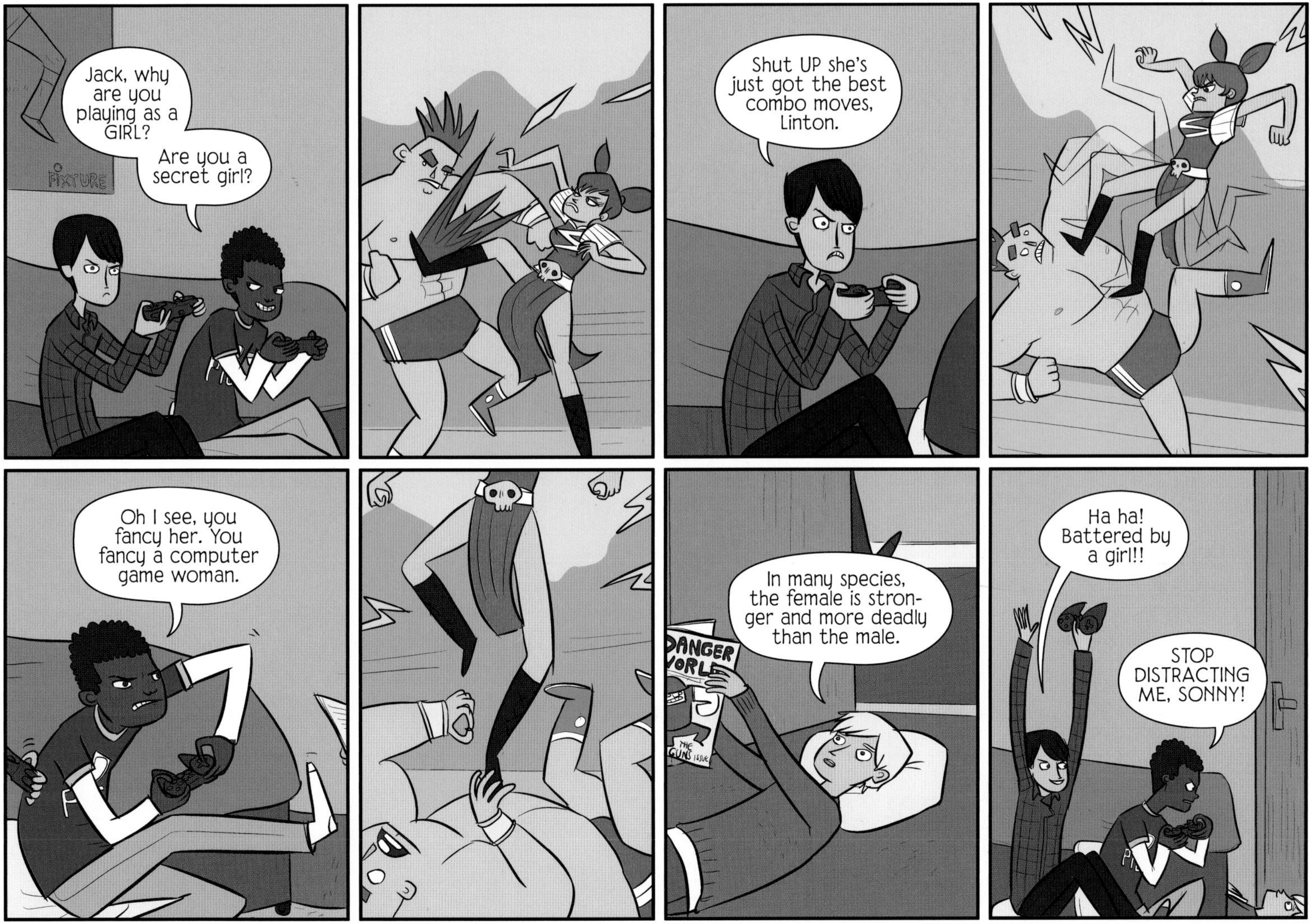
Jack, why are you playing as a GIRL?
Are you a secret girl?
FIXTURE
Shut UP she's just got the best combo moves, Linton.
Oh I see, you fancy her. You fancy a computer game woman.
In many species, the female is stronger and more deadly than the male.
DANGER WORLD
THE GUNS ISSUE
Ha ha! Battered by a girl!!
STOP DISTRACTING ME, SONNY!

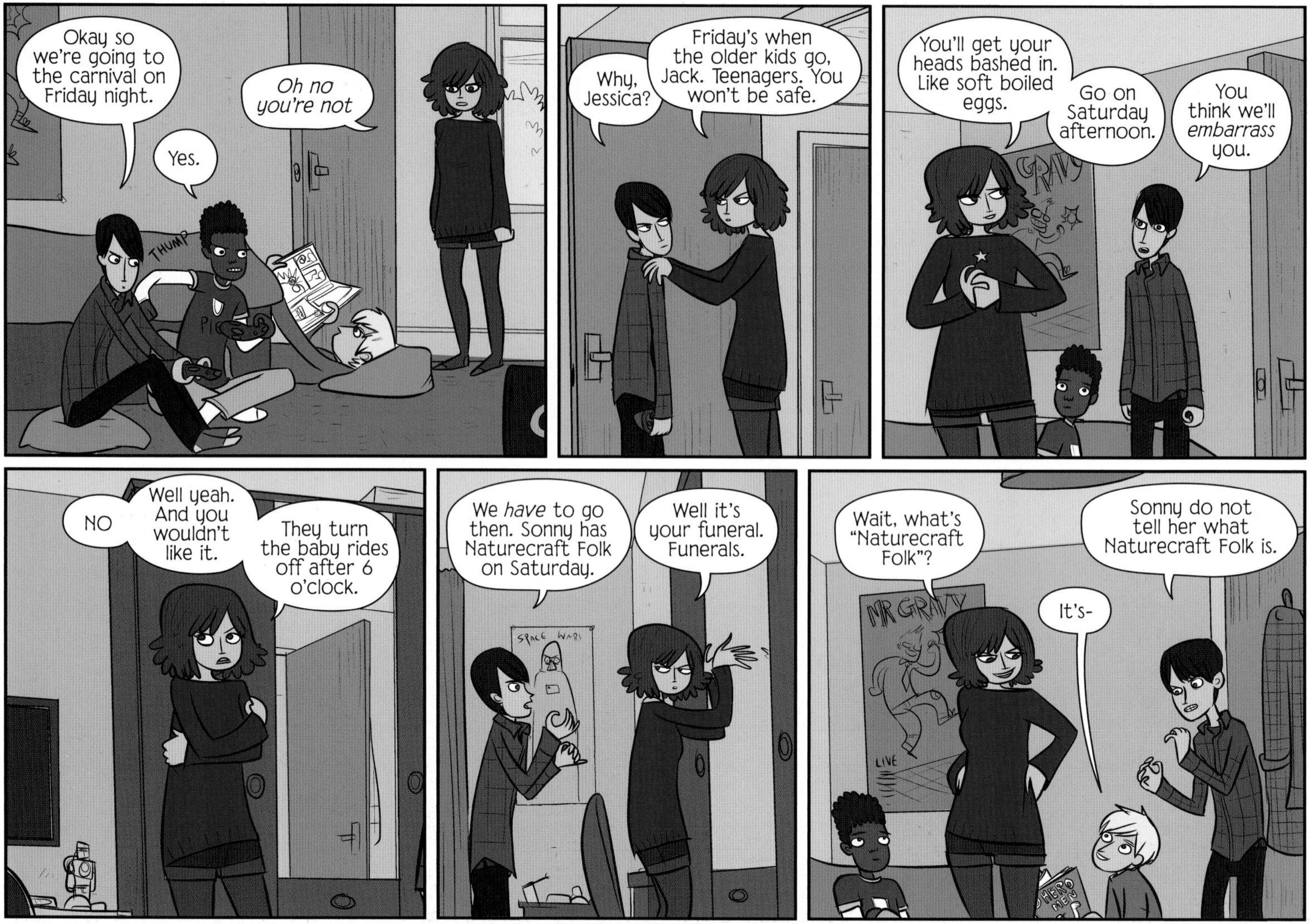
Okay so we're going to the carnival on Friday night.
Yes.
Oh no you're not
THUMP
Why, Jessica?
Friday's when the older kids go, Jack. Teenagers. You won't be safe.
You'll get your heads bashed in. Like soft boiled eggs.
Go on Saturday afternoon.
You think we'll *embarrass* you.
NO
Well yeah. And you wouldn't like it.
They turn the baby rides off after 6 o'clock.
We *have* to go then. Sonny has Naturecraft Folk on Saturday.
Well it's your funeral. Funerals.
SPACE WARS
Wait, what's "Naturecraft Folk"?
Sonny do not tell her what Naturecraft Folk is.
It's-
MR GRAVY
LIVE
HERO MEN

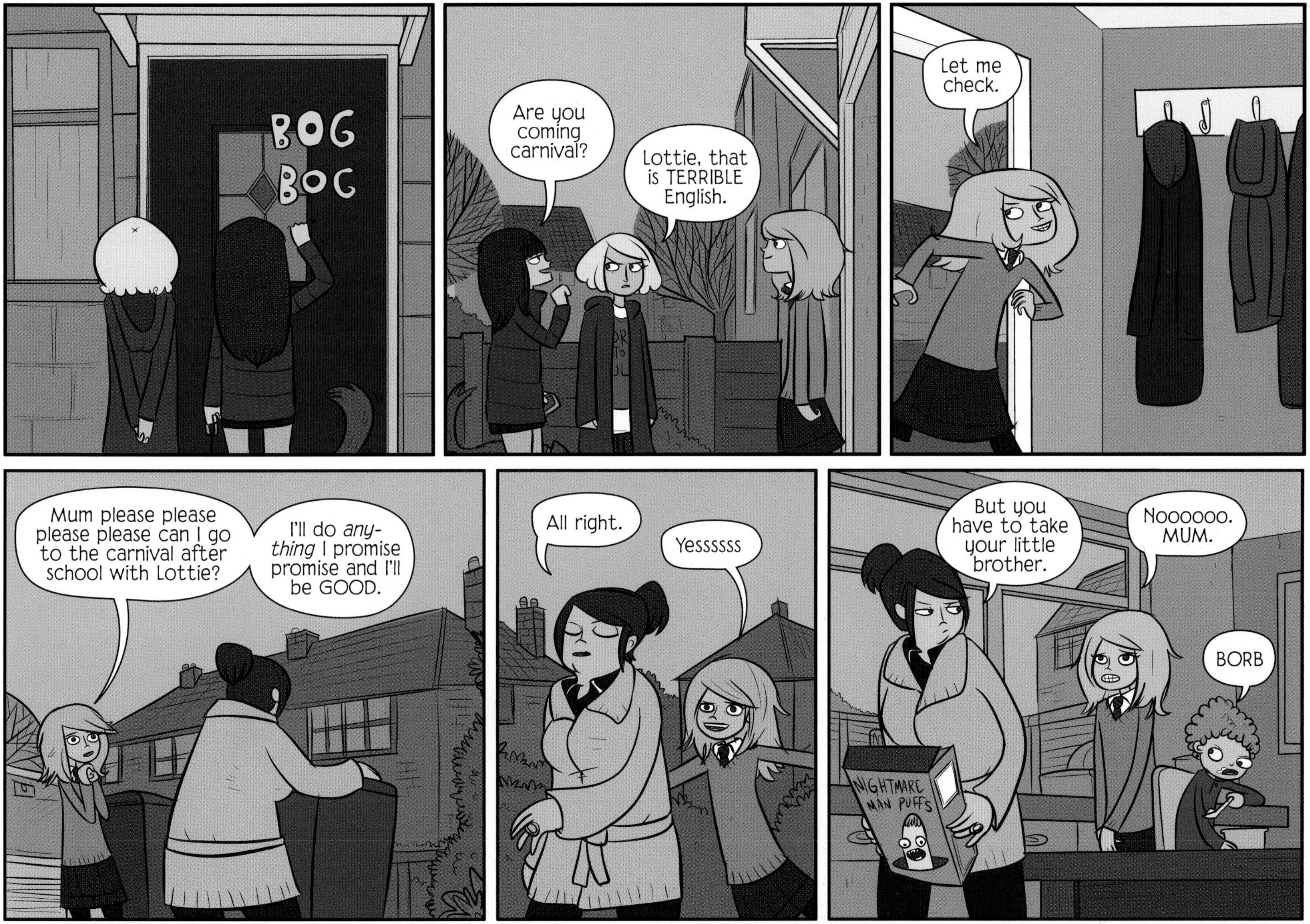
BOG
BOG
Are you coming carnival?
Lottie, that is TERRIBLE English.
Let me check.
Mum please please please please can I go to the carnival after school with Lottie?
I'll do *anything* I promise promise and I'll be GOOD.
All right.
Yessssss
But you have to take your little brother.
Noooooo. MUM.
BORB
NIGHTMARE MAN PUFFS

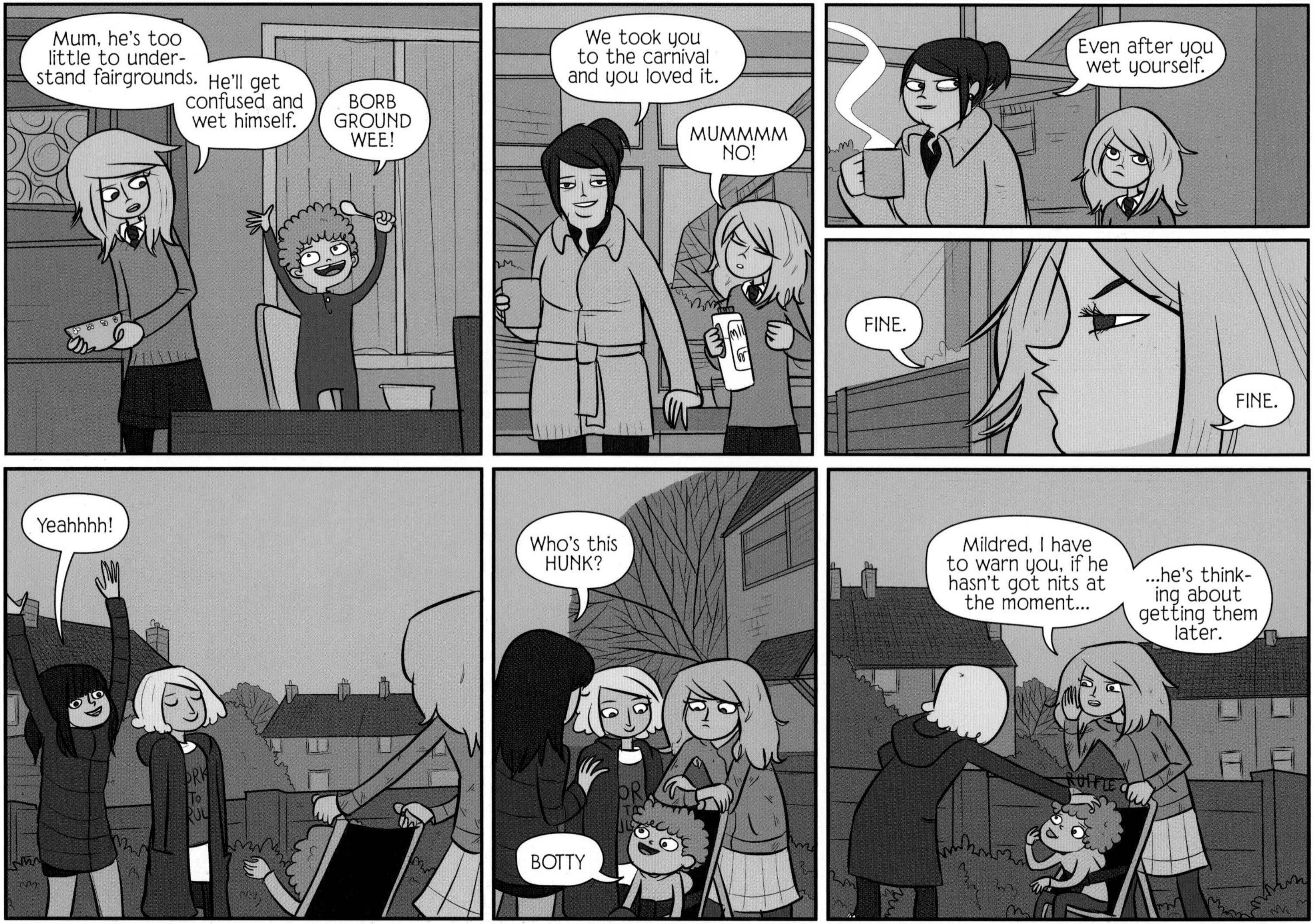
Mum, he's too little to under-stand fairgrounds.
He'll get confused and wet himself.
BORB GROUND WEE!
We took you to the carnival and you loved it.
MUMMMM NO!
Even after you wet yourself.
FINE.
FINE.
Yeahhhh!
Who's this HUNK?
BOTTY
Mildred, I have to warn you, if he hasn't got nits at the moment...
...he's think-ing about getting them later.
RUFFLE

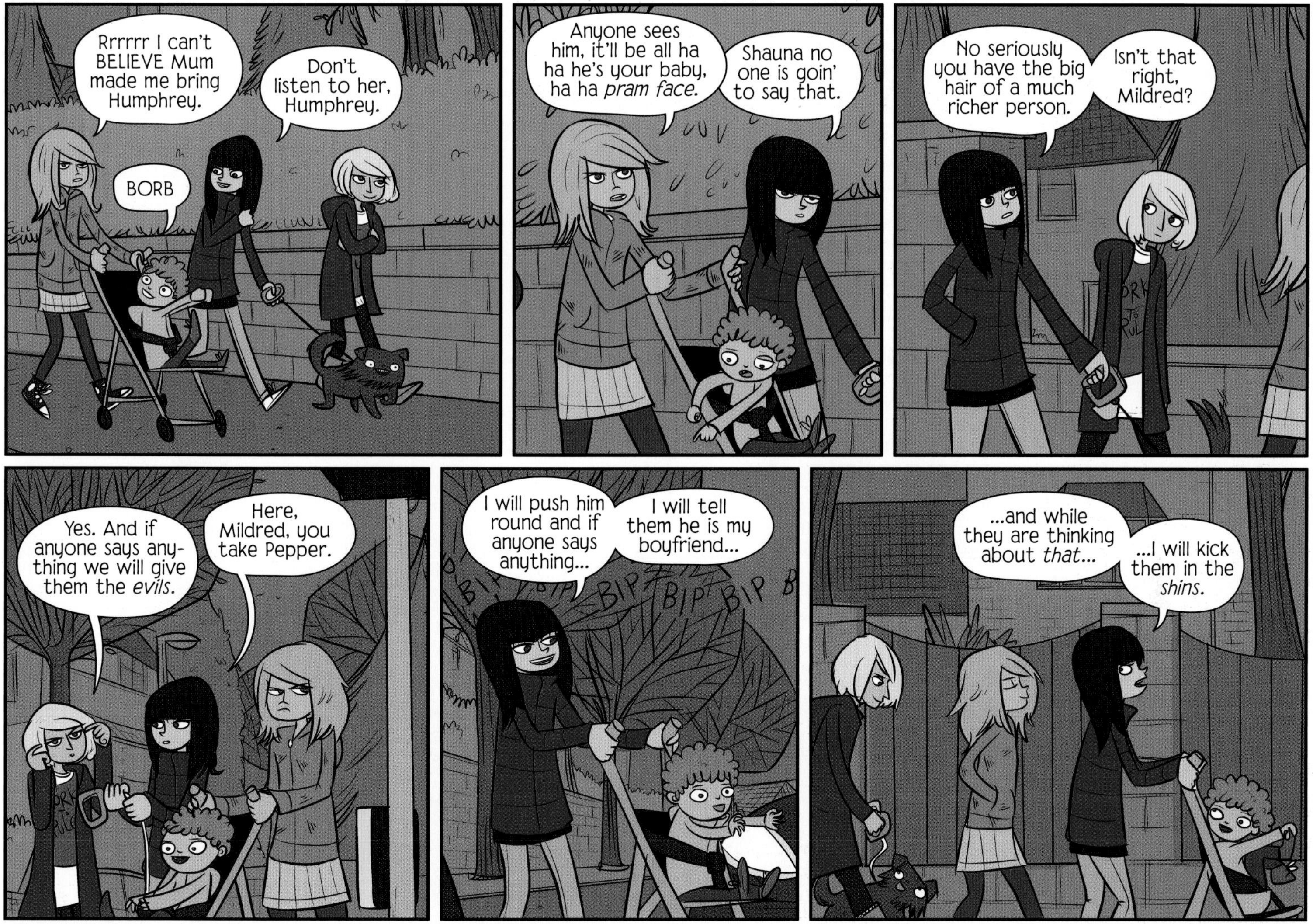
Rrrrrr I can't BELIEVE Mum made me bring Humphrey.
Don't listen to her, Humphrey.
BORB
Anyone sees him, it'll be all ha ha he's your baby, ha ha *pram face.*
Shauna no one is goin' to say that.
No seriously you have the big hair of a much richer person.
Isn't that right, Mildred?
Yes. And if anyone says anything we will give them the *evils.*
Here, Mildred, you take Pepper.
I will push him round and if anyone says anything...
I will tell them he is my boyfriend...
BIP BIP BIP BIP
...and while they are thinking about *that*...
...I will kick them in the *shins.*

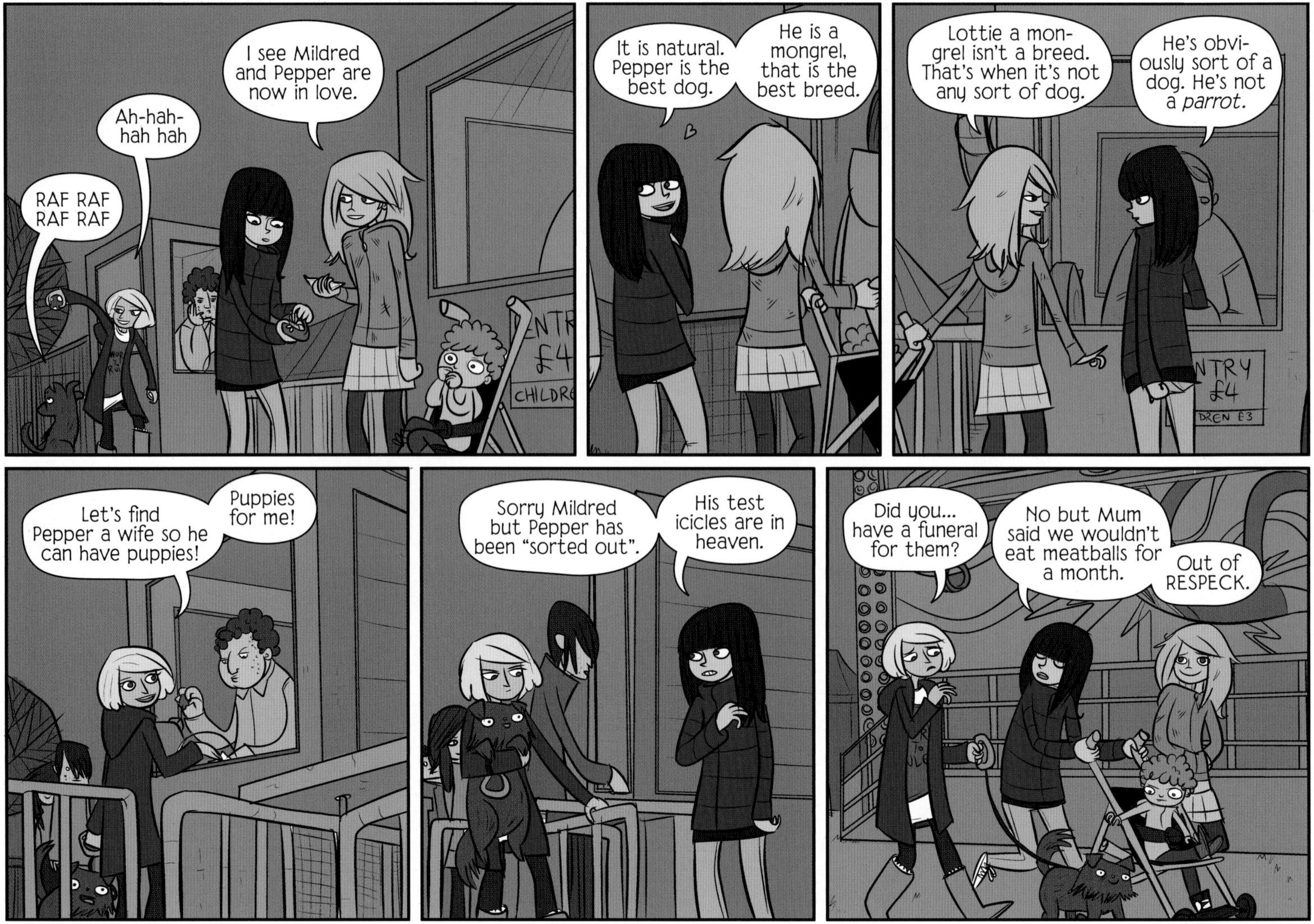

RAF RAF RAF RAF
Ah-hah-hah hah
I see Mildred and Pepper are now in love.
It is natural. Pepper is the best dog.
He is a mongrel, that is the best breed.
Lottie a mon-grel isn't a breed. That's when it's not any sort of dog.
He's obvi-ously sort of a dog. He's not a *parrot*.
Let's find Pepper a wife so he can have puppies!
Puppies for me!
Sorry Mildred but Pepper has been "sorted out".
His test icicles are in heaven.
Did you... have a funeral for them?
No but Mum said we wouldn't eat meatballs for a month.
Out of RESPECK.

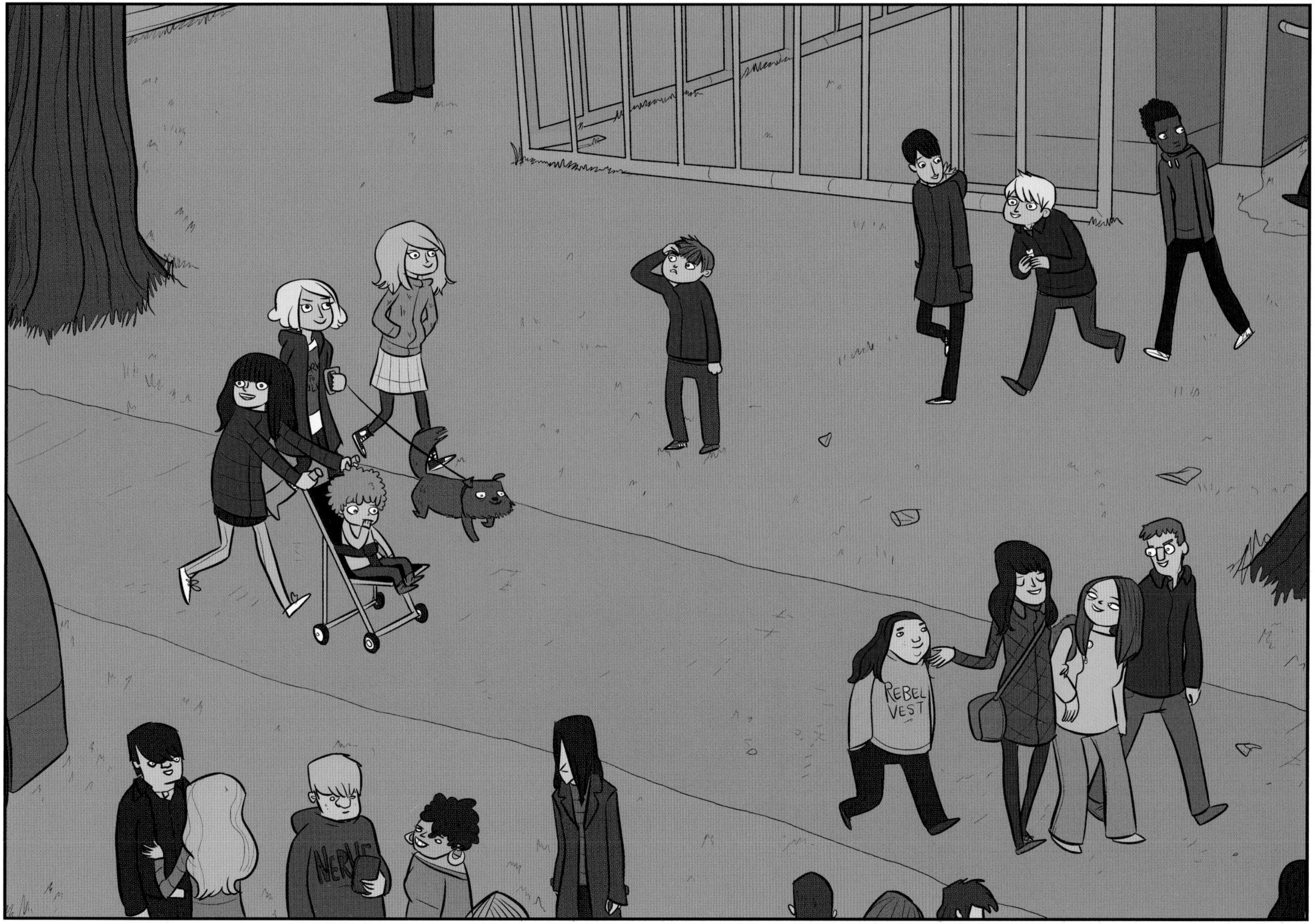
REBEL VEST

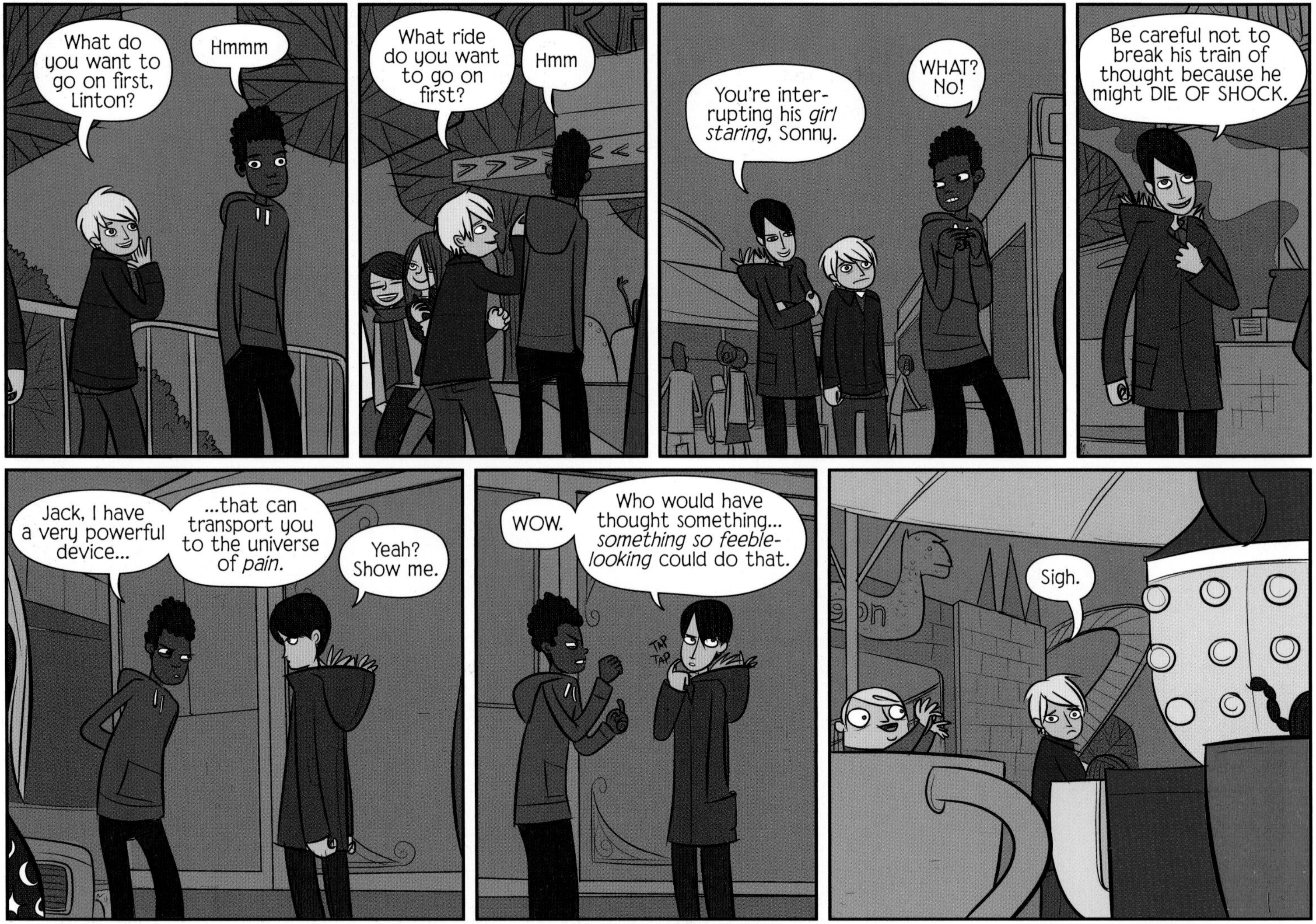

What do you want to go on first, Linton?
Hmmm
What ride do you want to go on first?
Hmm
You're inter-rupting his *girl staring*, Sonny.
WHAT? No!
Be careful not to break his train of thought because he might DIE OF SHOCK.
Jack, I have a very powerful device...
...that can transport you to the universe of *pain*.
Yeah? Show me.
WOW.
Who would have thought something... *something so feeble-looking* could do that.
TAP TAP
Sigh.

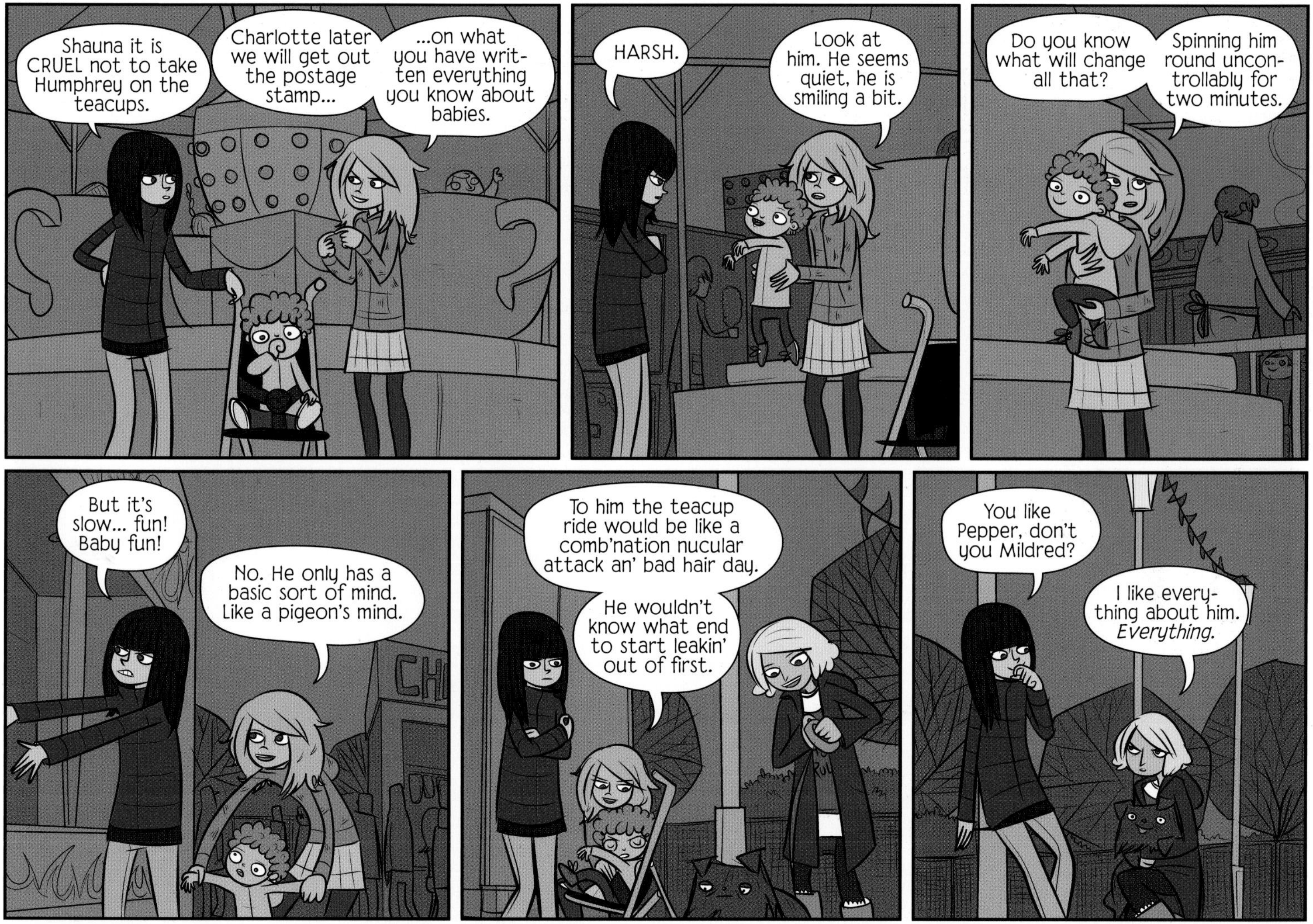
Shauna it is CRUEL not to take Humphrey on the teacups.
Charlotte later we will get out the postage stamp...
...on what you have written everything you know about babies.
HARSH.
Look at him. He seems quiet, he is smiling a bit.
Do you know what will change all that?
Spinning him round uncontrollably for two minutes.
But it's slow... fun! Baby fun!
No. He only has a basic sort of mind. Like a pigeon's mind.
To him the teacup ride would be like a comb'nation nucular attack an' bad hair day.
He wouldn't know what end to start leakin' out of first.
You like Pepper, don't you Mildred?
I like everything about him. *Everything.*

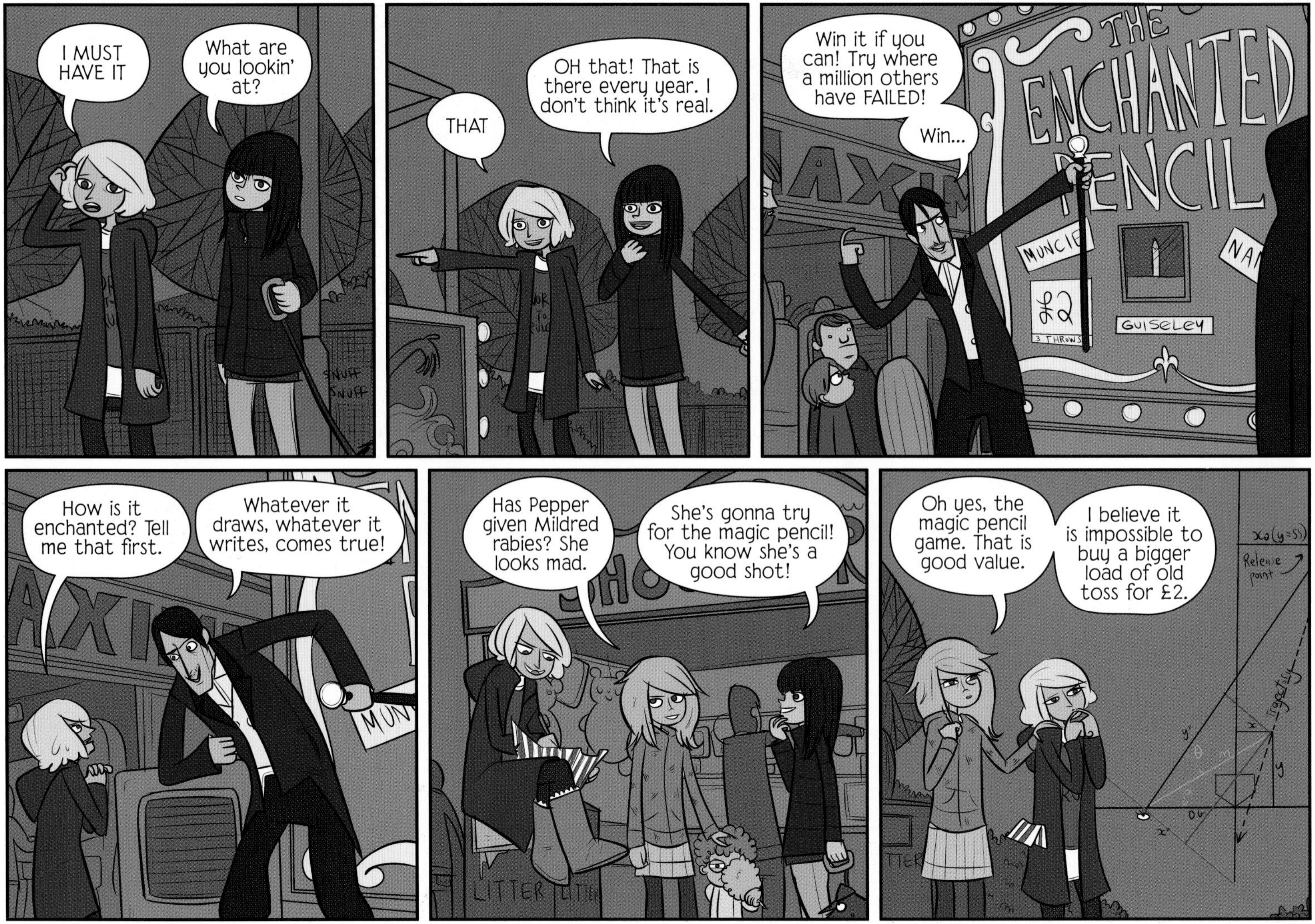
I MUST HAVE IT
What are you lookin' at?
SNUFF
SNUFF
THAT
OH that! That is there every year. I don't think it's real.
Win it if you can! Try where a million others have FAILED!
Win...
THE ENCHANTED PENCIL
MUNCIE
£2
3 THROWS
GUISELEY
How is it enchanted? Tell me that first.
Whatever it draws, whatever it writes, comes true!
Has Pepper given Mildred rabies? She looks mad.
She's gonna try for the magic pencil! You know she's a good shot!
LITTER
LITTER
Oh yes, the magic pencil game. That is good value.
I believe it is impossible to buy a bigger load of old toss for £2.
Release point
Trajectory

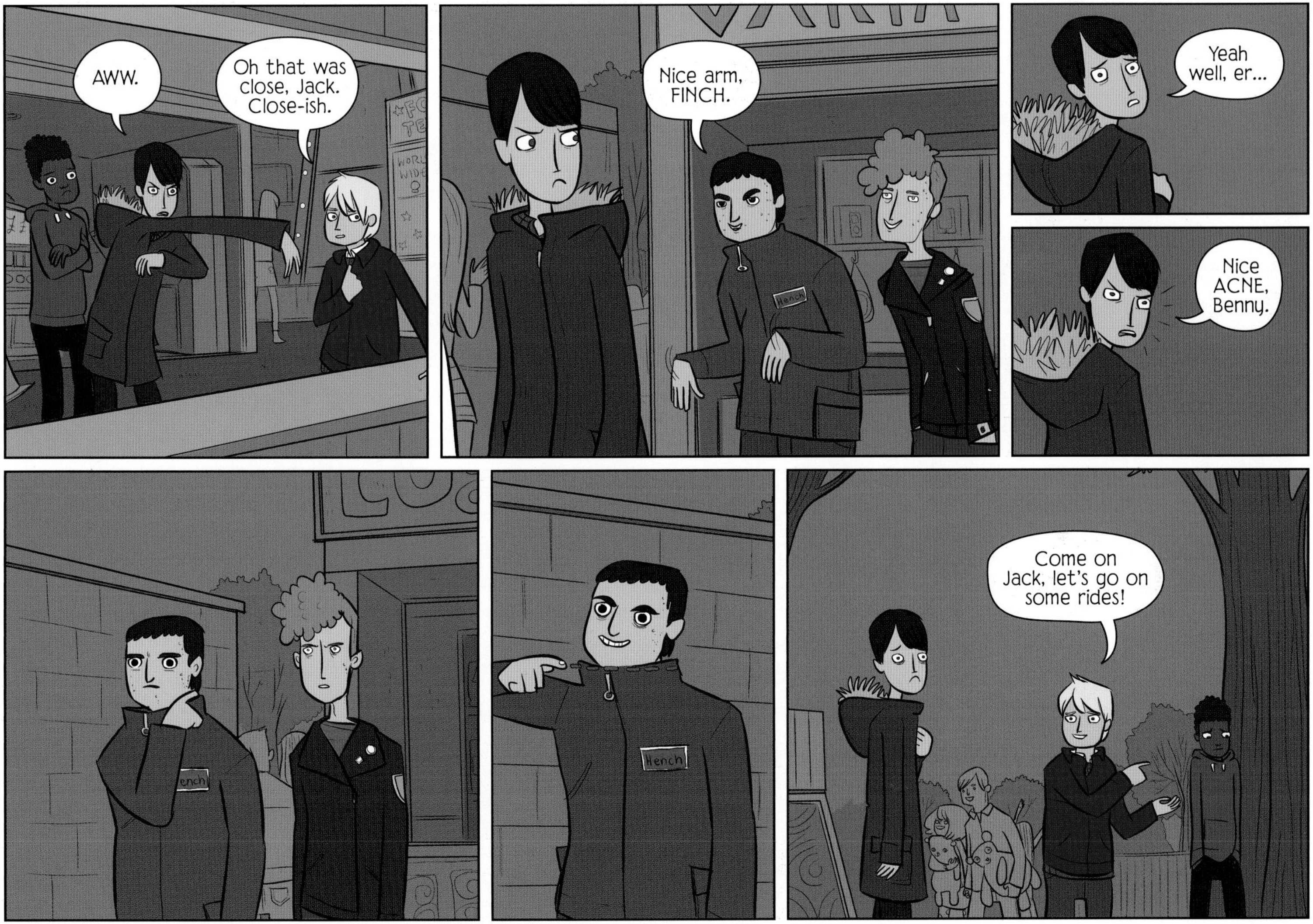
AWW.
Oh that was close, Jack. Close-ish.
Nice arm, FINCH.
Yeah well, er...
Nice ACNE, Benny.
Come on Jack, let's go on some rides!

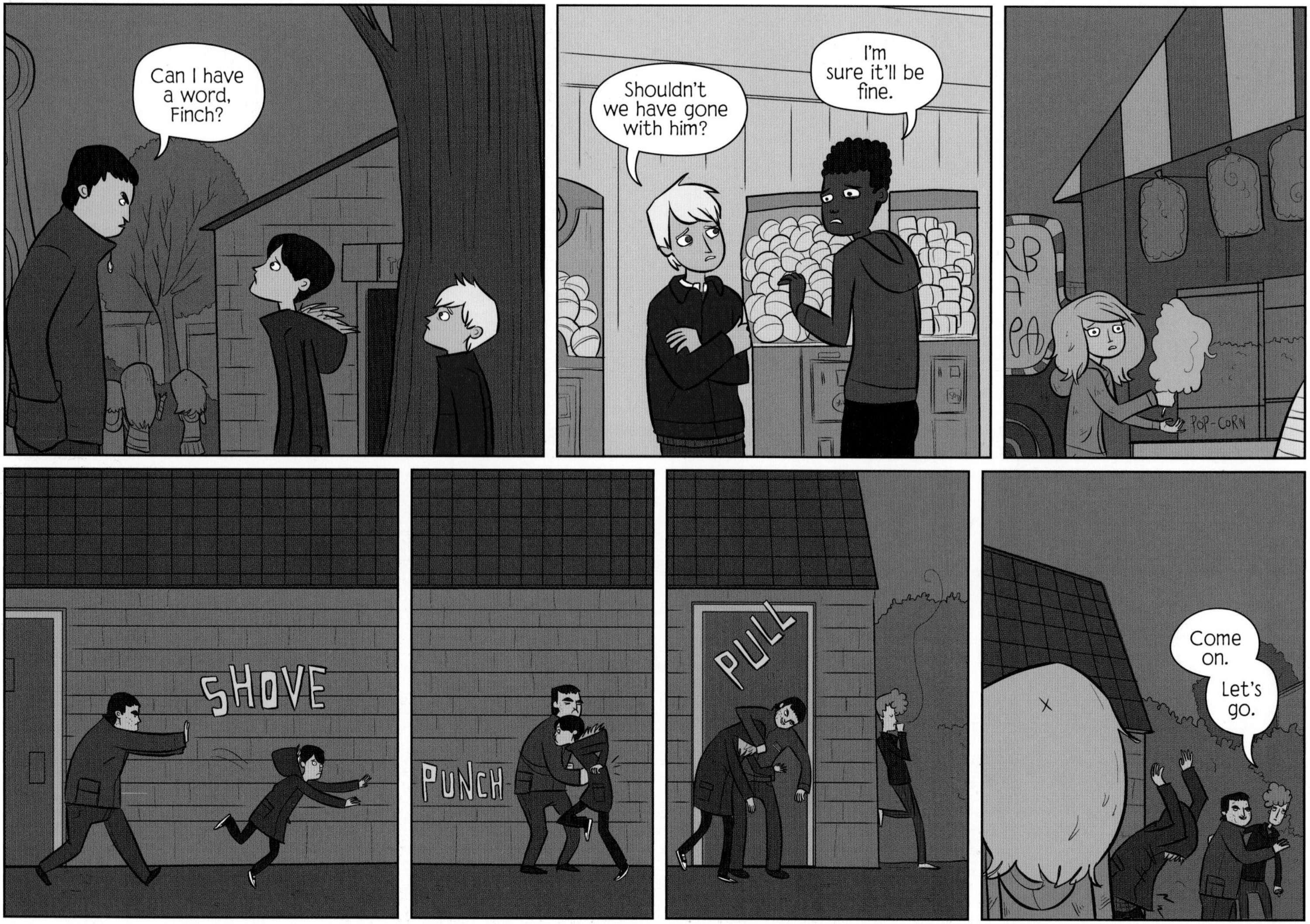
Can I have a word, Finch?
Shouldn't we have gone with him?
I'm sure it'll be fine.
POP-CORN
SHOVE
PUNCH
PULL
Come on.
Let's go.

Yeh I'm thinking about giving up the magic pencil.

No money in it any more.

My grandpa had this attraction, and my dad.

People just don't believe in the power of an enchanted pencil any more.

But I've got PLANS.

Hillbilly Simulater

I know, stick to the pencil.

Sigh.

Roll up! Roll up!

I WANT TO PLAY

PLOP

VEP

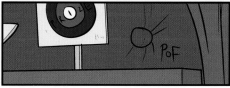

POF

What.

I think it might be fixed, Mildred.

I WANT TO PLAY AGAIN.

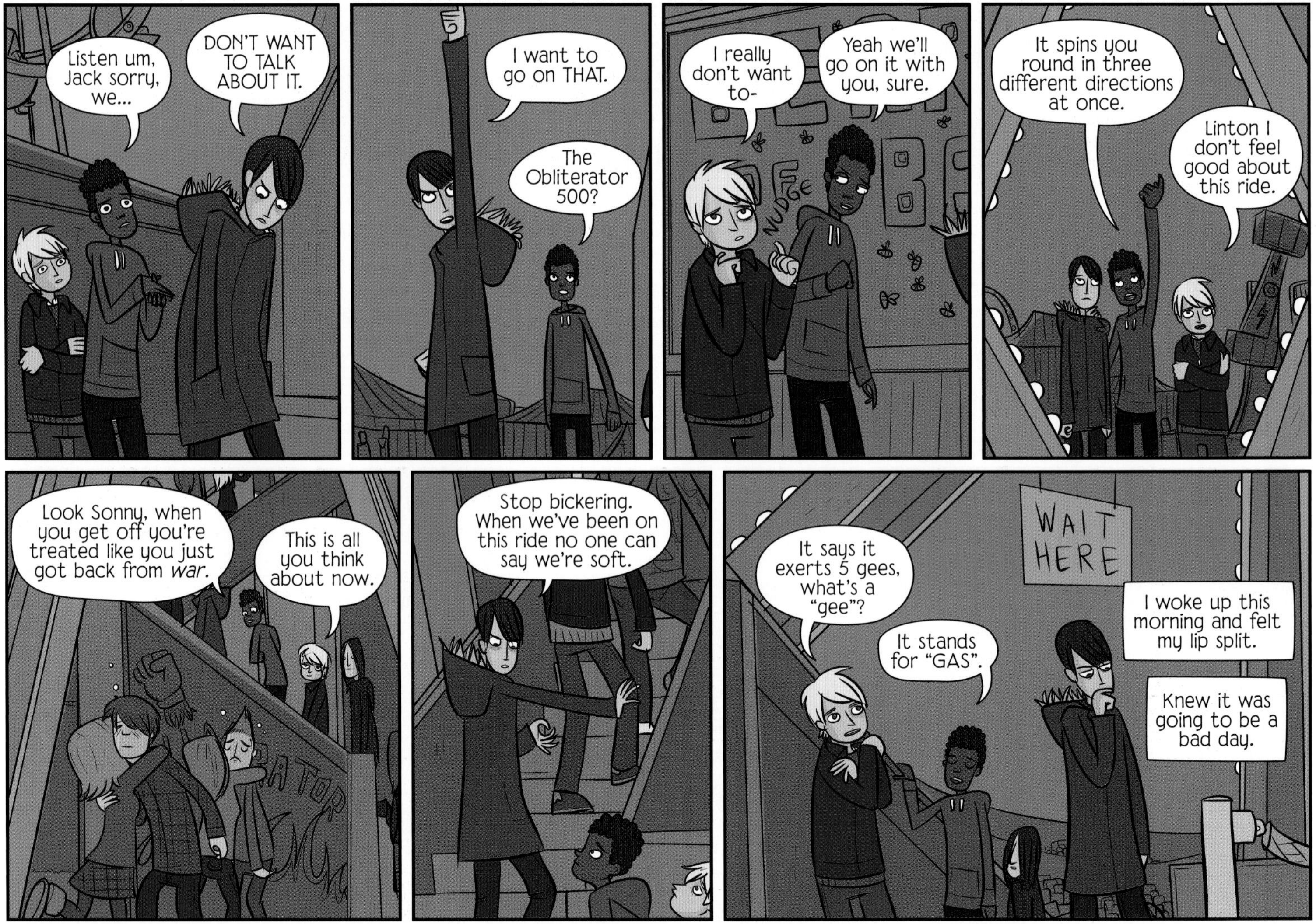
Listen um, Jack sorry, we...
DON'T WANT TO TALK ABOUT IT.
I want to go on THAT.
The Obliterator 500?
I really don't want to-
Yeah we'll go on it with you, sure.
NUDGE
It spins you round in three different directions at once.
Linton I don't feel good about this ride.
Look Sonny, when you get off you're treated like you just got back from *war*.
This is all you think about now.
Stop bickering. When we've been on this ride no one can say we're soft.
WAIT HERE
It says it exerts 5 gees, what's a "gee"?
It stands for "GAS".
I woke up this morning and felt my lip split.
Knew it was going to be a bad day.

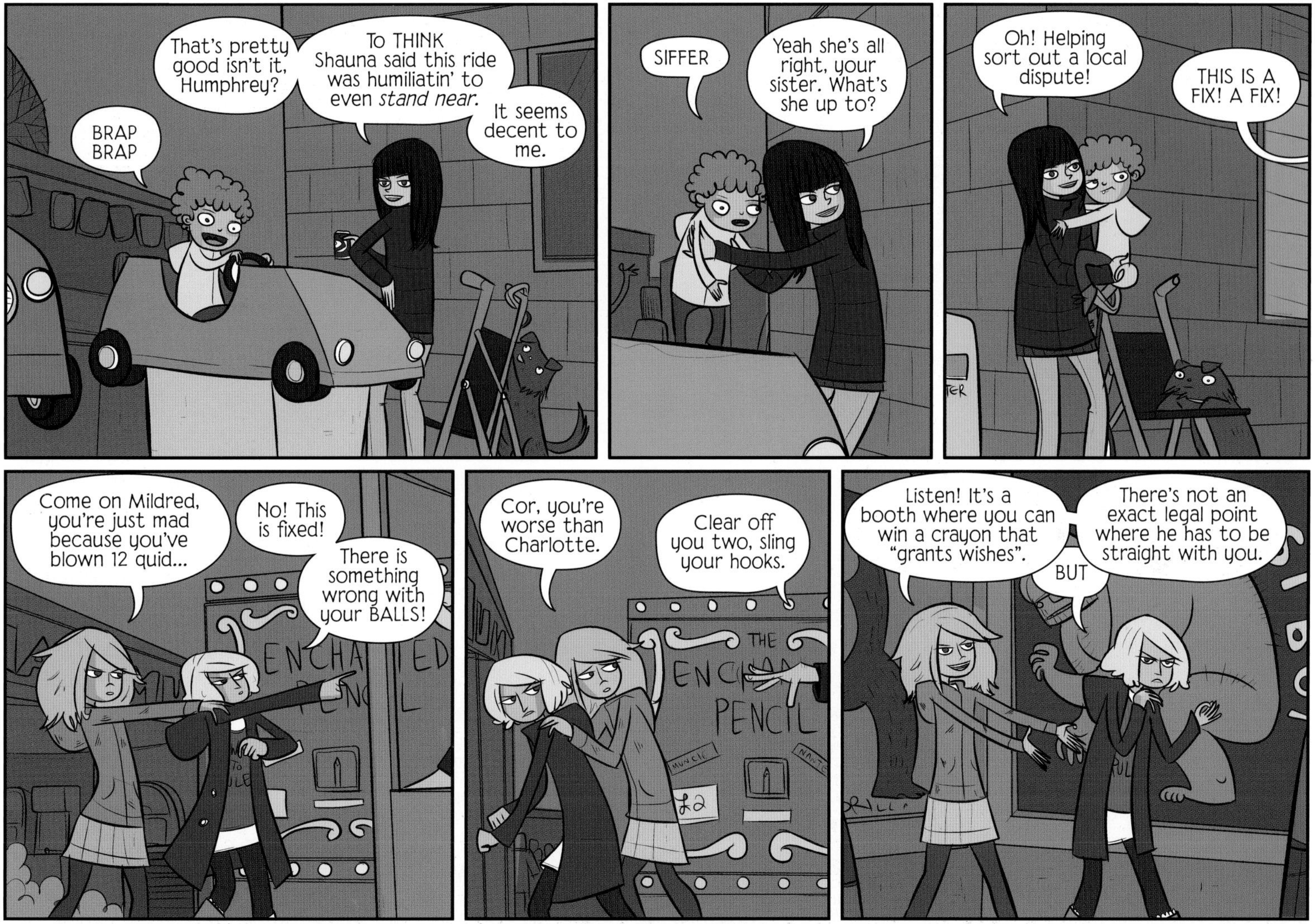
BRAP BRAP
That's pretty good isn't it, Humphrey?
To THINK Shauna said this ride was humiliatin' to even *stand near.*
It seems decent to me.
SIFFER
Yeah she's all right, your sister. What's she up to?
Oh! Helping sort out a local dispute!
THIS IS A FIX! A FIX!
Come on Mildred, you're just mad because you've blown 12 quid...
No! This is fixed!
There is something wrong with your BALLS!
Cor, you're worse than Charlotte.
Clear off you two, sling your hooks.
Listen! It's a booth where you can win a crayon that "grants wishes".
BUT
There's not an exact legal point where he has to be straight with you.

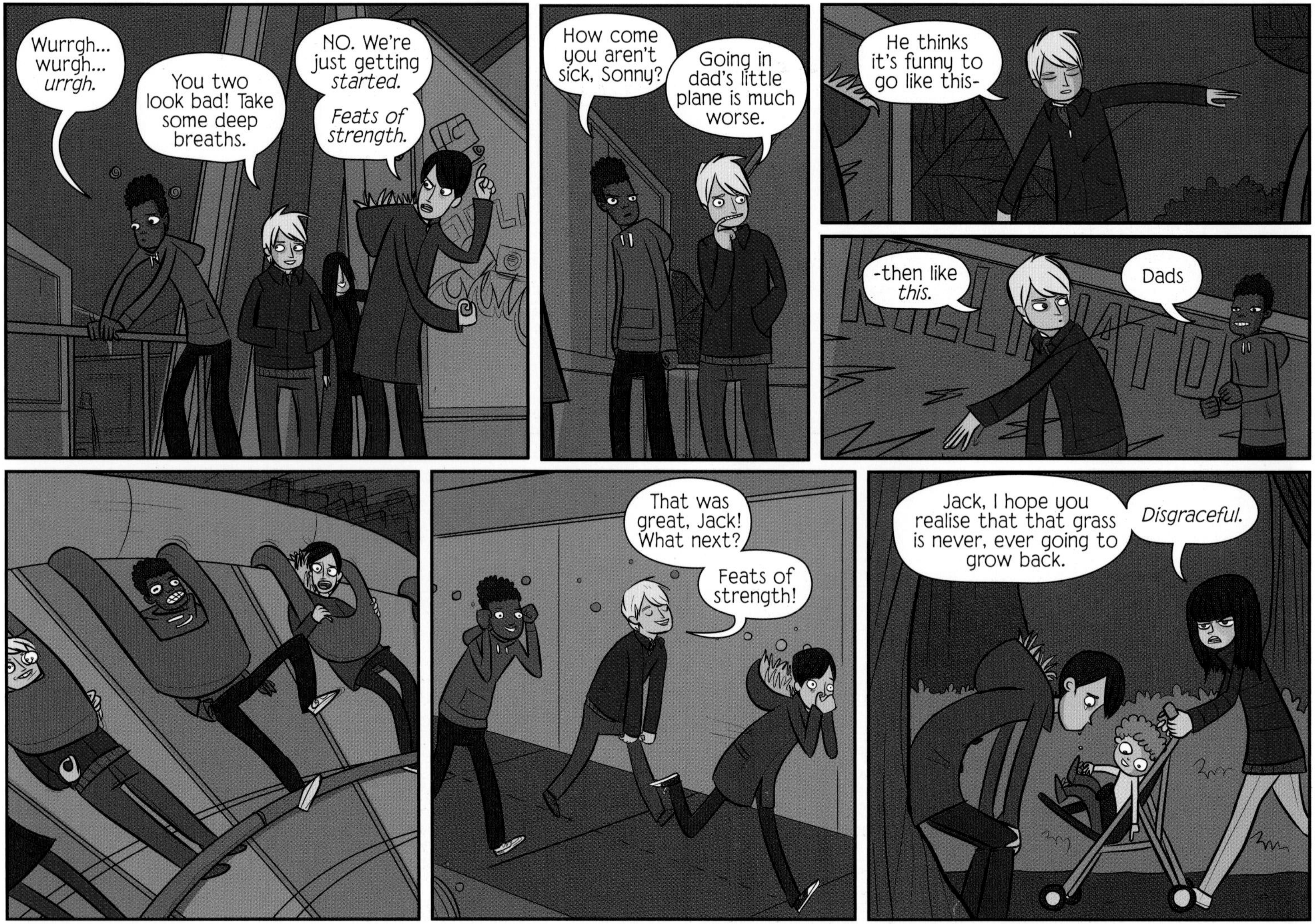
Wurrgh... wurgh... *urrgh.*
You two look bad! Take some deep breaths.
NO. We're just getting *started.*
Feats of strength.
How come you aren't sick, Sonny?
Going in dad's little plane is much worse.
He thinks it's funny to go like this-
-then like *this.*
Dads
That was great, Jack! What next?
Feats of strength!
Jack, I hope you realise that that grass is never, ever going to grow back.
Disgraceful.

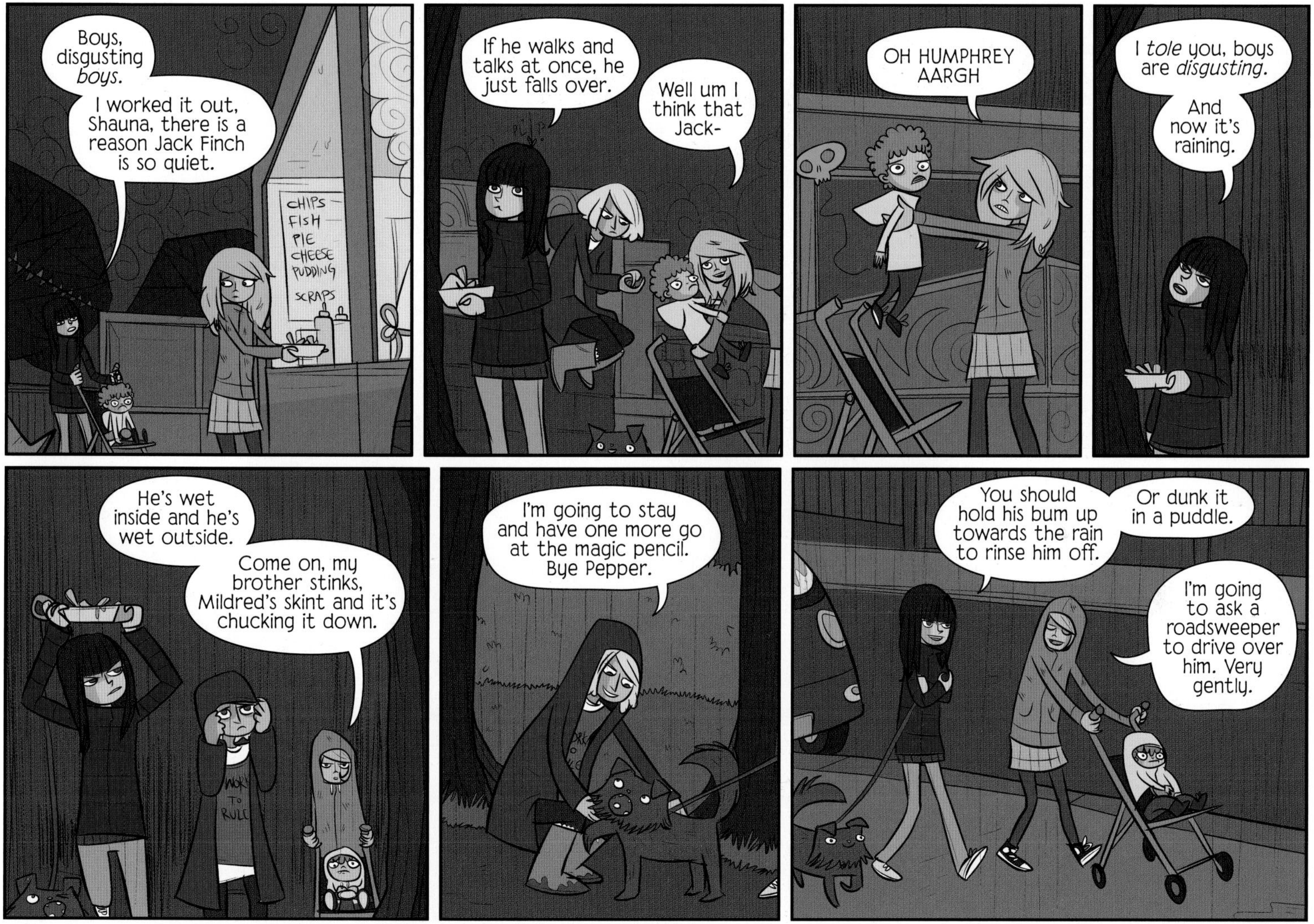
Boys, disgusting *boys*.
I worked it out, Shauna, there is a reason Jack Finch is so quiet.
CHIPS
FISH
PIE
CHEESE
PUDDING
SCRAPS
If he walks and talks at once, he just falls over.
Well um I think that Jack-
OH HUMPHREY AARGH
I *tole* you, boys are *disgusting*.
And now it's raining.
He's wet inside and he's wet outside.
Come on, my brother stinks, Mildred's skint and it's chucking it down.
I'm going to stay and have one more go at the magic pencil. Bye Pepper.
You should hold his bum up towards the rain to rinse him off.
Or dunk it in a puddle.
I'm going to ask a roadsweeper to drive over him. Very gently.

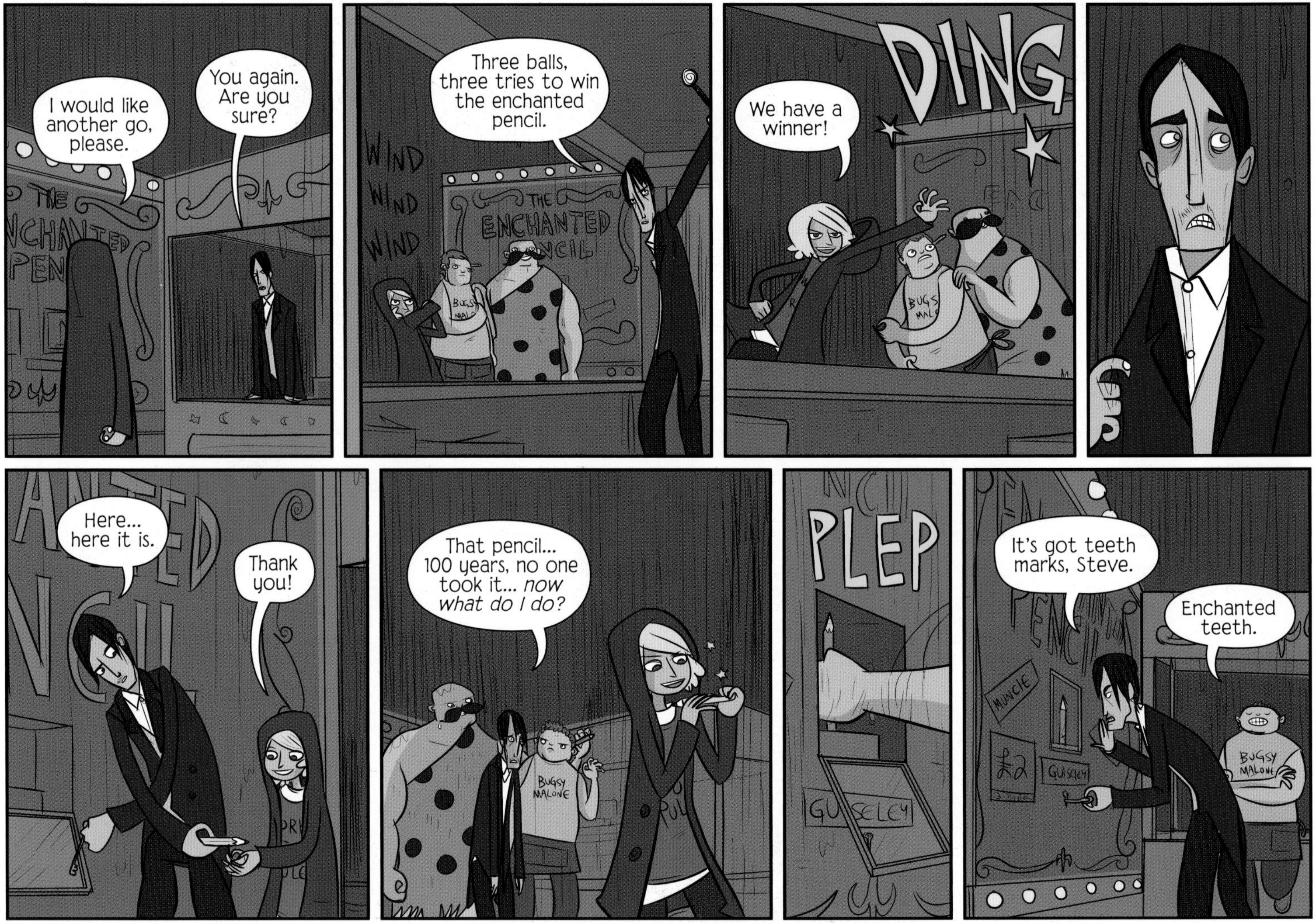
I would like another go, please.
You again. Are you sure?
WIND
WIND
WIND
Three balls, three tries to win the enchanted pencil.
We have a winner!
DING
Here... here it is.
Thank you!
That pencil... 100 years, no one took it... *now what do I do?*
PLEP
It's got teeth marks, Steve.
Enchanted teeth.
BUGSY MALONE

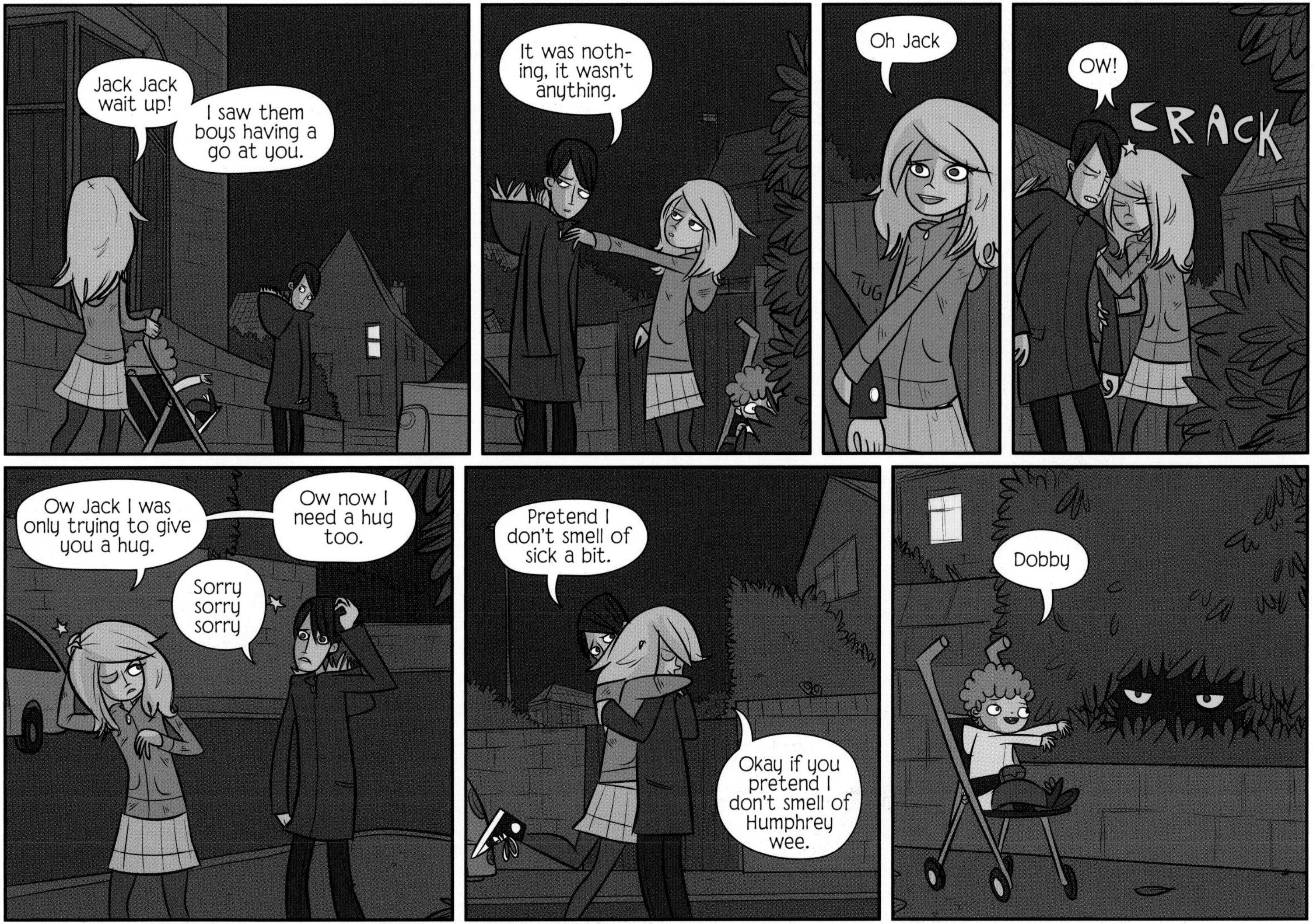
Jack Jack wait up!
I saw them boys having a go at you.
It was noth-ing, it wasn't anything.
Oh Jack
TUG
OW!
CRACK
Ow Jack I was only trying to give you a hug.
Ow now I need a hug too.
Sorry sorry sorry
Pretend I don't smell of sick a bit.
Okay if you pretend I don't smell of Humphrey wee.
Dobby

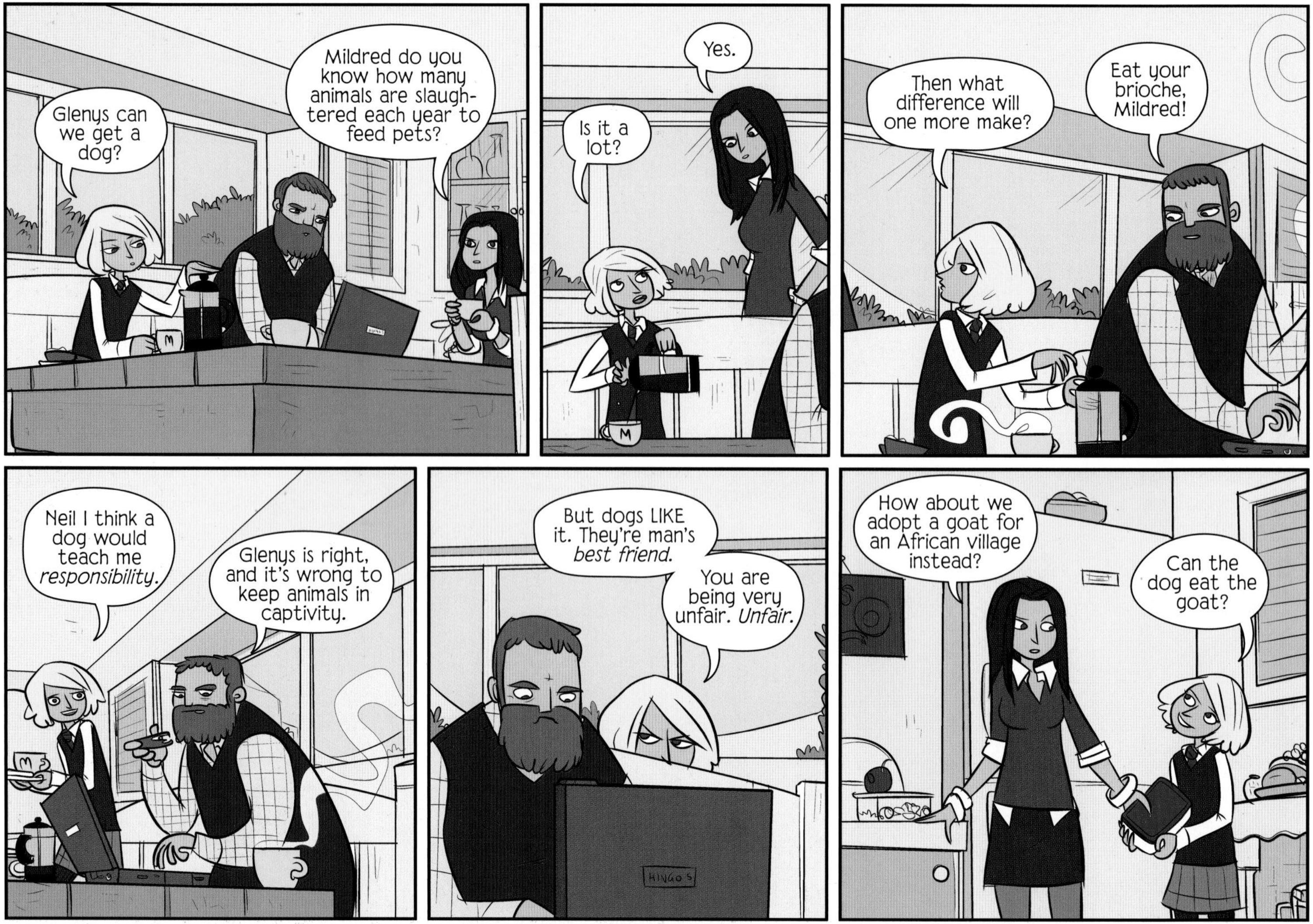
Glenys can we get a dog?
Mildred do you know how many animals are slaughtered each year to feed pets?
Is it a lot?
Yes.
Then what difference will one more make?
Eat your brioche, Mildred!
Neil I think a dog would teach me *responsibility.*
Glenys is right, and it's wrong to keep animals in captivity.
But dogs LIKE it. They're man's *best friend.*
You are being very unfair. *Unfair.*
How about we adopt a goat for an African village instead?
Can the dog eat the goat?

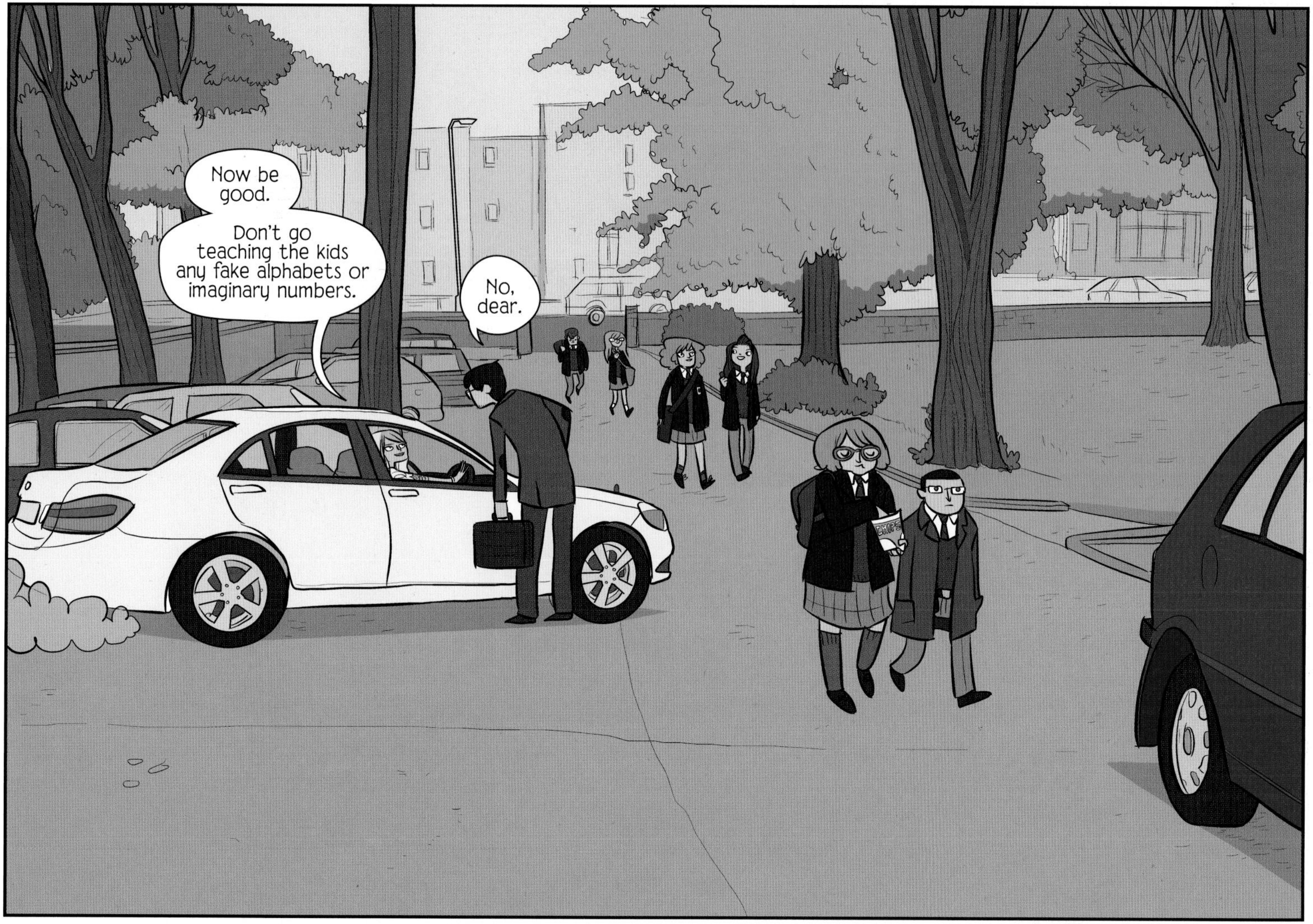
Now be good.
Don't go teaching the kids any fake alphabets or imaginary numbers.
No, dear.
CHIPS

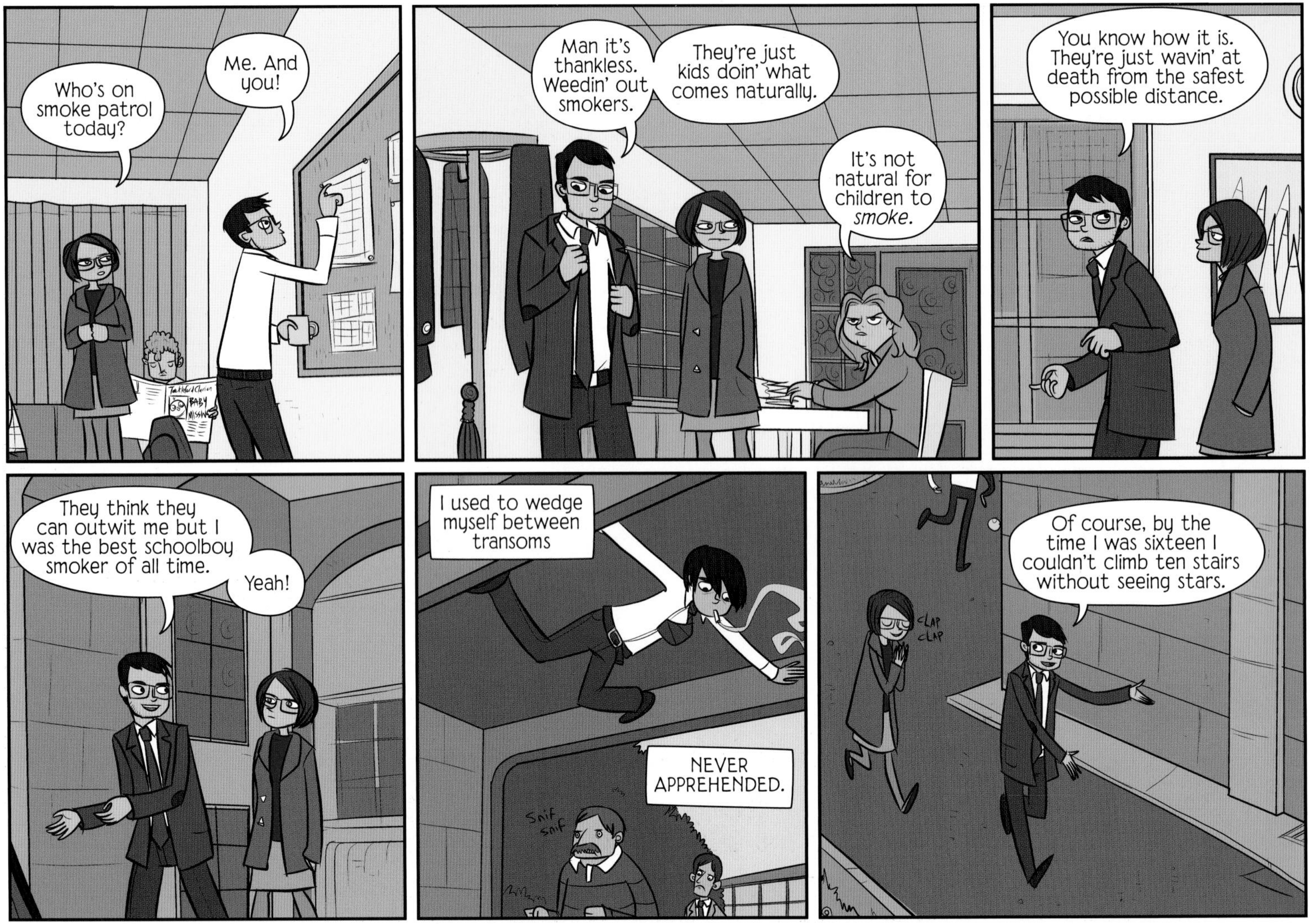
Who's on smoke patrol today?
Me. And you!
Man it's thankless. Weedin' out smokers.
They're just kids doin' what comes naturally.
It's not natural for children to *smoke*.
You know how it is. They're just wavin' at death from the safest possible distance.
They think they can outwit me but I was the best schoolboy smoker of all time.
Yeah!
I used to wedge myself between transoms
Snif snif
NEVER APPREHENDED.
CLAP CLAP
Of course, by the time I was sixteen I couldn't climb ten stairs without seeing stars.

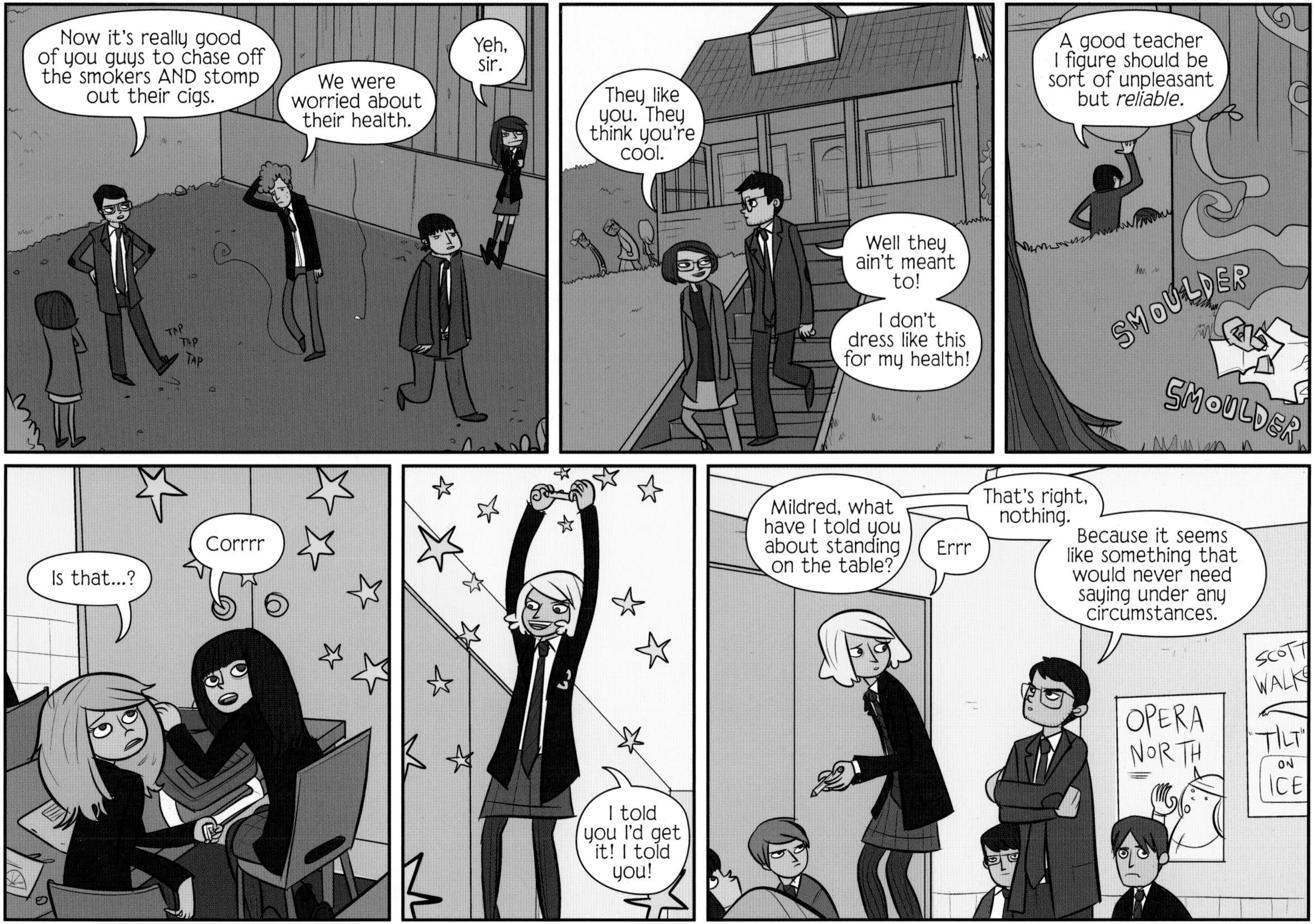
Now it's really good of you guys to chase off the smokers AND stomp out their cigs.
We were worried about their health.
Yeh, sir.
TAP TAP TAP
They like you. They think you're cool.
Well they ain't meant to!
I don't dress like this for my health!
A good teacher I figure should be sort of unpleasant but *reliable*.
SMOULDER
SMOULDER
Is that...?
Corrrr
I told you I'd get it! I told you!
Mildred, what have I told you about standing on the table?
Errr
That's right, nothing.
Because it seems like something that would never need saying under any circumstances.
OPERA NORTH
"TILT" ON ICE

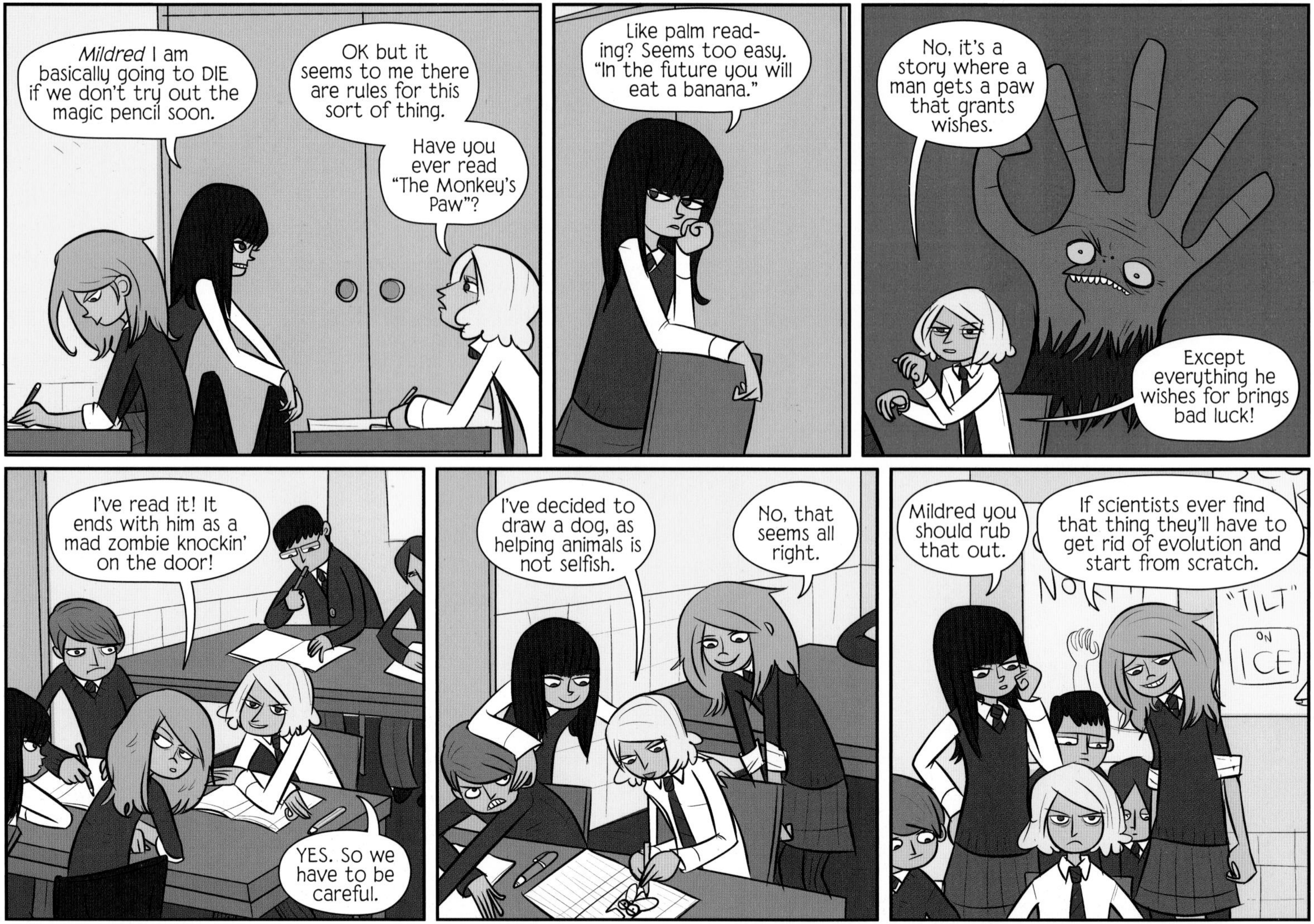
Mildred I am basically going to DIE if we don't try out the magic pencil soon.
OK but it seems to me there are rules for this sort of thing.
Have you ever read "The Monkey's Paw"?
Like palm reading? Seems too easy. "In the future you will eat a banana."
No, it's a story where a man gets a paw that grants wishes.
Except everything he wishes for brings bad luck!
I've read it! It ends with him as a mad zombie knockin' on the door!
YES. So we have to be careful.
I've decided to draw a dog, as helping animals is not selfish.
No, that seems all right.
Mildred you should rub that out.
If scientists ever find that thing they'll have to get rid of evolution and start from scratch.
"TILT" ON ICE

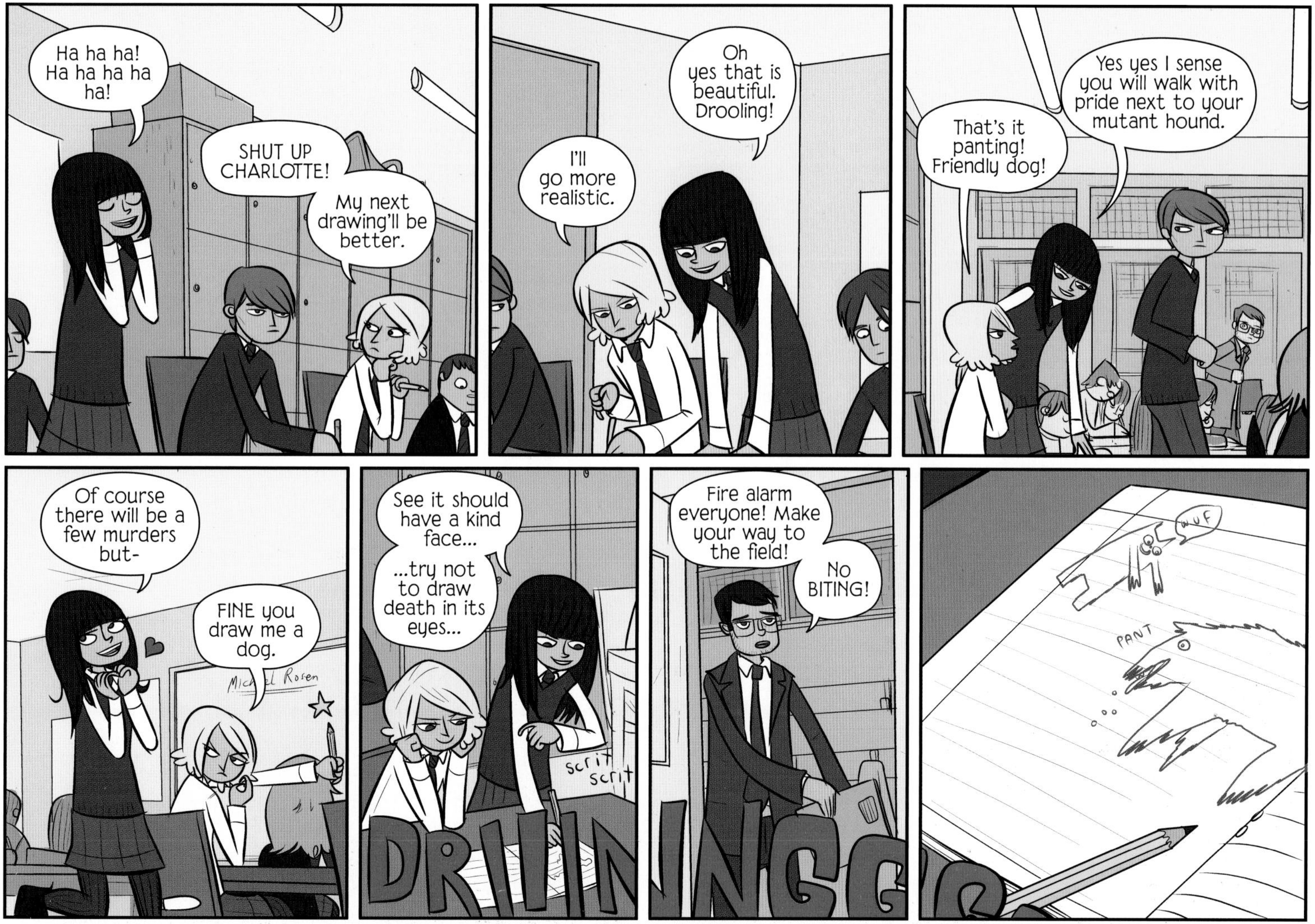

Ha ha ha! Ha ha ha ha ha!
SHUT UP CHARLOTTE!
My next drawing'll be better.
Oh yes that is beautiful. Drooling!
I'll go more realistic.
Yes yes I sense you will walk with pride next to your mutant hound.
That's it panting! Friendly dog!
Of course there will be a few murders but-
FINE you draw me a dog.
See it should have a kind face...
...try not to draw death in its eyes...
scrit scrit
Fire alarm everyone! Make your way to the field!
No BITING!
DRIIINNGGG
WUF
PANT

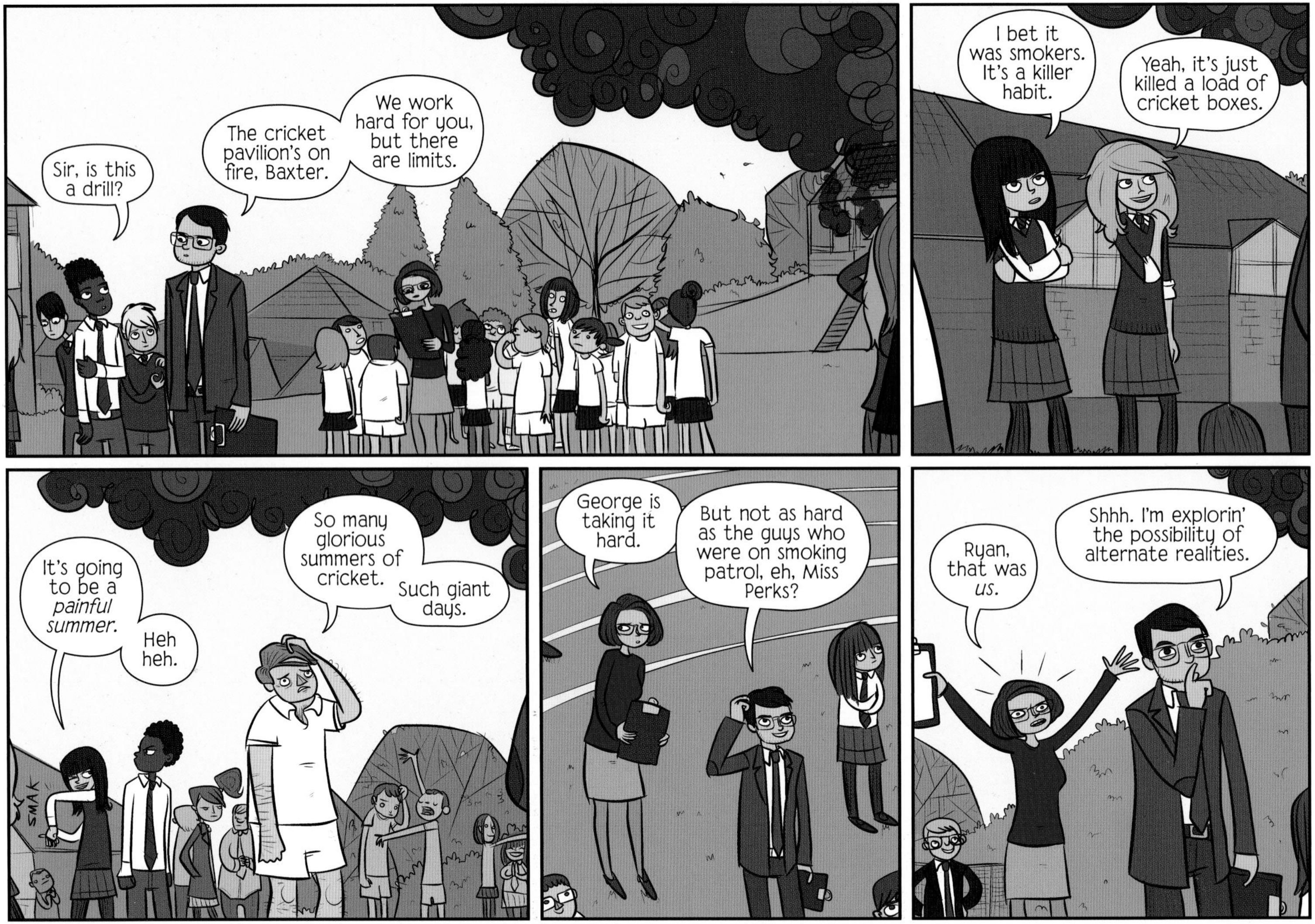
Sir, is this a drill?
The cricket pavilion's on fire, Baxter.
We work hard for you, but there are limits.
I bet it was smokers. It's a killer habit.
Yeah, it's just killed a load of cricket boxes.
It's going to be a *painful summer.*
Heh heh.
SMAK
So many glorious summers of cricket.
Such giant days.
George is taking it hard.
But not as hard as the guys who were on smoking patrol, eh, Miss Perks?
Ryan, that was *us.*
Shhh. I'm explorin' the possibility of alternate realities.

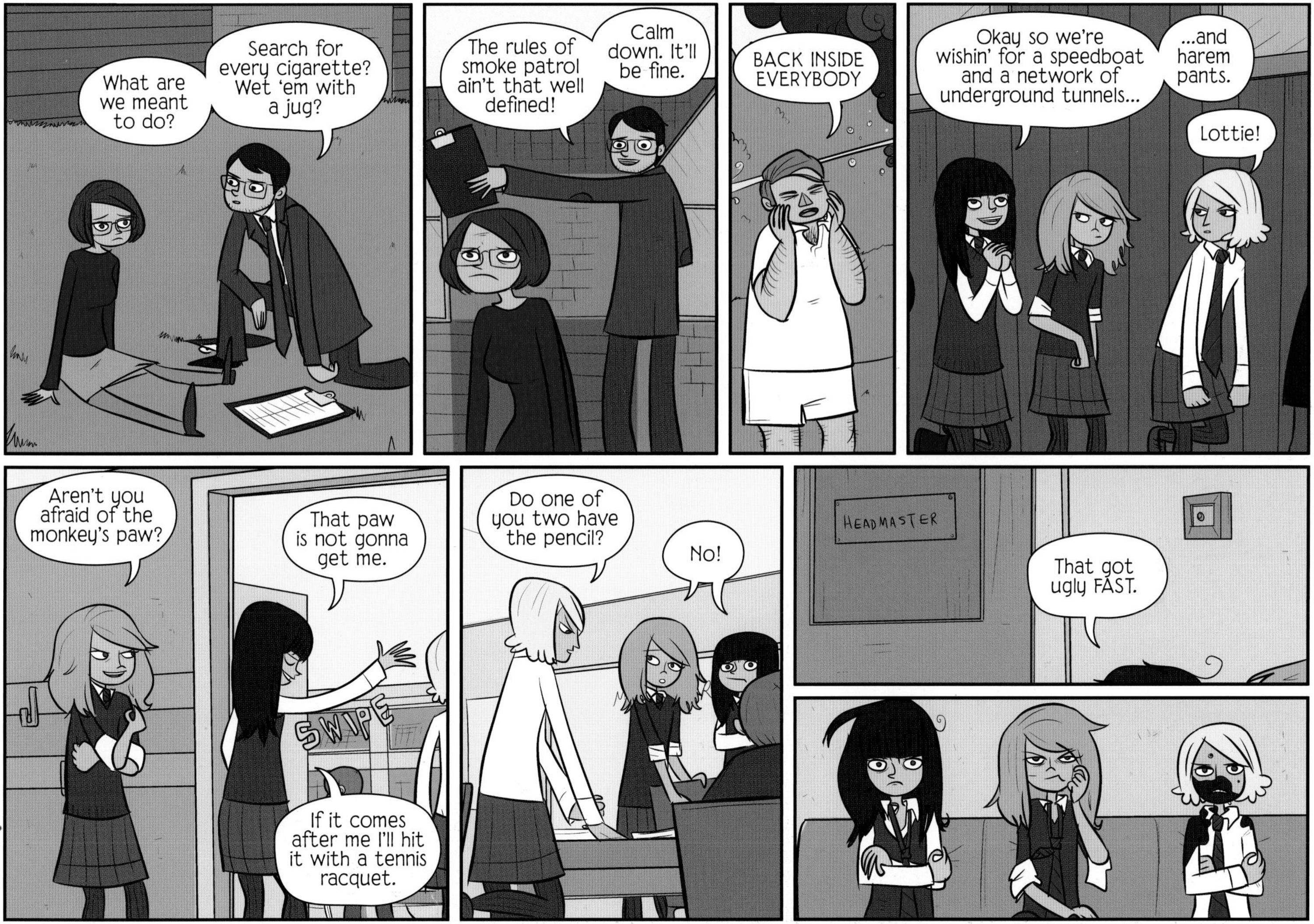
What are we meant to do?
Search for every cigarette? Wet 'em with a jug?
The rules of smoke patrol ain't that well defined!
Calm down. It'll be fine.
BACK INSIDE EVERYBODY
Okay so we're wishin' for a speedboat and a network of underground tunnels...
...and harem pants.
Lottie!
Aren't you afraid of the monkey's paw?
That paw is not gonna get me.
SWIPE
If it comes after me I'll hit it with a tennis racquet.
Do one of you two have the pencil?
No!
HEADMASTER
That got ugly FAST.

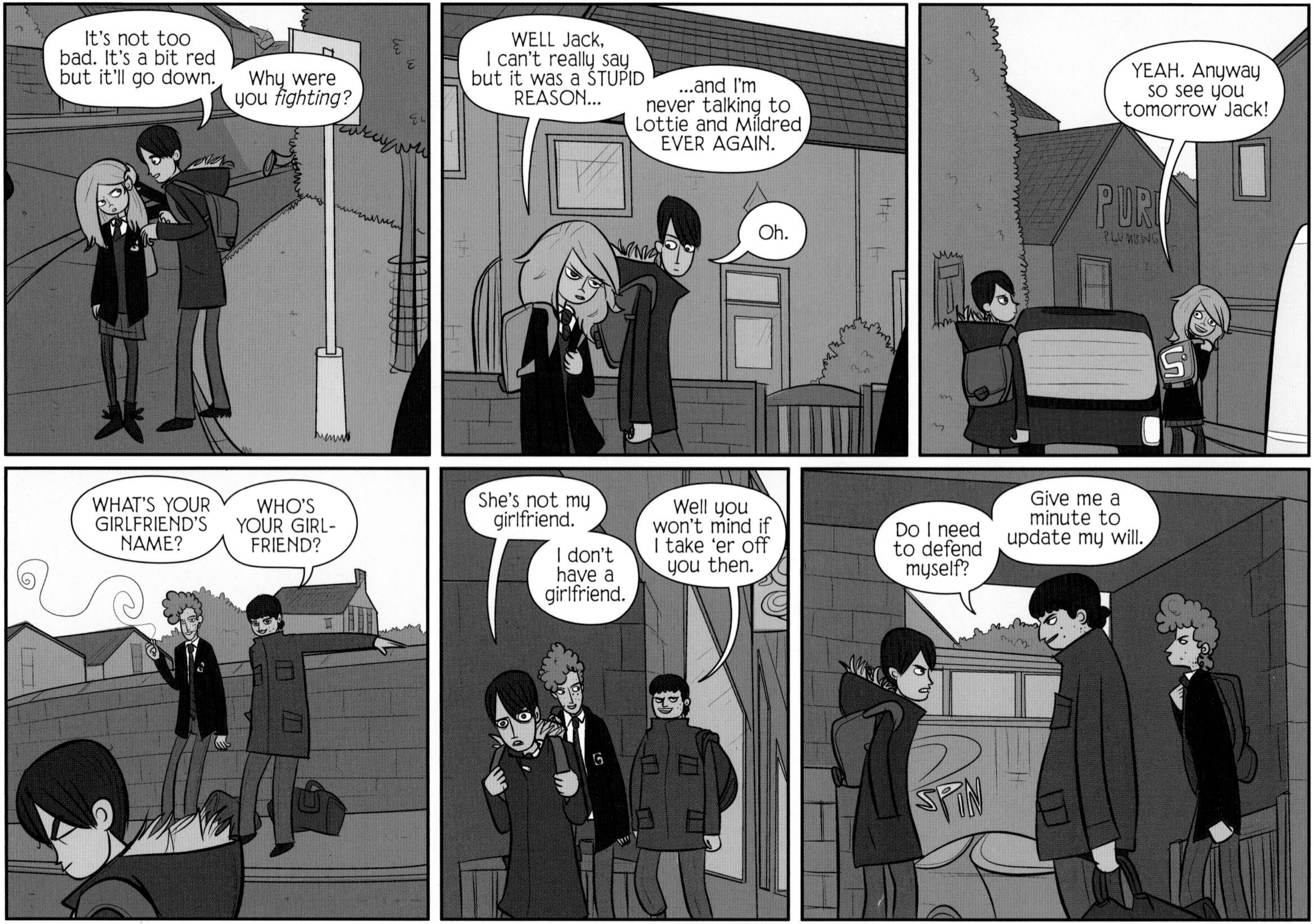
It's not too bad. It's a bit red but it'll go down.
Why were you *fighting*?
WELL Jack, I can't really say but it was a STUPID REASON...
...and I'm never talking to Lottie and Mildred EVER AGAIN.
Oh.
YEAH. Anyway so see you tomorrow Jack!
WHAT'S YOUR GIRLFRIEND'S NAME?
WHO'S YOUR GIRL-FRIEND?
She's not my girlfriend.
I don't have a girlfriend.
Well you won't mind if I take 'er off you then.
Do I need to defend myself?
Give me a minute to update my will.
SPIN

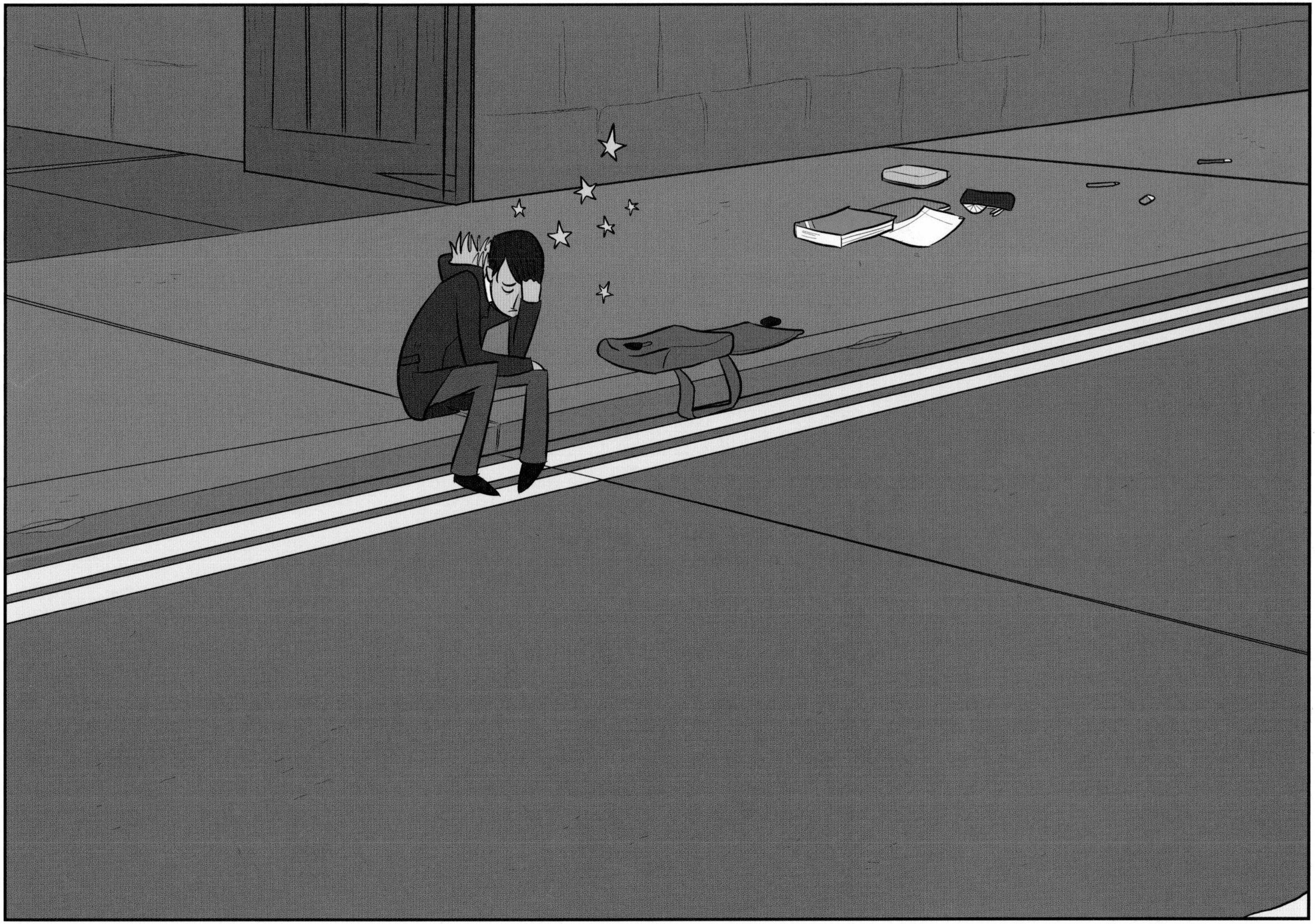

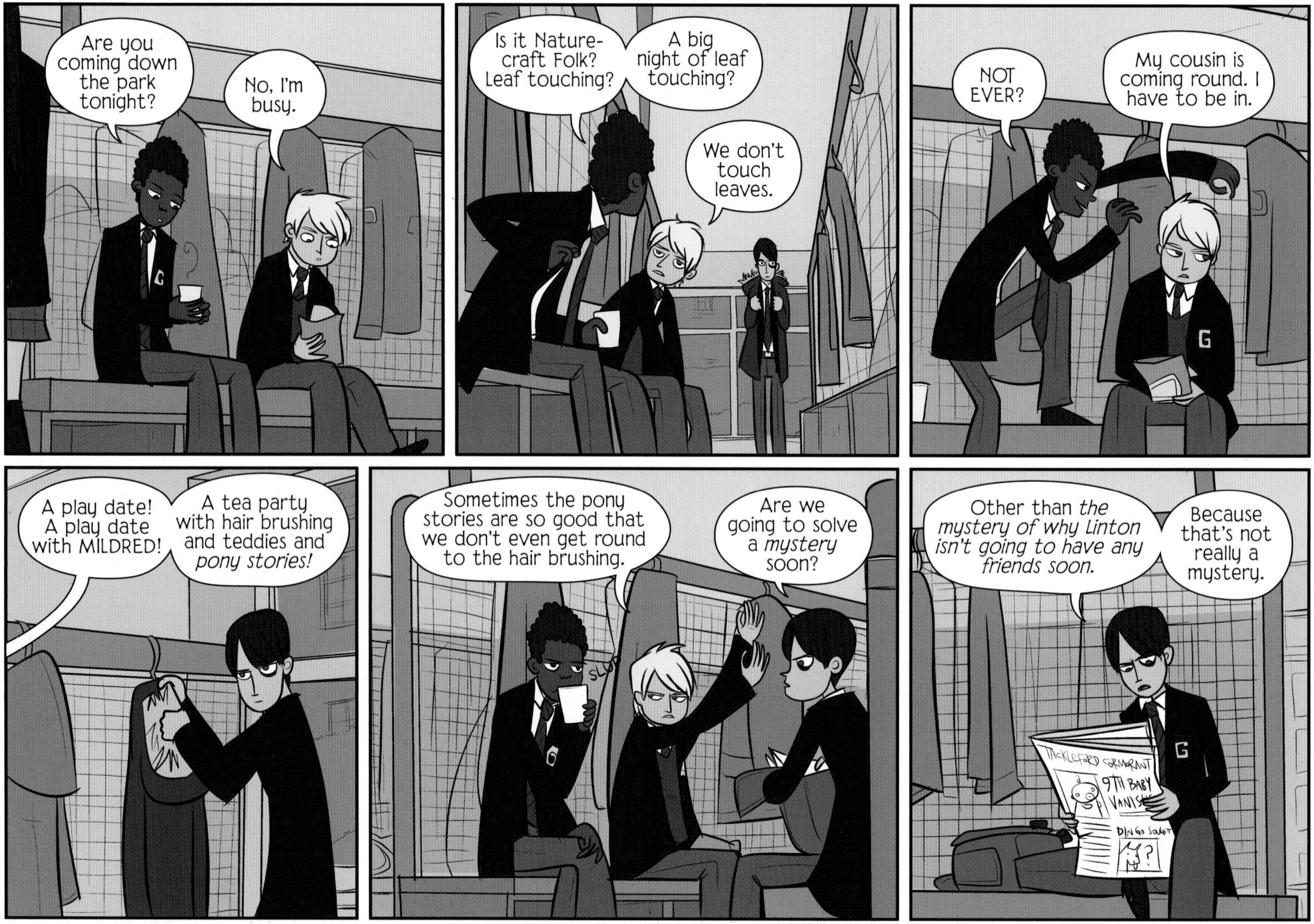
Are you coming down the park tonight?
No, I'm busy.
Is it Nature-craft Folk? Leaf touching?
A big night of leaf touching?
We don't touch leaves.
NOT EVER?
My cousin is coming round. I have to be in.
A play date! A play date with MILDRED!
A tea party with hair brushing and teddies and *pony stories!*
Sometimes the pony stories are so good that we don't even get round to the hair brushing.
Are we going to solve a *mystery* soon?
Other than *the mystery of why Linton isn't going to have any friends soon.*
Because that's not really a mystery.
TACKLEFORD CORMORANT
9TH BABY
DINGO SOUGHT

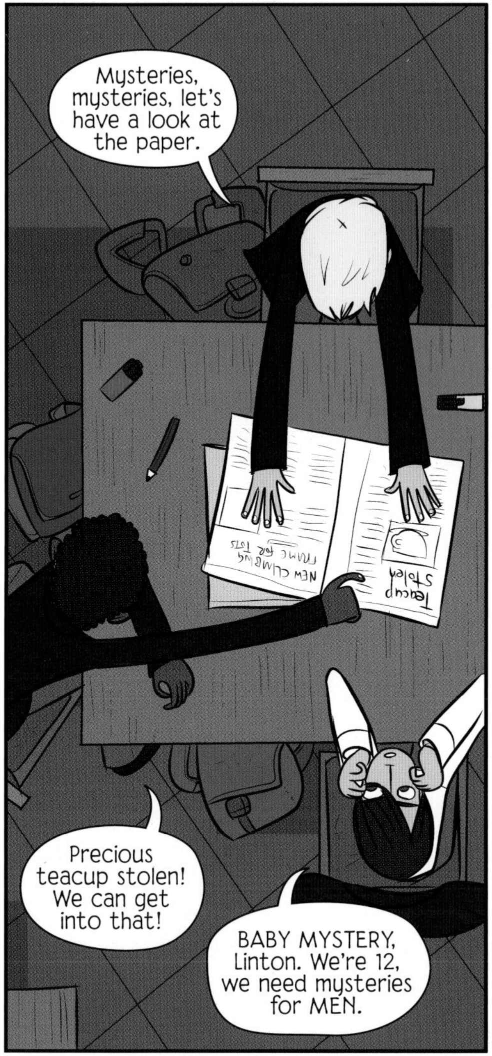
Mysteries, mysteries, let's have a look at the paper.
Precious teacup stolen! We can get into that!
BABY MYSTERY, Linton. We're 12, we need mysteries for MEN.

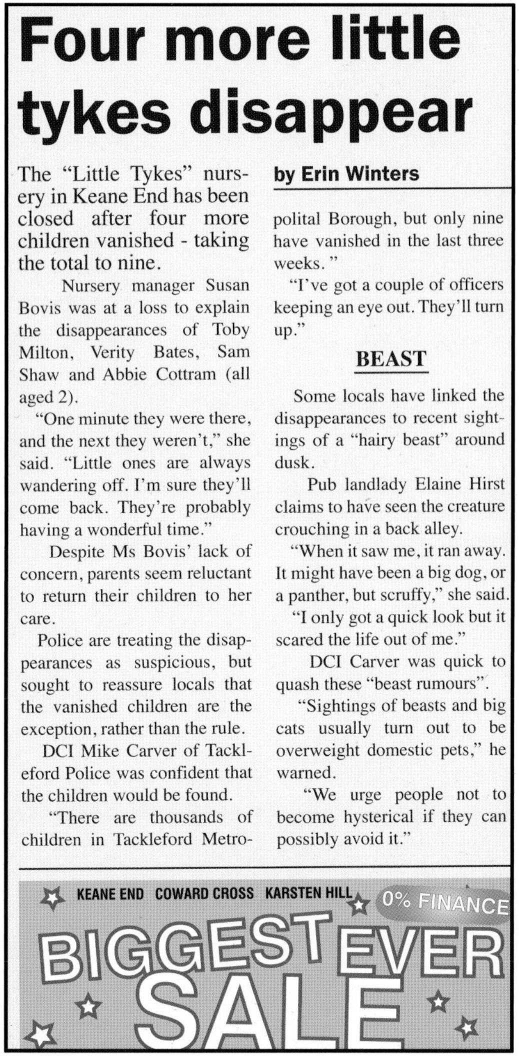

Four more little tykes disappear

by Erin Winters

The "Little Tykes" nursery in Keane End has been closed after four more children vanished - taking the total to nine.

Nursery manager Susan Bovis was at a loss to explain the disappearances of Toby Milton, Verity Bates, Sam Shaw and Abbie Cottram (all aged 2).

"One minute they were there, and the next they weren't," she said. "Little ones are always wandering off. I'm sure they'll come back. They're probably having a wonderful time."

Despite Ms Bovis' lack of concern, parents seem reluctant to return their children to her care.

Police are treating the disappearances as suspicious, but sought to reassure locals that the vanished children are the exception, rather than the rule.

DCI Mike Carver of Tackleford Police was confident that the children would be found.

"There are thousands of children in Tackleford Metropolital Borough, but only nine have vanished in the last three weeks."

"I've got a couple of officers keeping an eye out. They'll turn up."

BEAST

Some locals have linked the disappearances to recent sightings of a "hairy beast" around dusk.

Pub landlady Elaine Hirst claims to have seen the creature crouching in a back alley.

"When it saw me, it ran away. It might have been a big dog, or a panther, but scruffy," she said. "I only got a quick look but it scared the life out of me."

DCI Carver was quick to quash these "beast rumours".

"Sightings of beasts and big cats usually turn out to be overweight domestic pets," he warned.

"We urge people not to become hysterical if they can possibly avoid it."

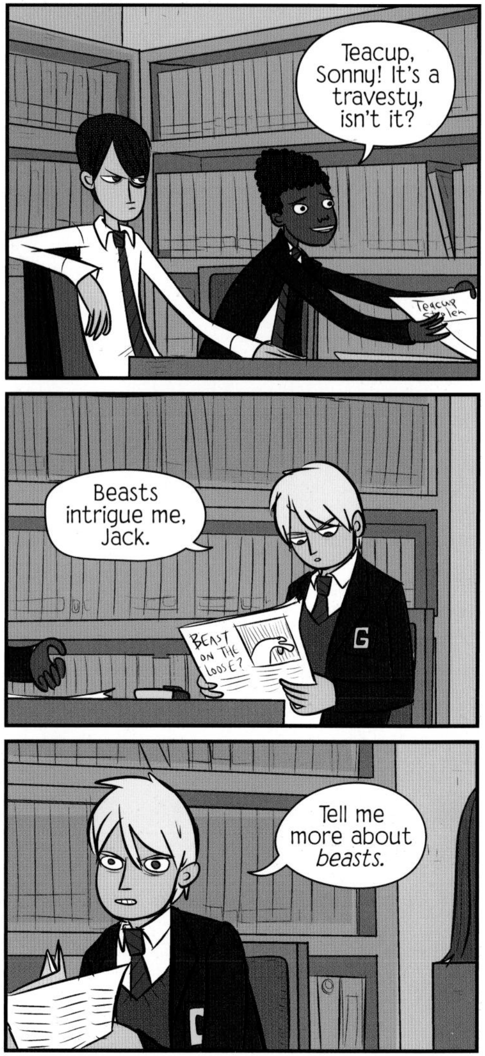
Teacup, Sonny! It's a travesty, isn't it?
Teacup stolen
Beasts intrigue me, Jack.
BEAST ON THE LOOSE?
Tell me more about beasts.

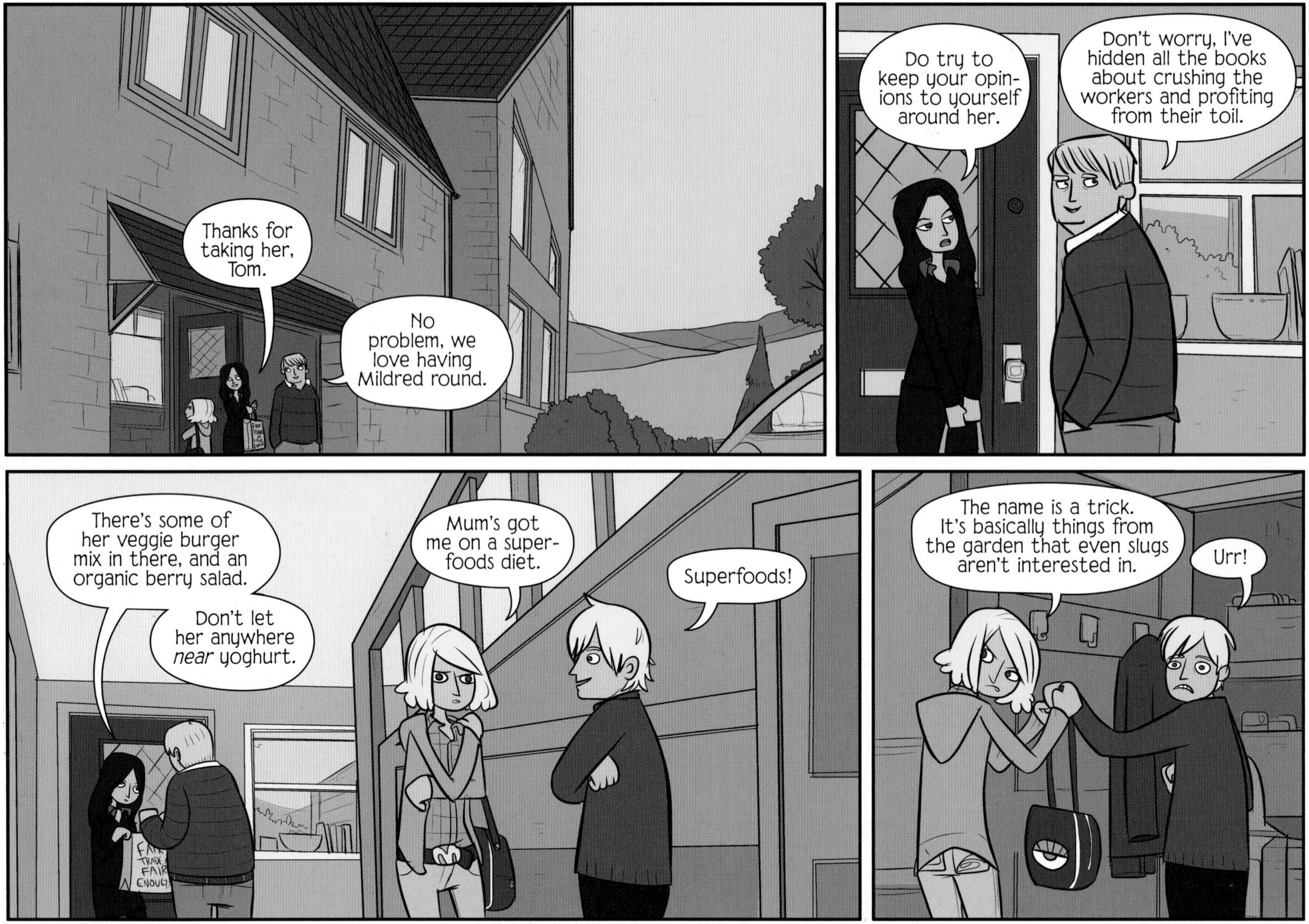
Thanks for taking her, Tom.
No problem, we love having Mildred round.
FAIR TRADE FAIR ENOUGH
Do try to keep your opinions to yourself around her.
Don't worry, I've hidden all the books about crushing the workers and profiting from their toil.
There's some of her veggie burger mix in there, and an organic berry salad.
Don't let her anywhere *near* yoghurt.
FAIR TRADE FAIR ENOUGH
Mum's got me on a superfoods diet.
Superfoods!
The name is a trick. It's basically things from the garden that even slugs aren't interested in.
Urr!

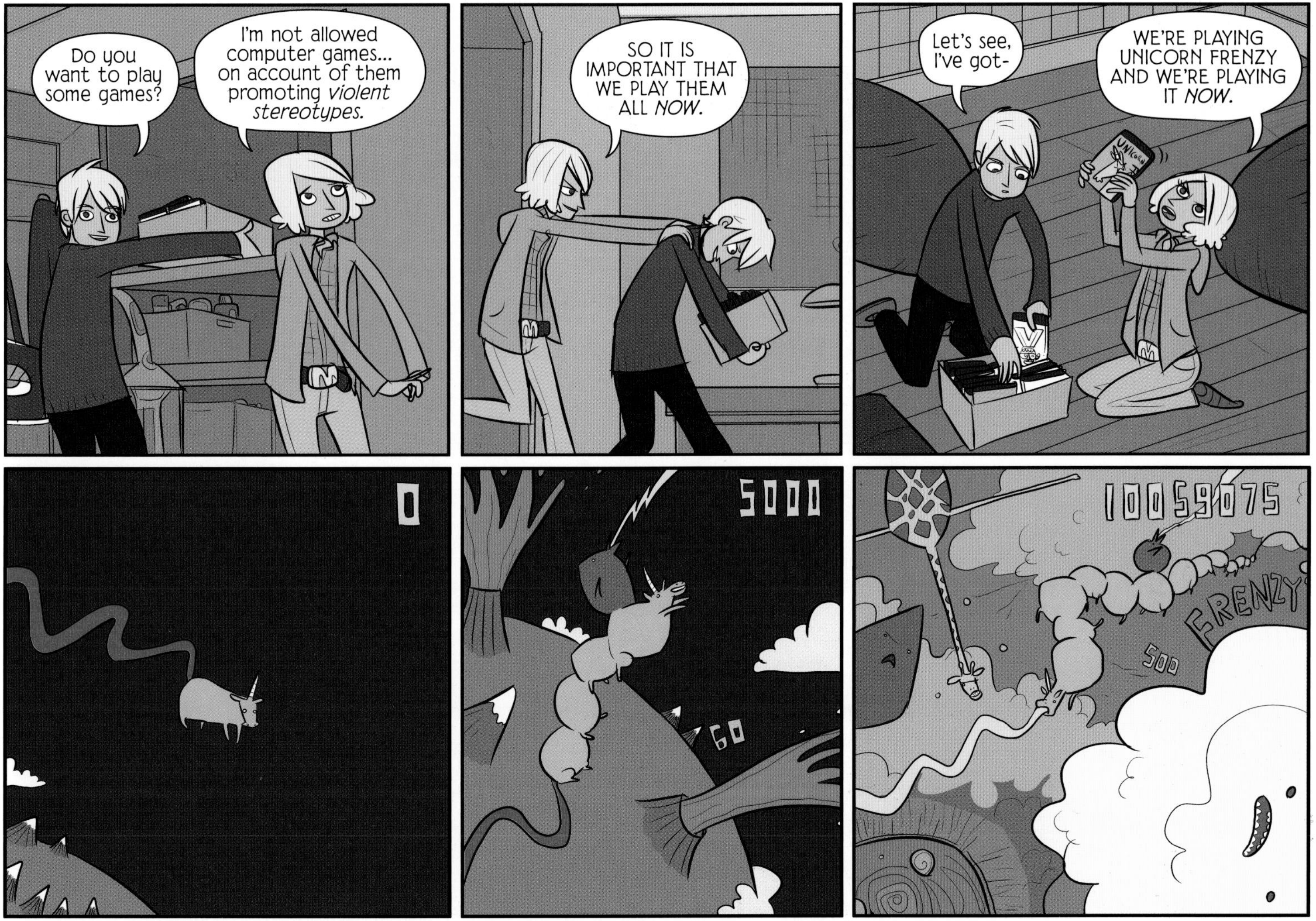
Do you want to play some games?
I'm not allowed computer games... on account of them promoting *violent stereotypes.*
SO IT IS IMPORTANT THAT WE PLAY THEM ALL *NOW.*
Let's see, I've got-
WE'RE PLAYING UNICORN FRENZY AND WE'RE PLAYING IT *NOW.*
0
5000
GO
10059075
FRENZY
500

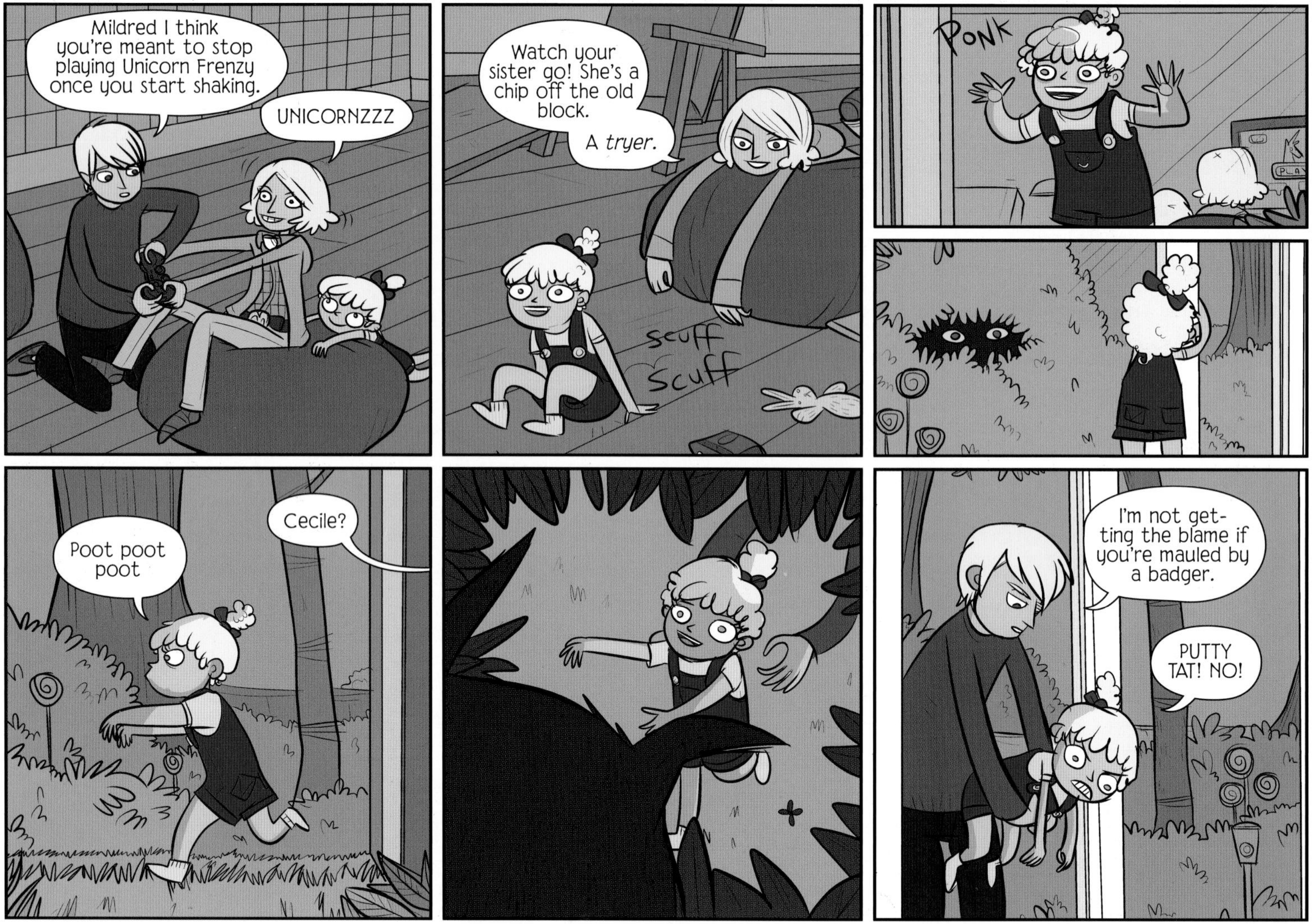
Mildred I think you're meant to stop playing Unicorn Frenzy once you start shaking.
UNICORNZZZ
Watch your sister go! She's a chip off the old block.
A *tryer.*
SCUFF
SCUFF
PONK
Cecile?
Poot poot poot
I'm not getting the blame if you're mauled by a badger.
PUTTY TAT! NO!

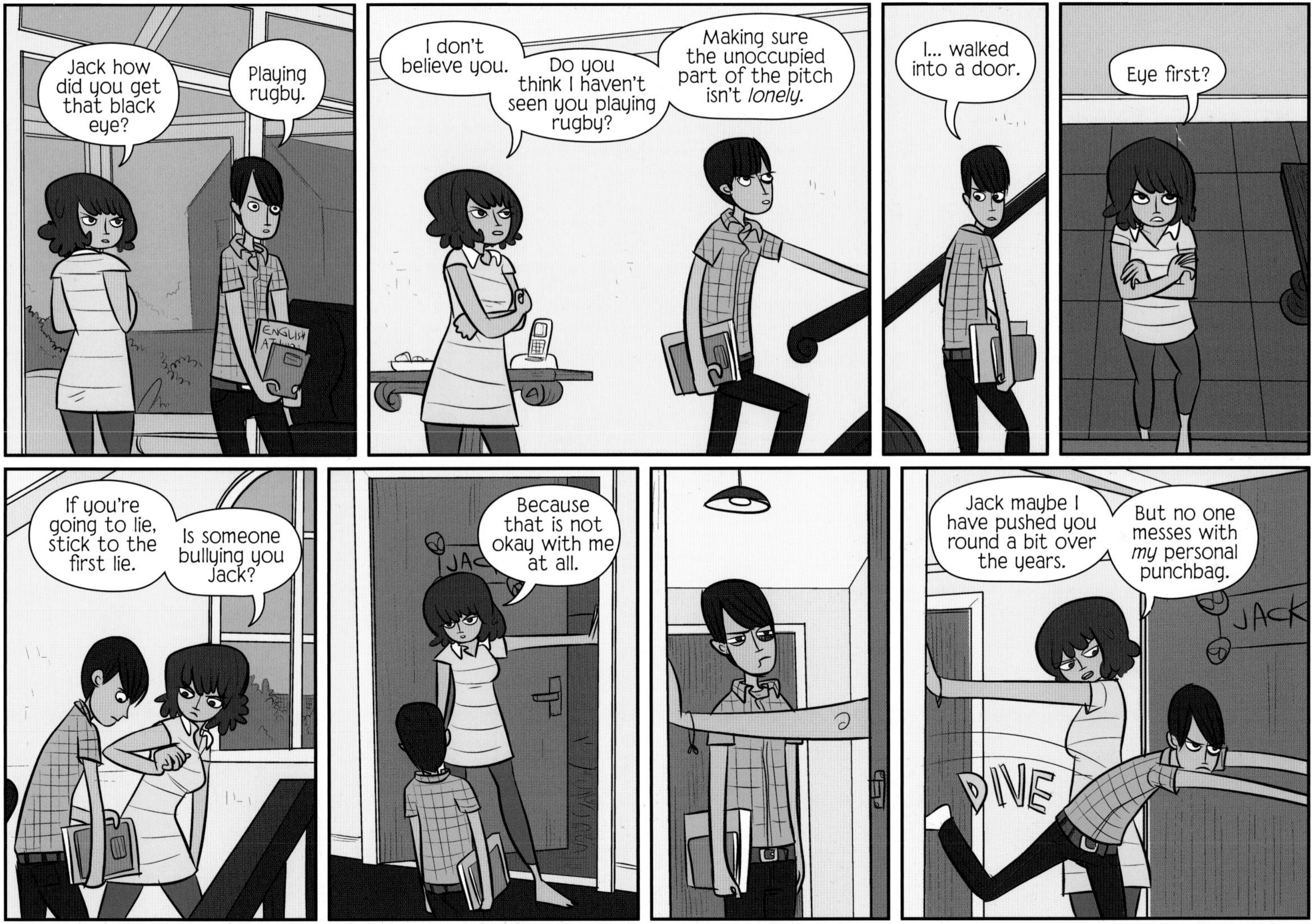

Jack how did you get that black eye?
Playing rugby.
ENGLISH
I don't believe you.
Do you think I haven't seen you playing rugby?
Making sure the unoccupied part of the pitch isn't *lonely*.
I... walked into a door.
Eye first?
If you're going to lie, stick to the first lie.
Is someone bullying you Jack?
Because that is not okay with me at all.
JACK
Jack maybe I have pushed you round a bit over the years.
But no one messes with *my* personal punchbag.
JACK
DIVE

Bad Machinery, Volume Two

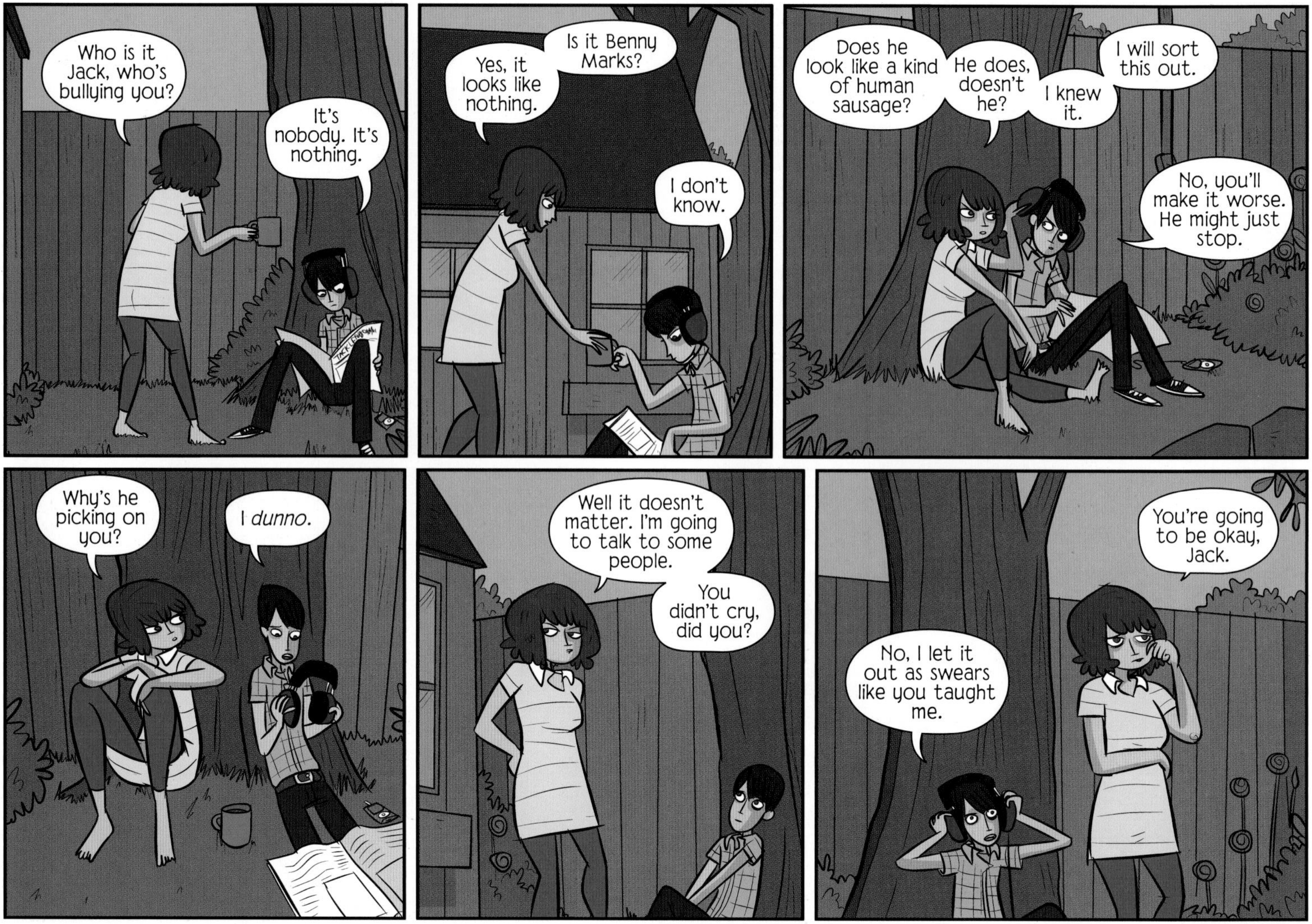
Who is it Jack, who's bullying you?
It's nobody. It's nothing.
Yes, it looks like nothing.
Is it Benny Marks?
I don't know.
Does he look like a kind of human sausage?
He does, doesn't he?
I knew it.
I will sort this out.
No, you'll make it worse. He might just stop.
Why's he picking on you?
I *dunno*.
Well it doesn't matter. I'm going to talk to some people.
You didn't cry, did you?
No, I let it out as swears like you taught me.
You're going to be okay, Jack.

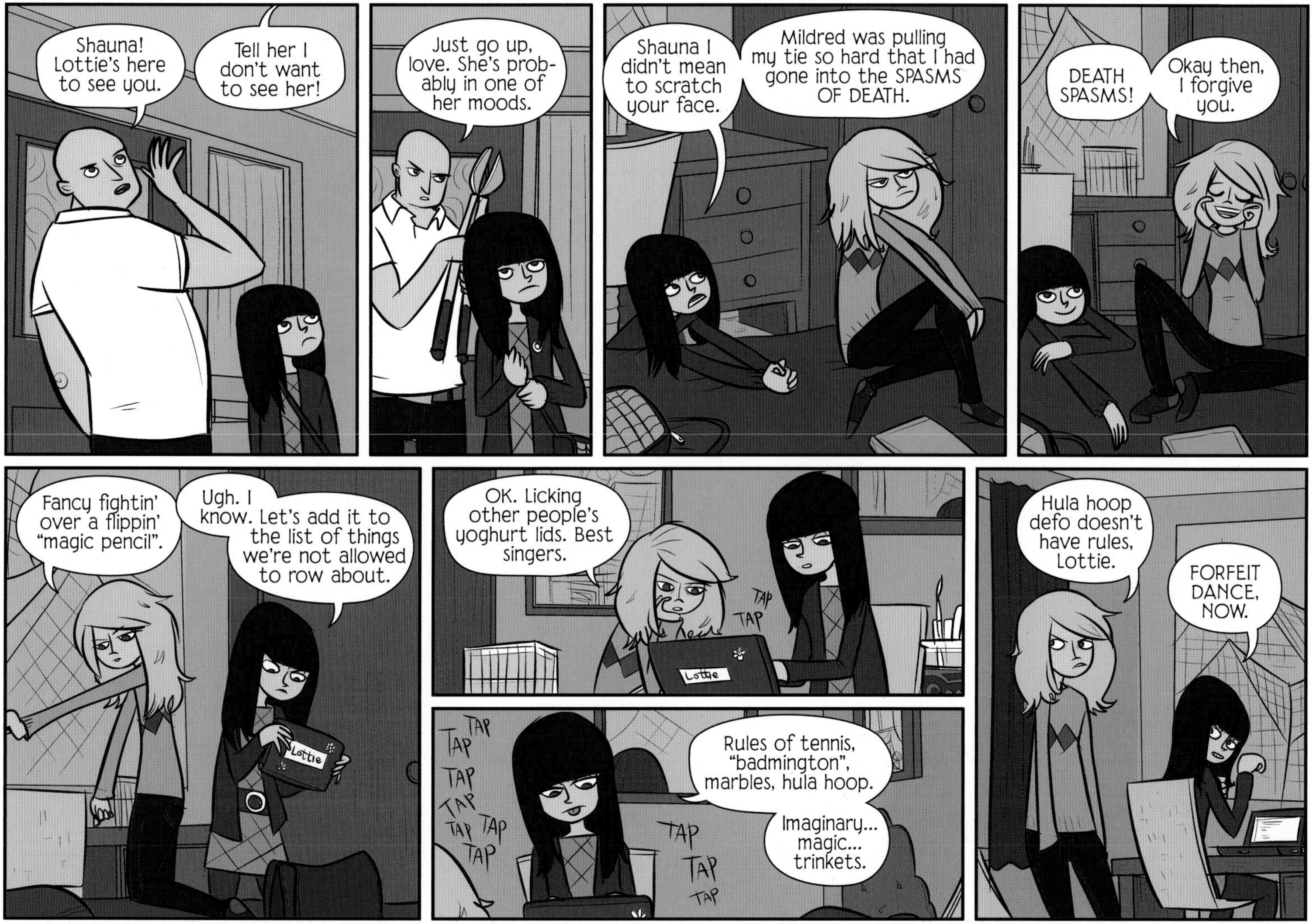
Shauna! Lottie's here to see you.
Tell her I don't want to see her!
Just go up, love. She's probably in one of her moods.
Shauna I didn't mean to scratch your face.
Mildred was pulling my tie so hard that I had gone into the SPASMS OF DEATH.
DEATH SPASMS!
Okay then, I forgive you.
Fancy fightin' over a flippin' "magic pencil".
Ugh. I know. Let's add it to the list of things we're not allowed to row about.
Lottie
OK. Licking other people's yoghurt lids. Best singers.
TAP TAP
Lottie
TAP TAP TAP TAP TAP TAP TAP
Rules of tennis, "badmington", marbles, hula hoop.
Imaginary... magic... trinkets.
TAP TAP TAP
Hula hoop defo doesn't have rules, Lottie.
FORFEIT DANCE, NOW.

Bad Machinery, Volume Two

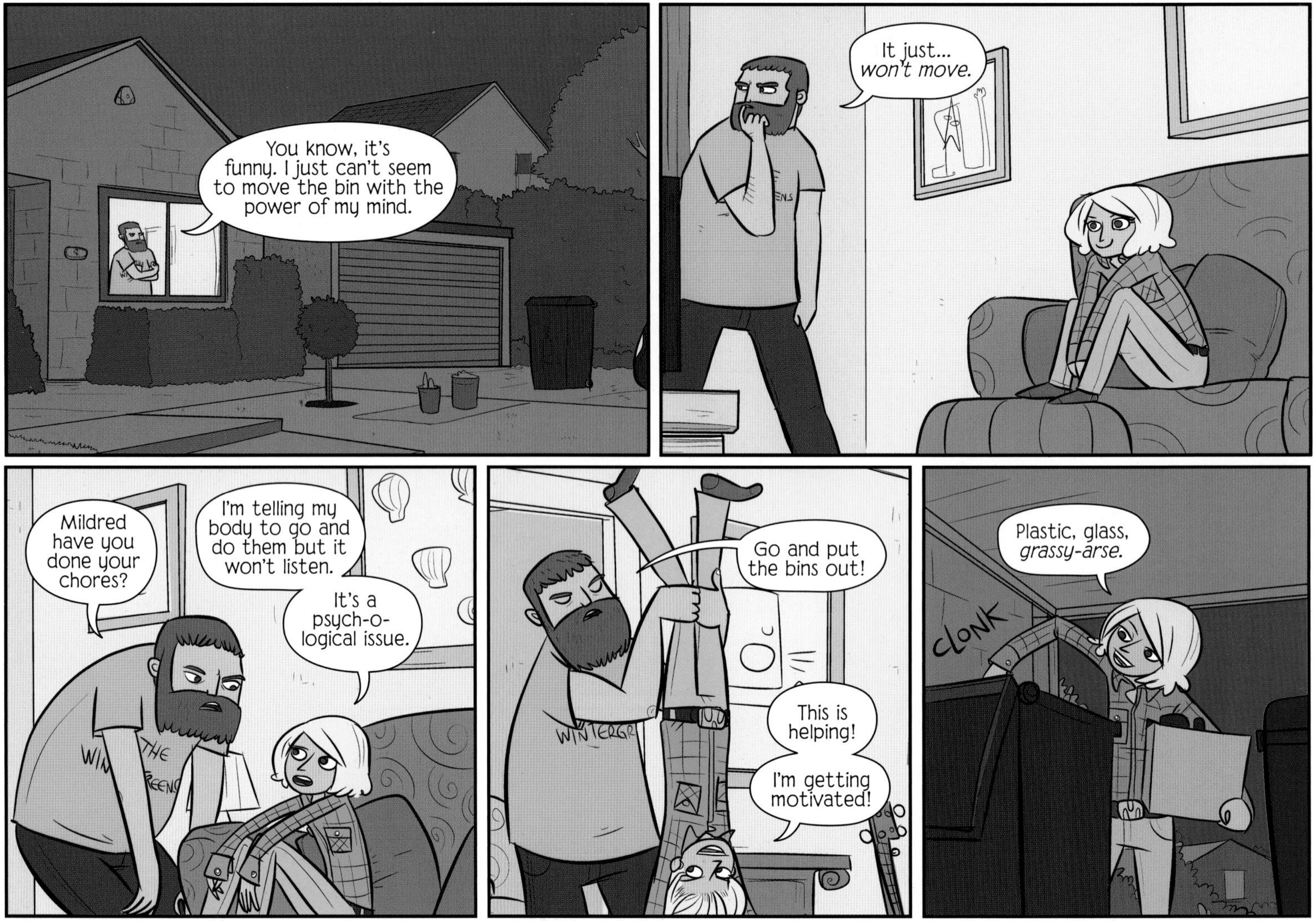
You know, it's funny. I just can't seem to move the bin with the power of my mind.
It just... *won't move.*
Mildred have you done your chores?
I'm telling my body to go and do them but it won't listen.
It's a psych-o-logical issue.
Go and put the bins out!
This is helping!
I'm getting motivated!
CLONK
Plastic, glass, *grassy-arse.*

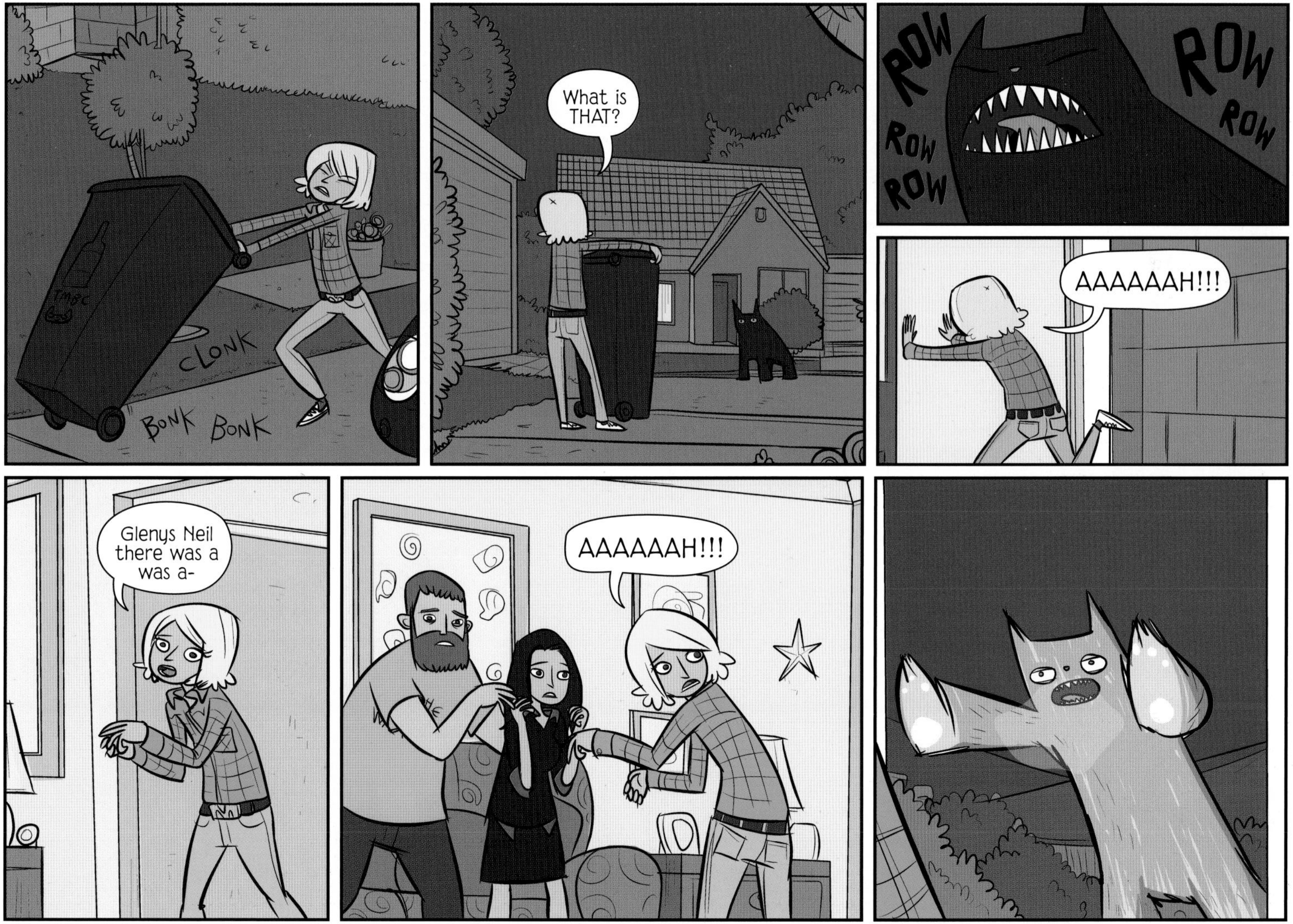
CLONK
BONK BONK
What is THAT?
ROW
ROW
ROW
ROW
ROW
ROW
AAAAAAH!!!
Glenys Neil there was a was a-
AAAAAAH!!!

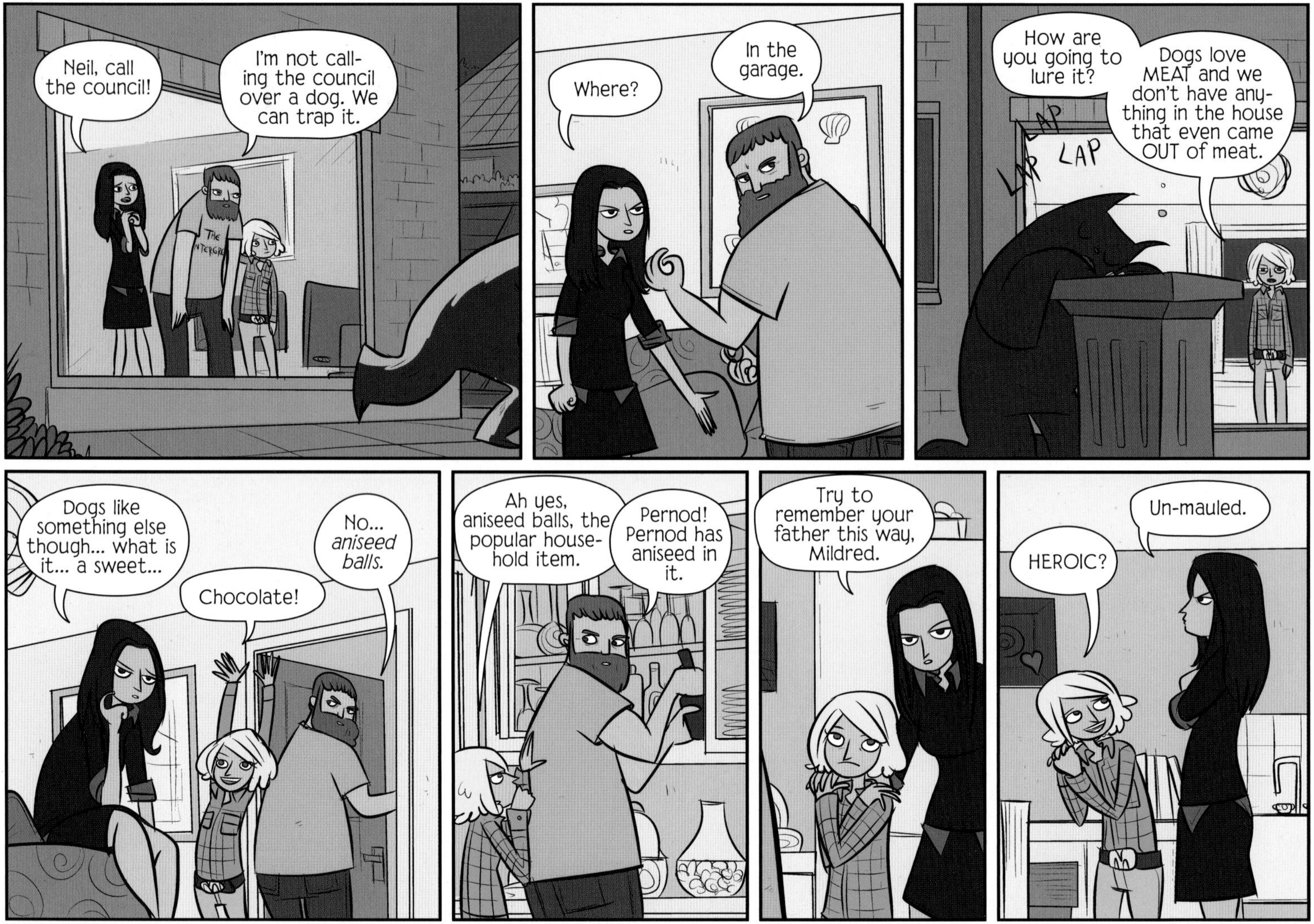
Neil, call the council!
I'm not calling the council over a dog. We can trap it.
Where?
In the garage.
How are you going to lure it?
LAP LAP LAP
Dogs love MEAT and we don't have anything in the house that even came OUT of meat.
Dogs like something else though... what is it... a sweet...
Chocolate!
No... *aniseed balls.*
Ah yes, aniseed balls, the popular household item.
Pernod! Pernod has aniseed in it.
Try to remember your father this way, Mildred.
HEROIC?
Un-mauled.

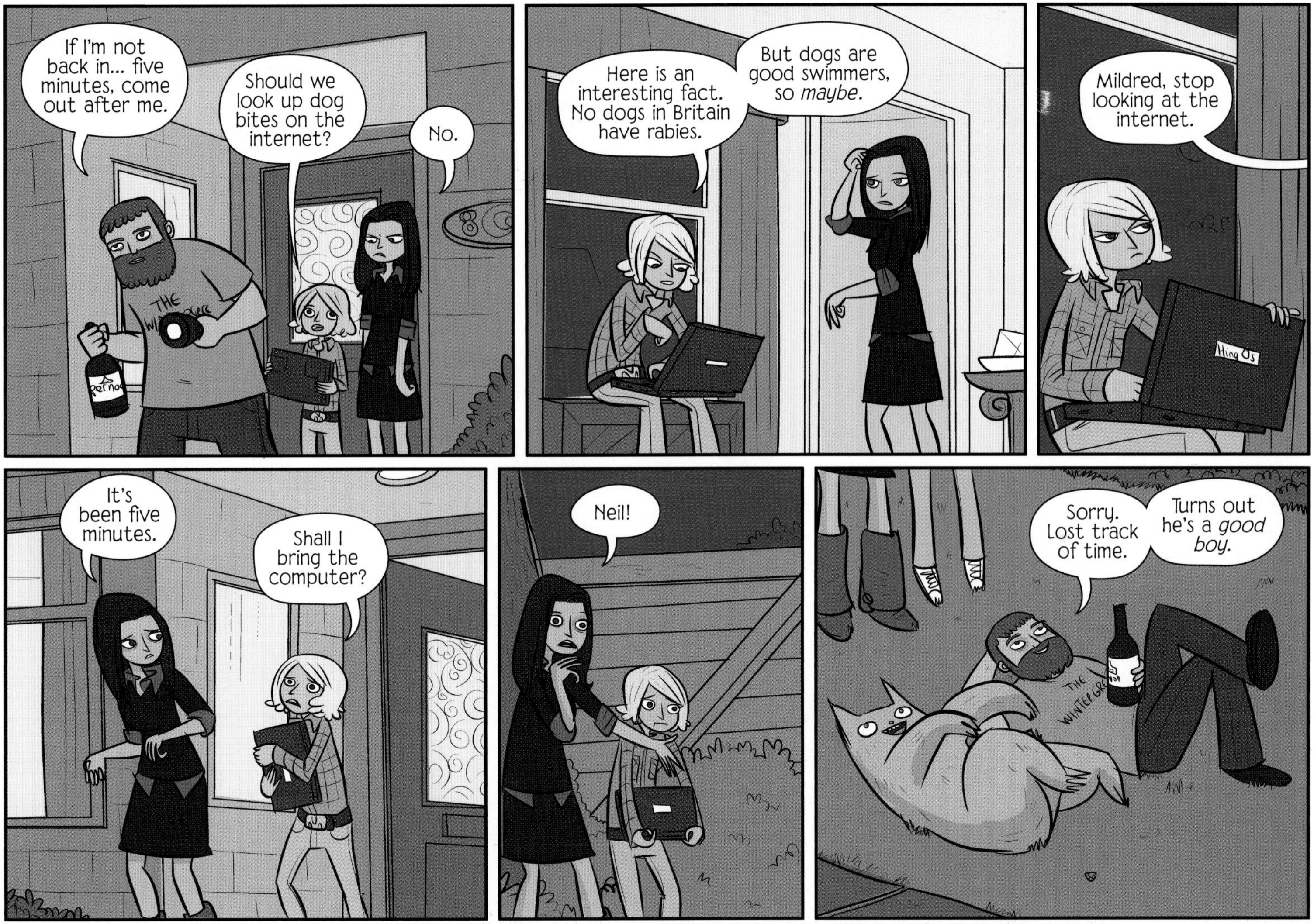

If I'm not back in... five minutes, come out after me.
Should we look up dog bites on the internet?
No.
Here is an interesting fact. No dogs in Britain have rabies.
But dogs are good swimmers, so *maybe*.
Mildred, stop looking at the internet.
It's been five minutes.
Shall I bring the computer?
Neil!
Sorry. Lost track of time.
Turns out he's a *good boy*.

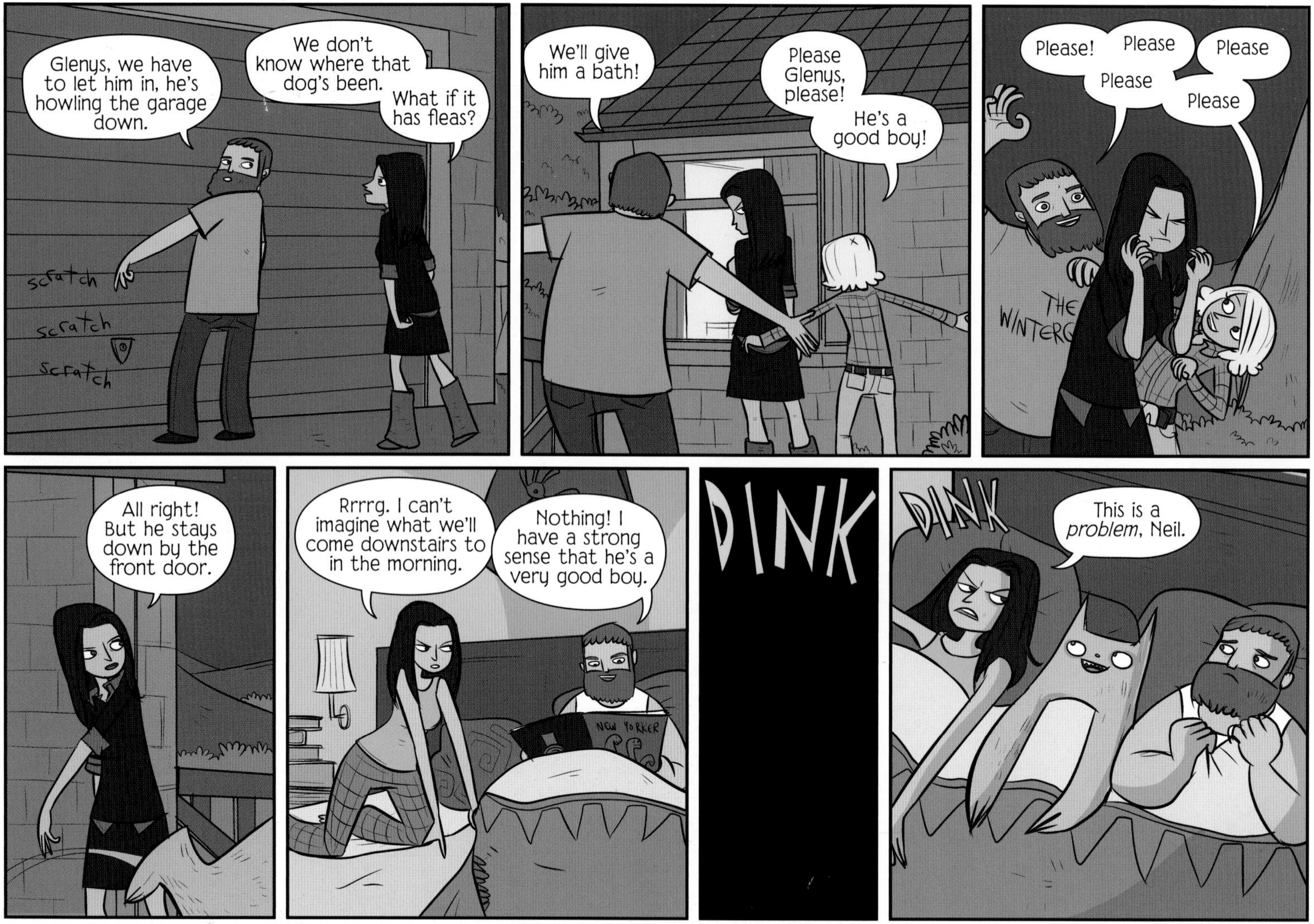
Glenys, we have to let him in, he's howling the garage down.
We don't know where that dog's been.
What if it has fleas?
scratch
scratch
scratch
We'll give him a bath!
Please Glenys, please!
He's a good boy!
Please!
Please
Please
Please
Please
All right! But he stays down by the front door.
Rrrrg. I can't imagine what we'll come downstairs to in the morning.
Nothing! I have a strong sense that he's a very good boy.
NEW YORKER
DINK
DINK
This is a *problem*, Neil.

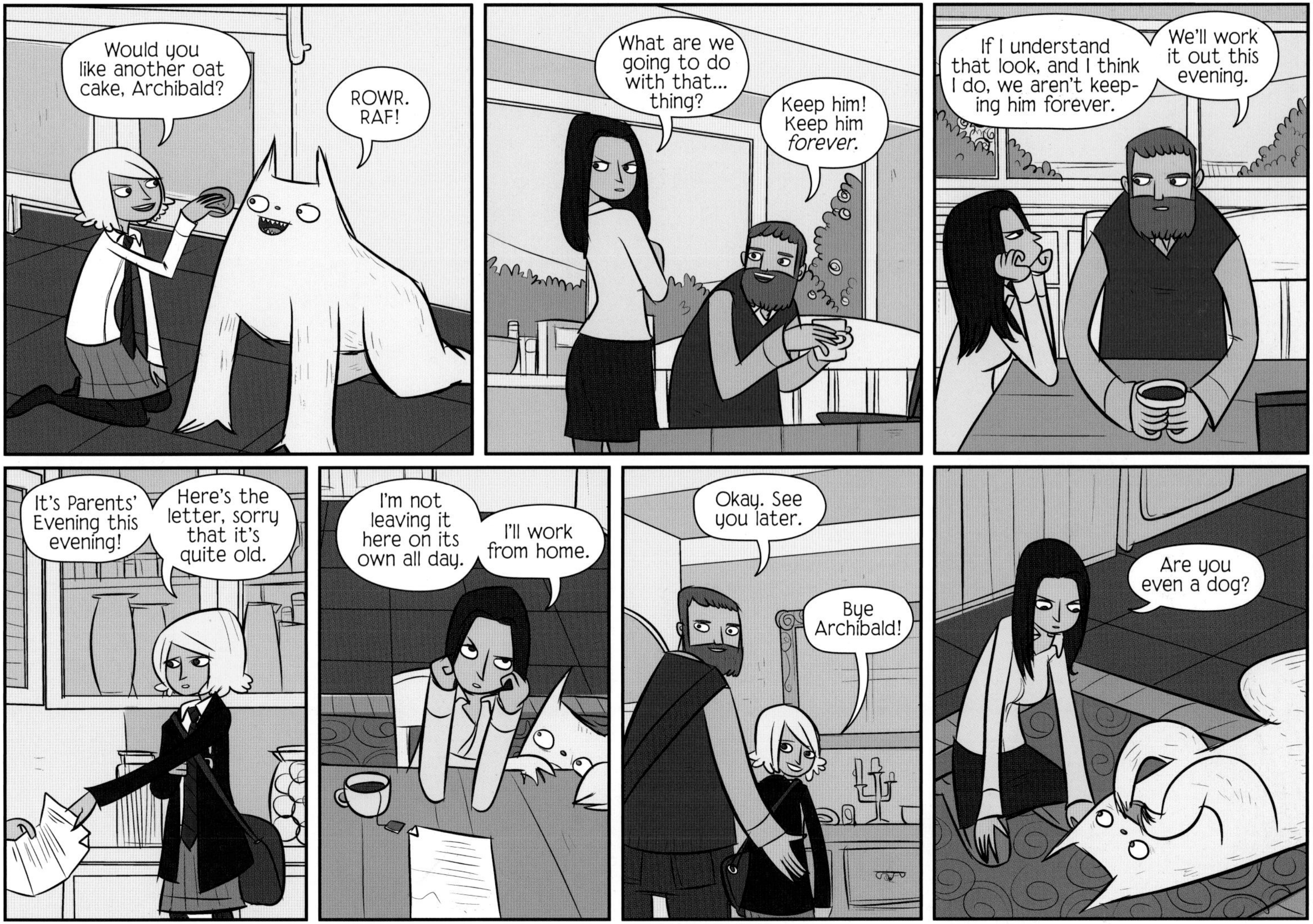
Would you like another oat cake, Archibald?
ROWR. RAF!
What are we going to do with that... thing?
Keep him! Keep him *forever.*
If I understand that look, and I think I do, we aren't keep-ing him forever.
We'll work it out this evening.
It's Parents' Evening this evening!
Here's the letter, sorry that it's quite old.
I'm not leaving it here on its own all day.
I'll work from home.
Okay. See you later.
Bye Archibald!
Are you even a dog?

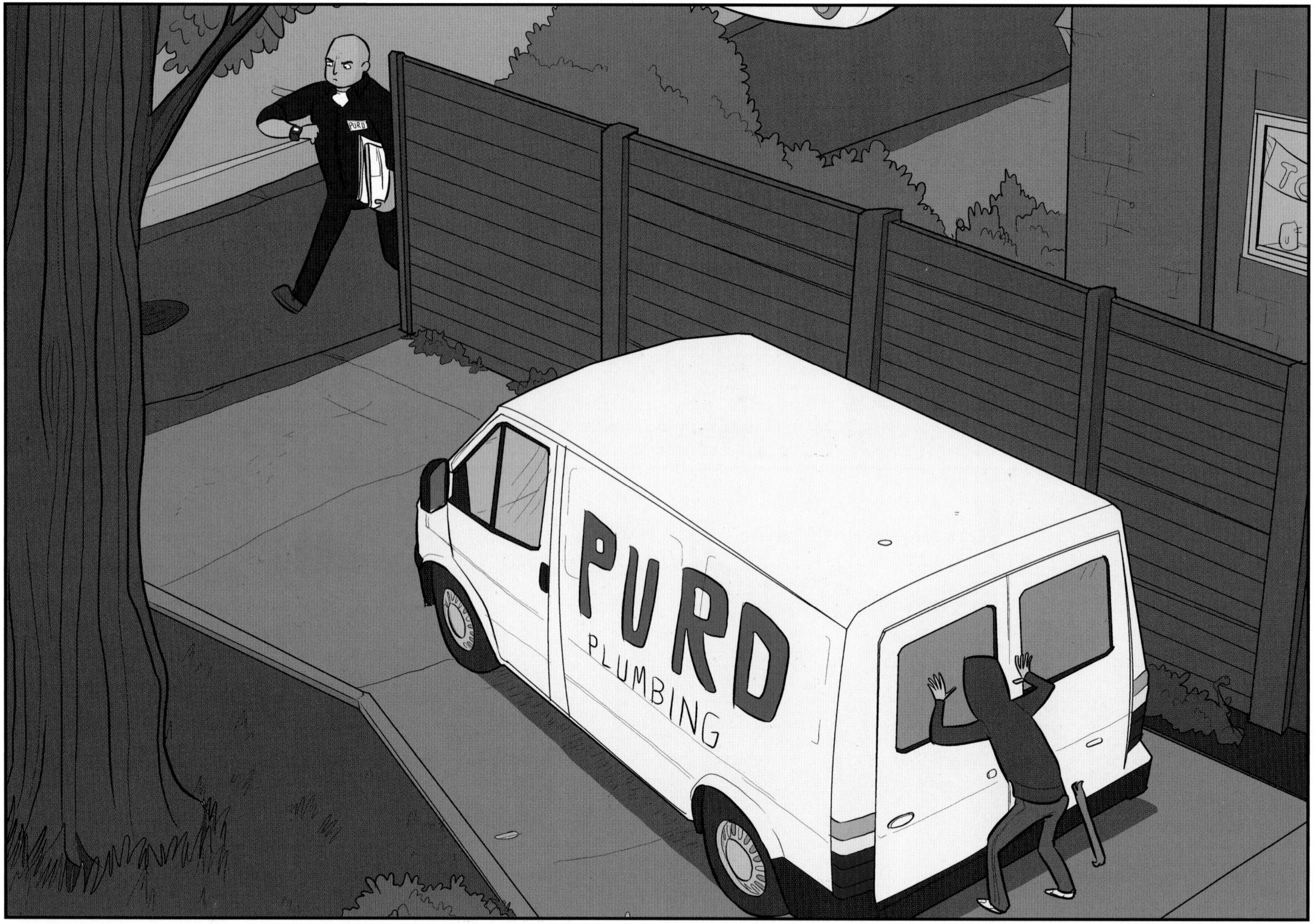
PURD
PURD
PLUMBING

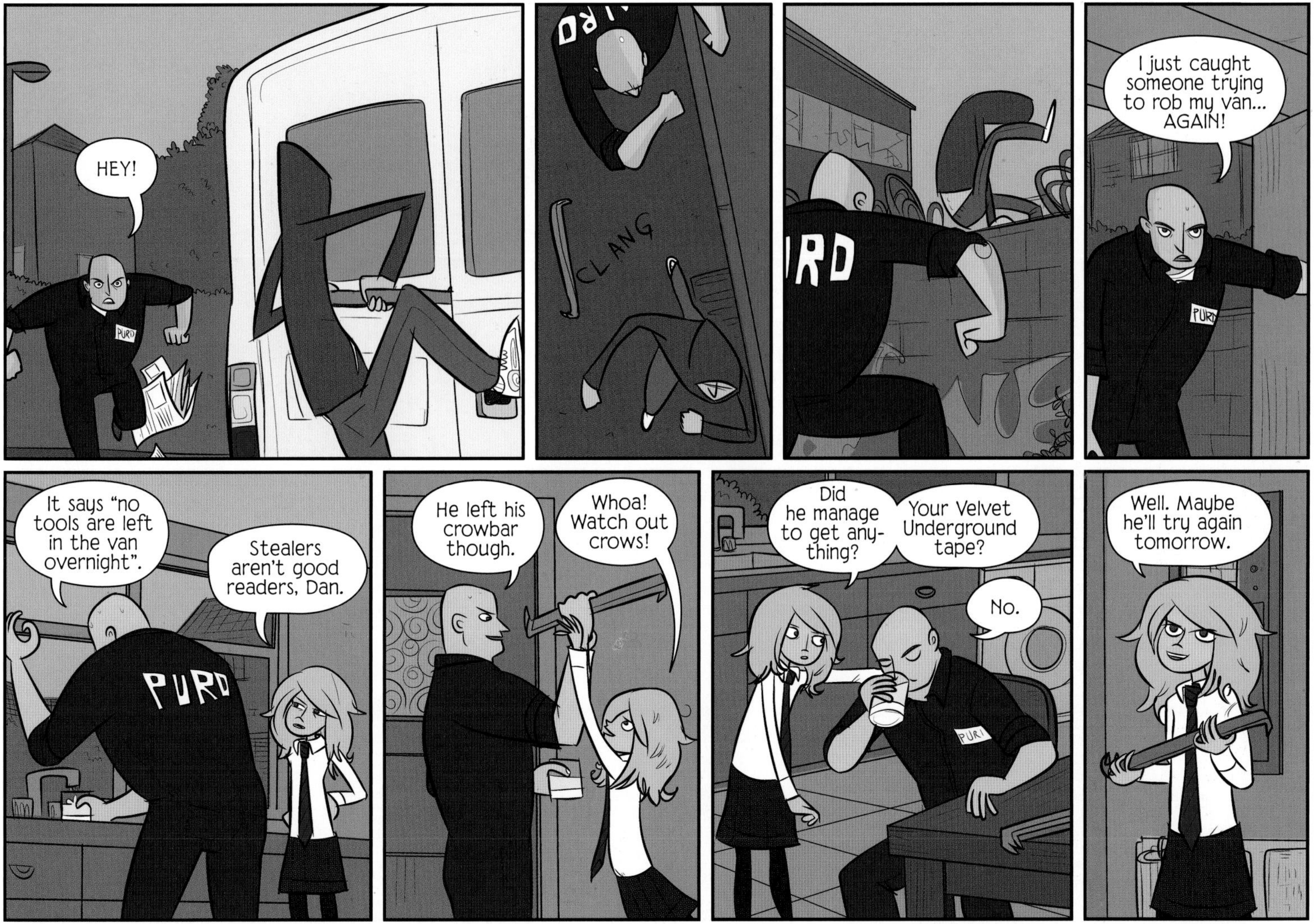
HEY!
CLANG
I just caught someone trying to rob my van... AGAIN!
It says "no tools are left in the van overnight".
Stealers aren't good readers, Dan.
He left his crowbar though.
Whoa! Watch out crows!
Did he manage to get any-thing?
Your Velvet Underground tape?
No.
Well. Maybe he'll try again tomorrow.

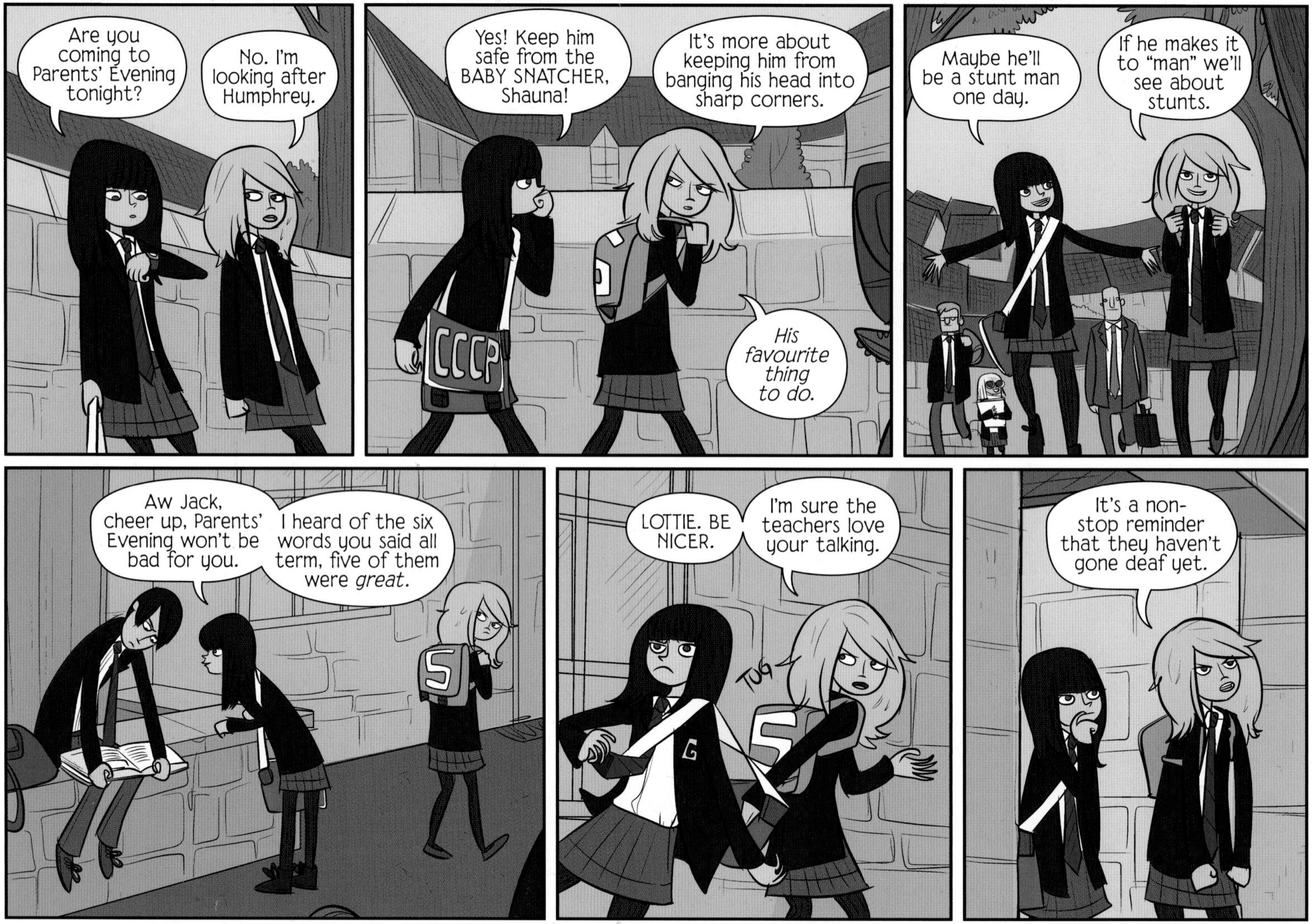

Are you coming to Parents' Evening tonight?
No. I'm looking after Humphrey.
Yes! Keep him safe from the BABY SNATCHER, Shauna!
It's more about keeping him from banging his head into sharp corners.
His favourite thing to do.
Maybe he'll be a stunt man one day.
If he makes it to "man" we'll see about stunts.
Aw Jack, cheer up, Parents' Evening won't be bad for you.
I heard of the six words you said all term, five of them were *great*.
LOTTIE. BE NICER.
I'm sure the teachers love your talking.
TUG
It's a non-stop reminder that they haven't gone deaf yet.

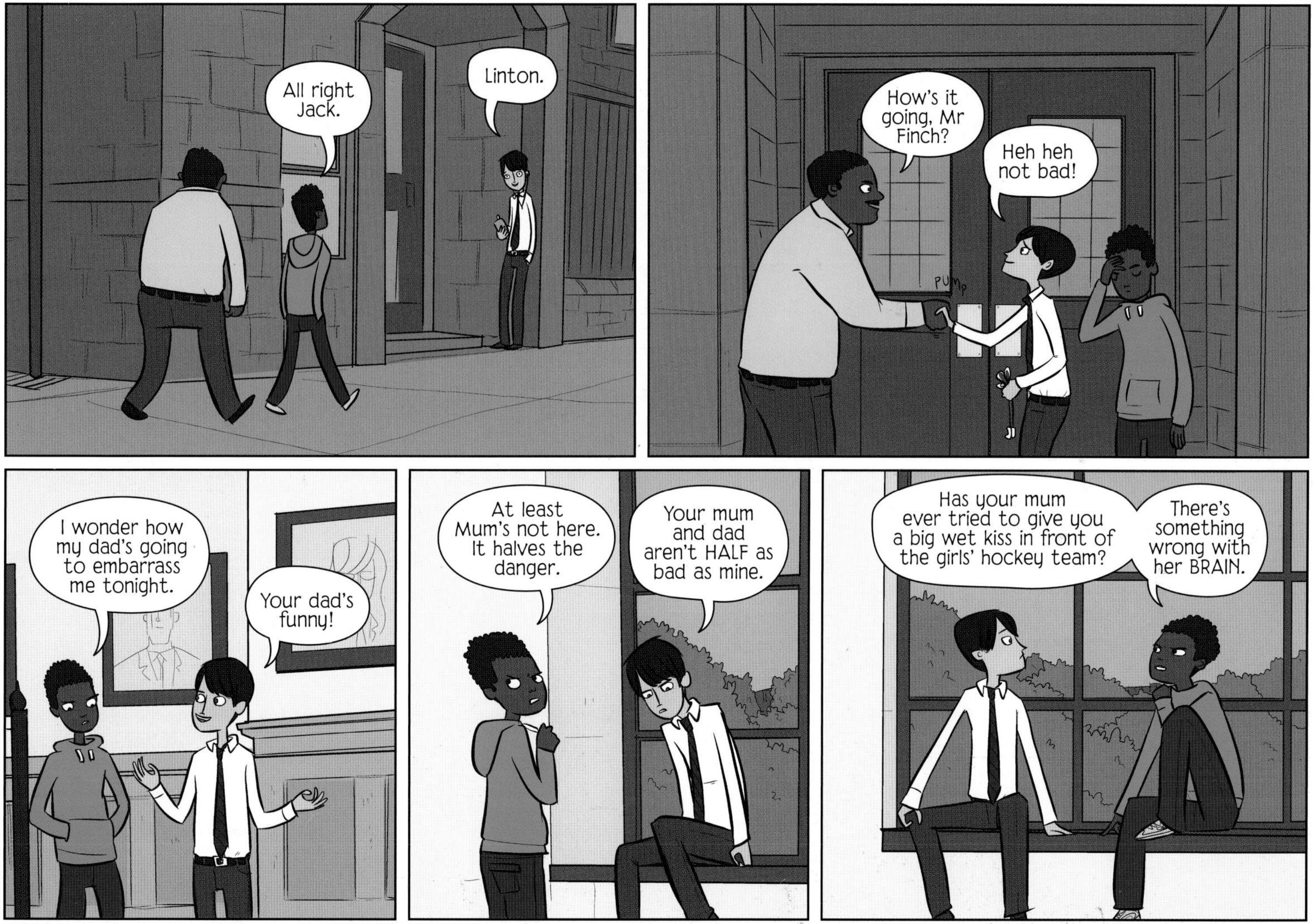
All right Jack.
Linton.
How's it going, Mr Finch?
Heh heh not bad!
PUMp
I wonder how my dad's going to embarrass me tonight.
Your dad's funny!
At least Mum's not here. It halves the danger.
Your mum and dad aren't HALF as bad as mine.
Has your mum ever tried to give you a big wet kiss in front of the girls' hockey team?
There's something wrong with her BRAIN.

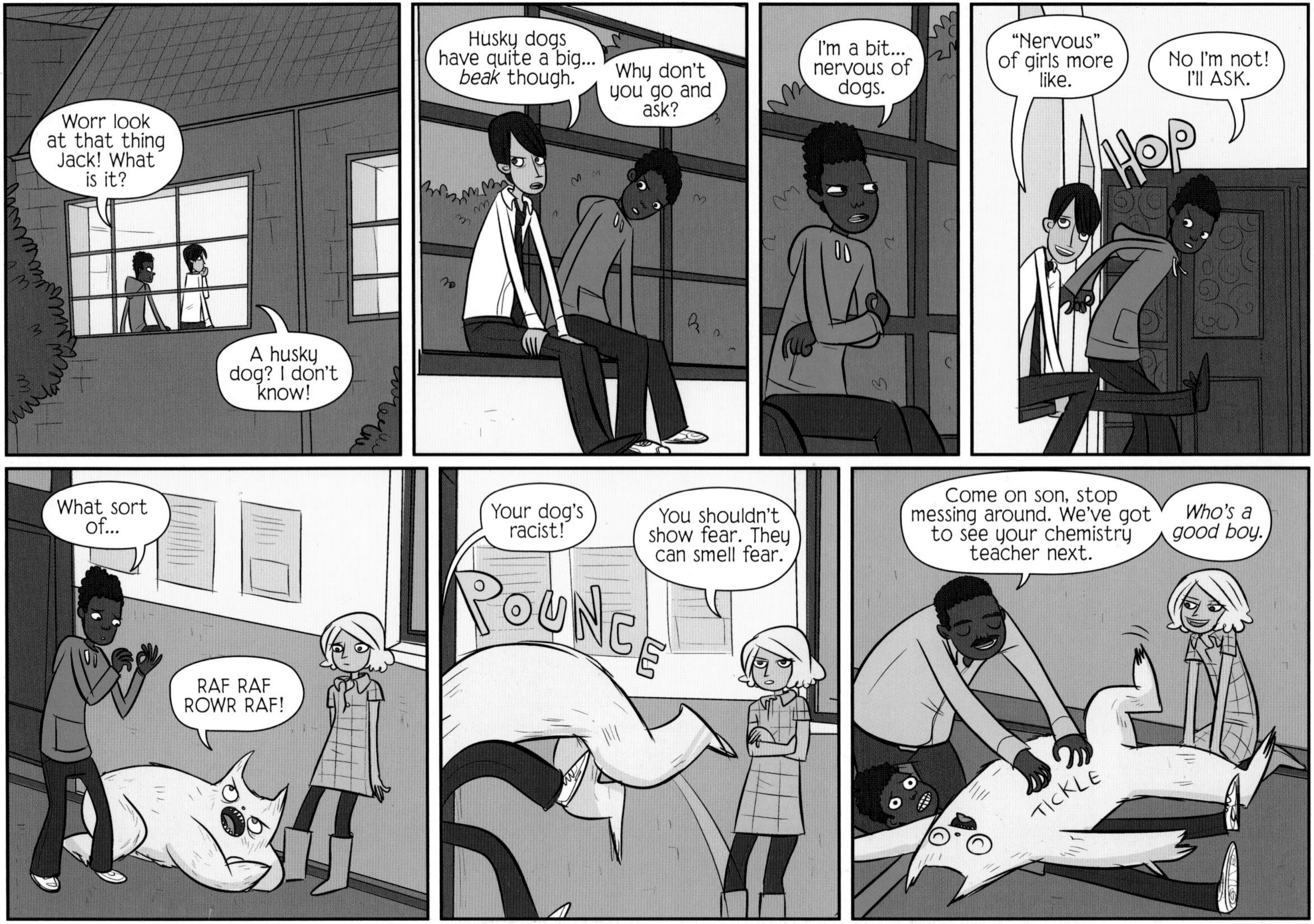
Worr look at that thing Jack! What is it?
A husky dog? I don't know!
Husky dogs have quite a big... *beak* though.
Why don't you go and ask?
I'm a bit... nervous of dogs.
"Nervous" of girls more like.
No I'm not! I'll ASK.
HOP
What sort of...
RAF RAF ROWR RAF!
Your dog's racist!
POUNCE
You shouldn't show fear. They can smell fear.
Come on son, stop messing around. We've got to see your chemistry teacher next.
Who's a good boy.
TICKLE

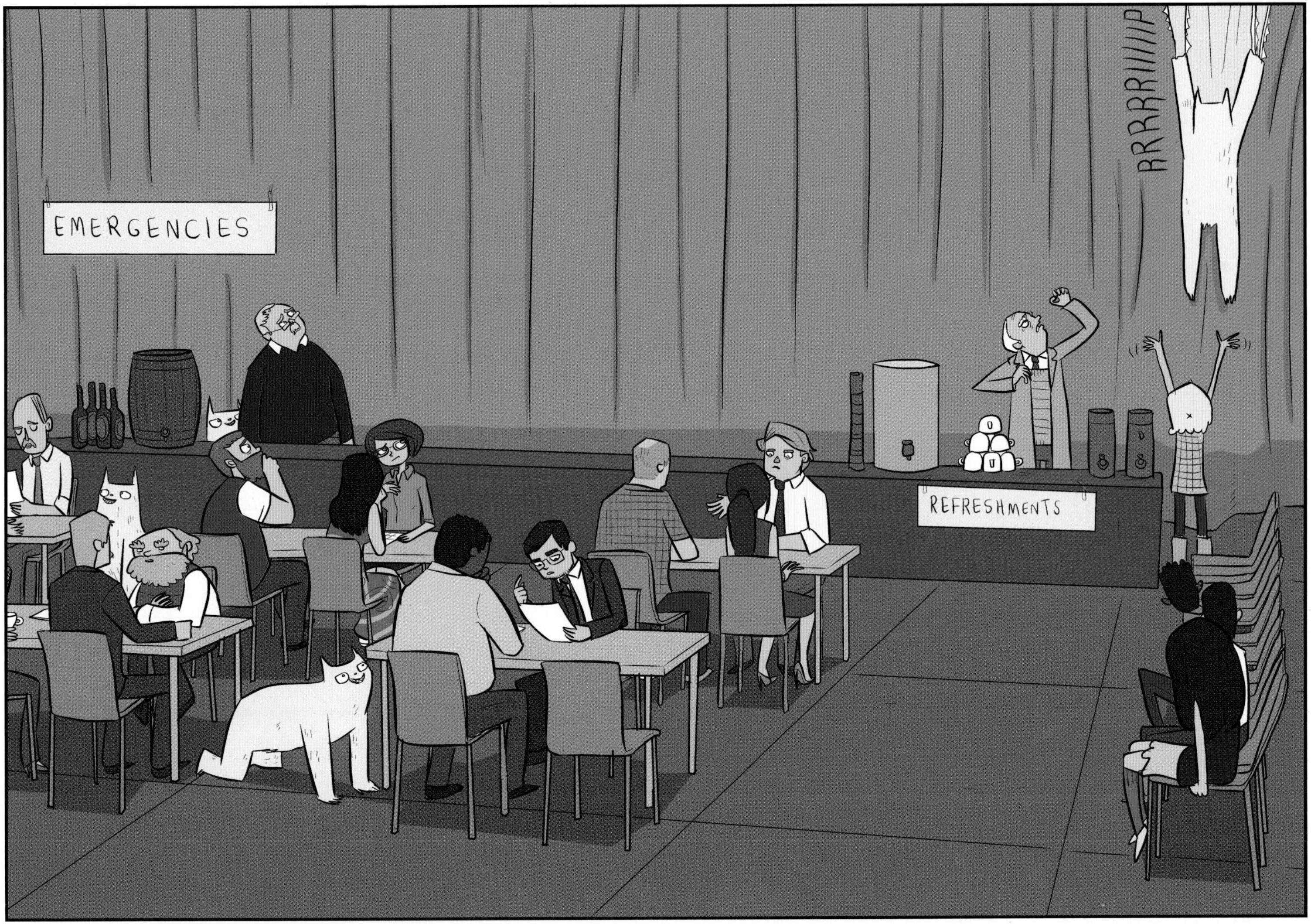
EMERGENCIES
REFRESHMENTS
BRRRRRIIIIIIIIP

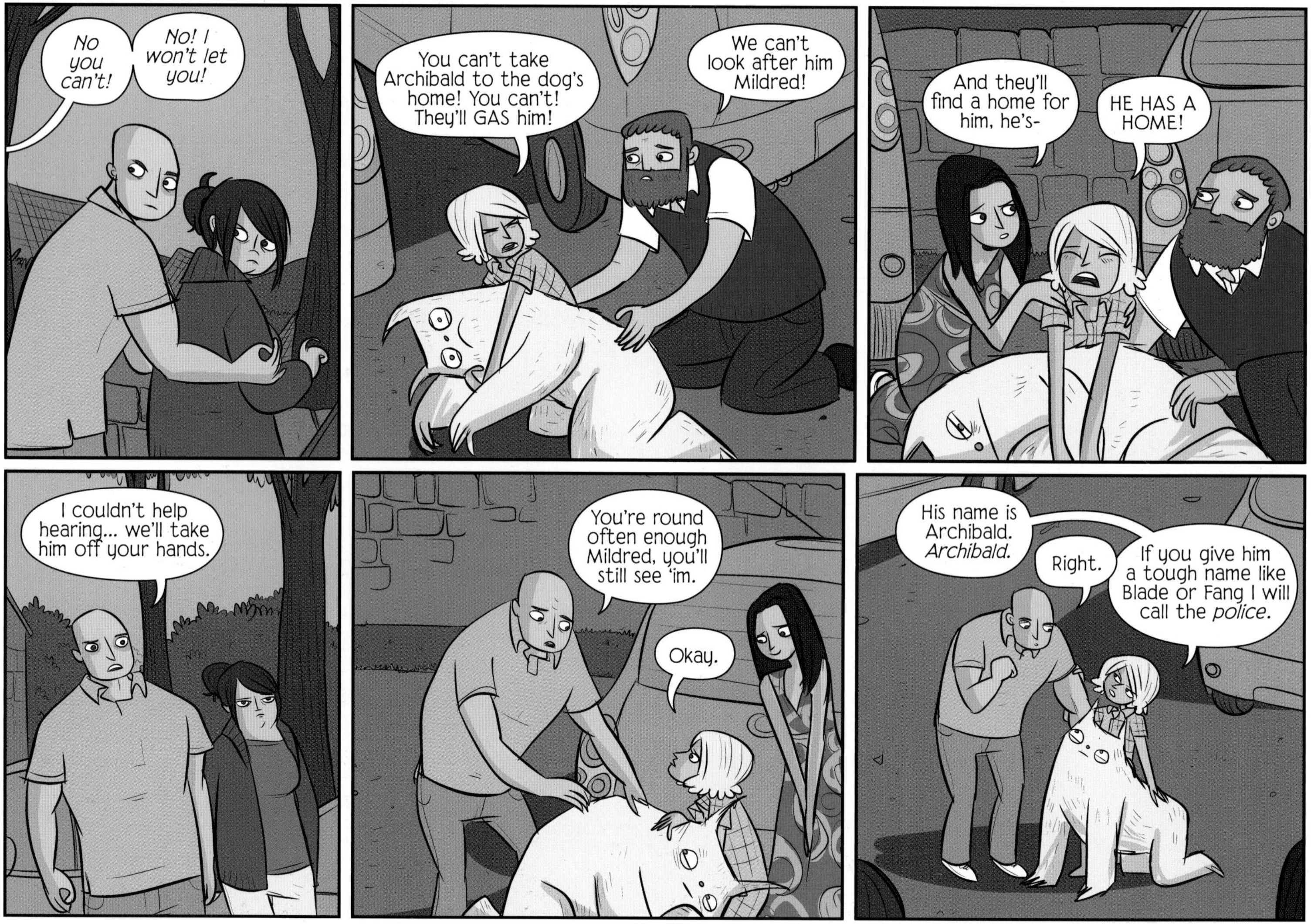
No you can't!
No! I won't let you!
You can't take Archibald to the dog's home! You can't! They'll GAS him!
We can't look after him Mildred!
And they'll find a home for him, he's-
HE HAS A HOME!
I couldn't help hearing... we'll take him off your hands.
You're round often enough Mildred, you'll still see 'im.
Okay.
His name is Archibald. *Archibald.*
Right.
If you give him a tough name like Blade or Fang I will call the *police*.

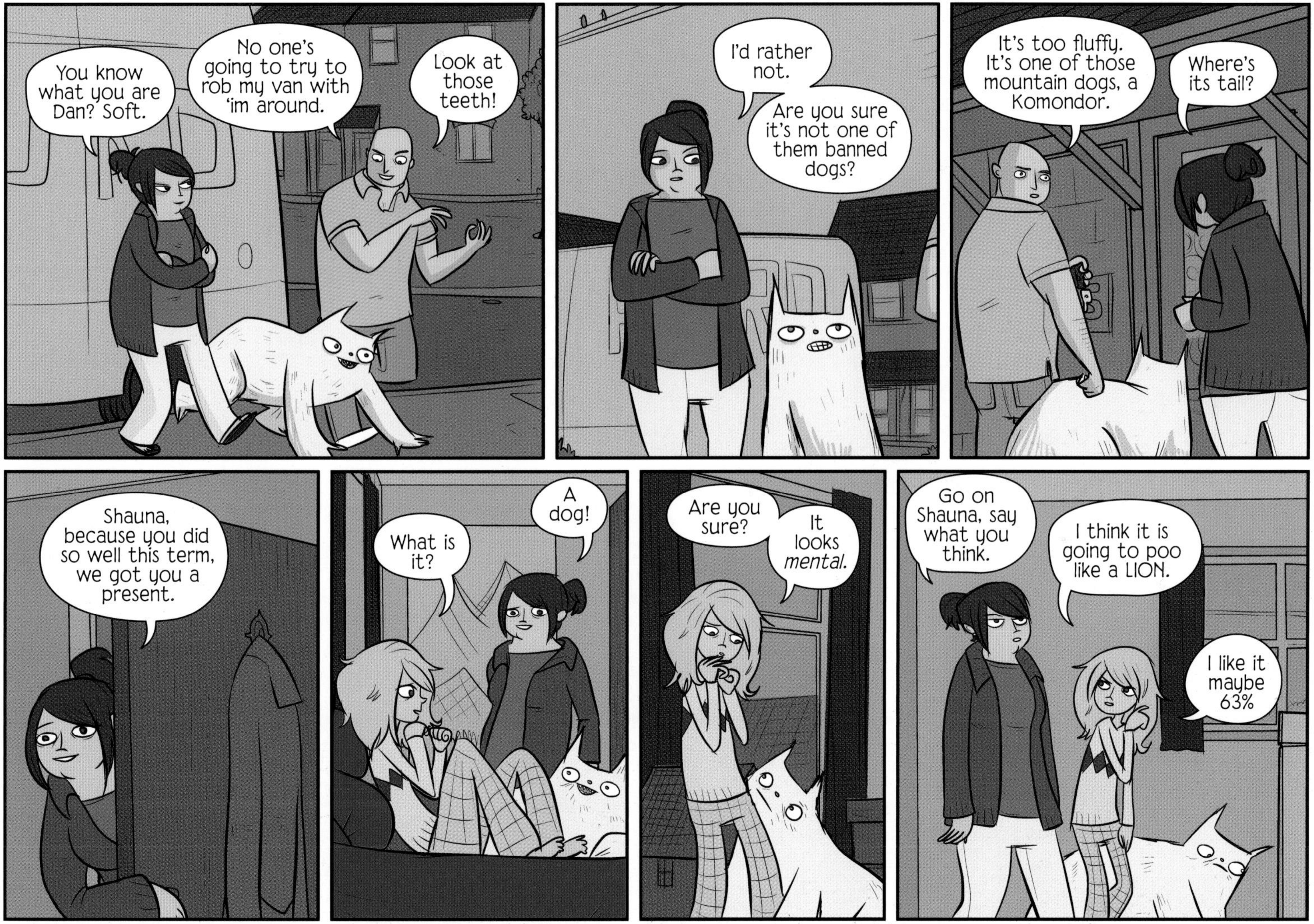
You know what you are Dan? Soft.
No one's going to try to rob my van with 'im around.
Look at those teeth!
I'd rather not.
Are you sure it's not one of them banned dogs?
It's too fluffy. It's one of those mountain dogs, a Komondor.
Where's its tail?
Shauna, because you did so well this term, we got you a present.
What is it?
A dog!
Are you sure?
It looks *mental.*
Go on Shauna, say what you think.
I think it is going to poo like a LION.
I like it maybe 63%

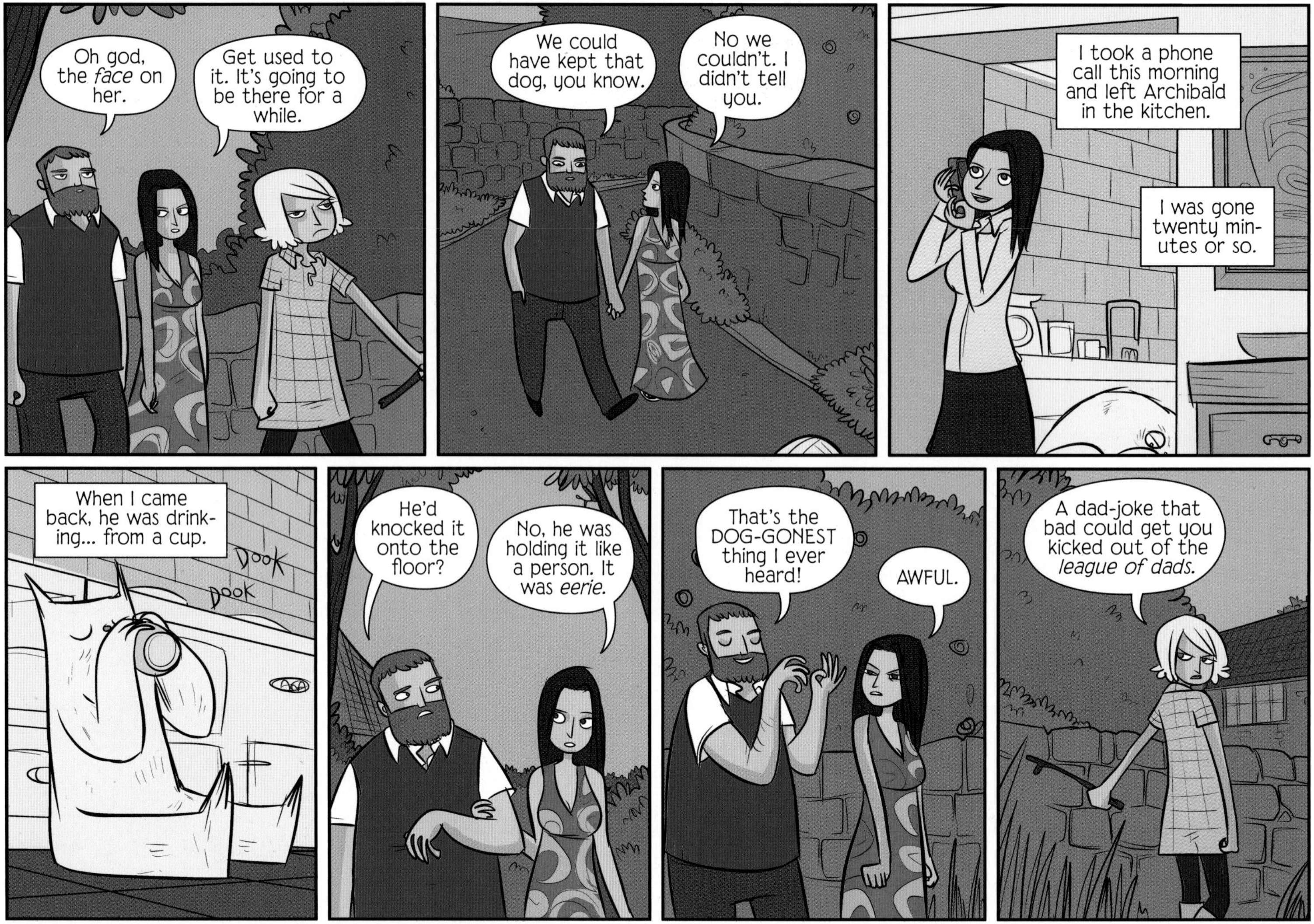
Oh god, the *face* on her.
Get used to it. It's going to be there for a while.
We could have kept that dog, you know.
No we couldn't. I didn't tell you.
I took a phone call this morning and left Archibald in the kitchen.
I was gone twenty minutes or so.
When I came back, he was drinking... from a cup.
DOOK
DOOK
He'd knocked it onto the floor?
No, he was holding it like a person. It was *eerie.*
That's the DOG-GONEST thing I ever heard!
AWFUL.
A dad-joke that bad could get you kicked out of the *league of dads.*

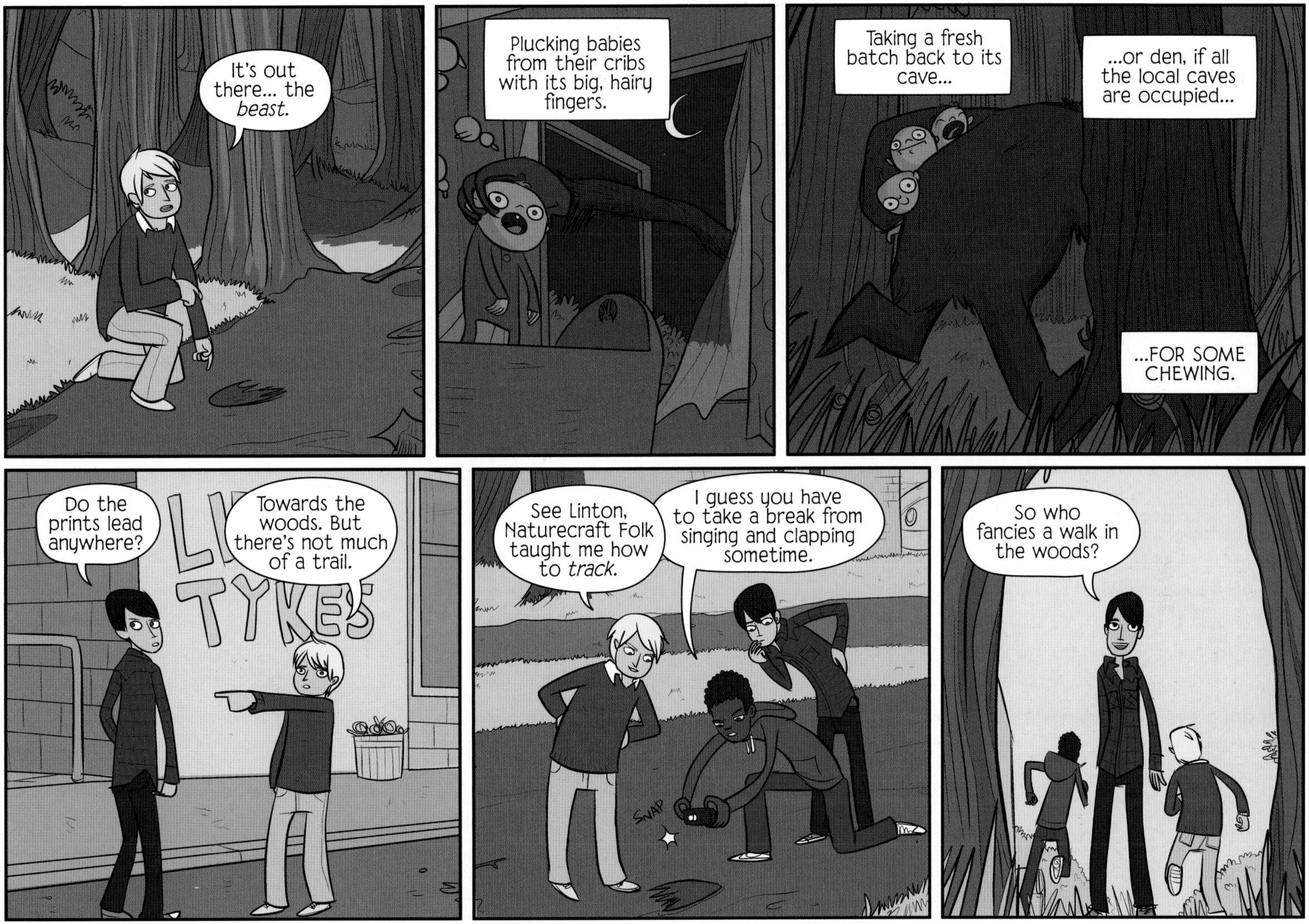
It's out there... the *beast.*
Plucking babies from their cribs with its big, hairy fingers.
Taking a fresh batch back to its cave...
...or den, if all the local caves are occupied...
...FOR SOME CHEWING.
Do the prints lead anywhere?
LI
TYKES
Towards the woods. But there's not much of a trail.
See Linton, Naturecraft Folk taught me how to *track.*
I guess you have to take a break from singing and clapping sometime.
SNAP
So who fancies a walk in the woods?

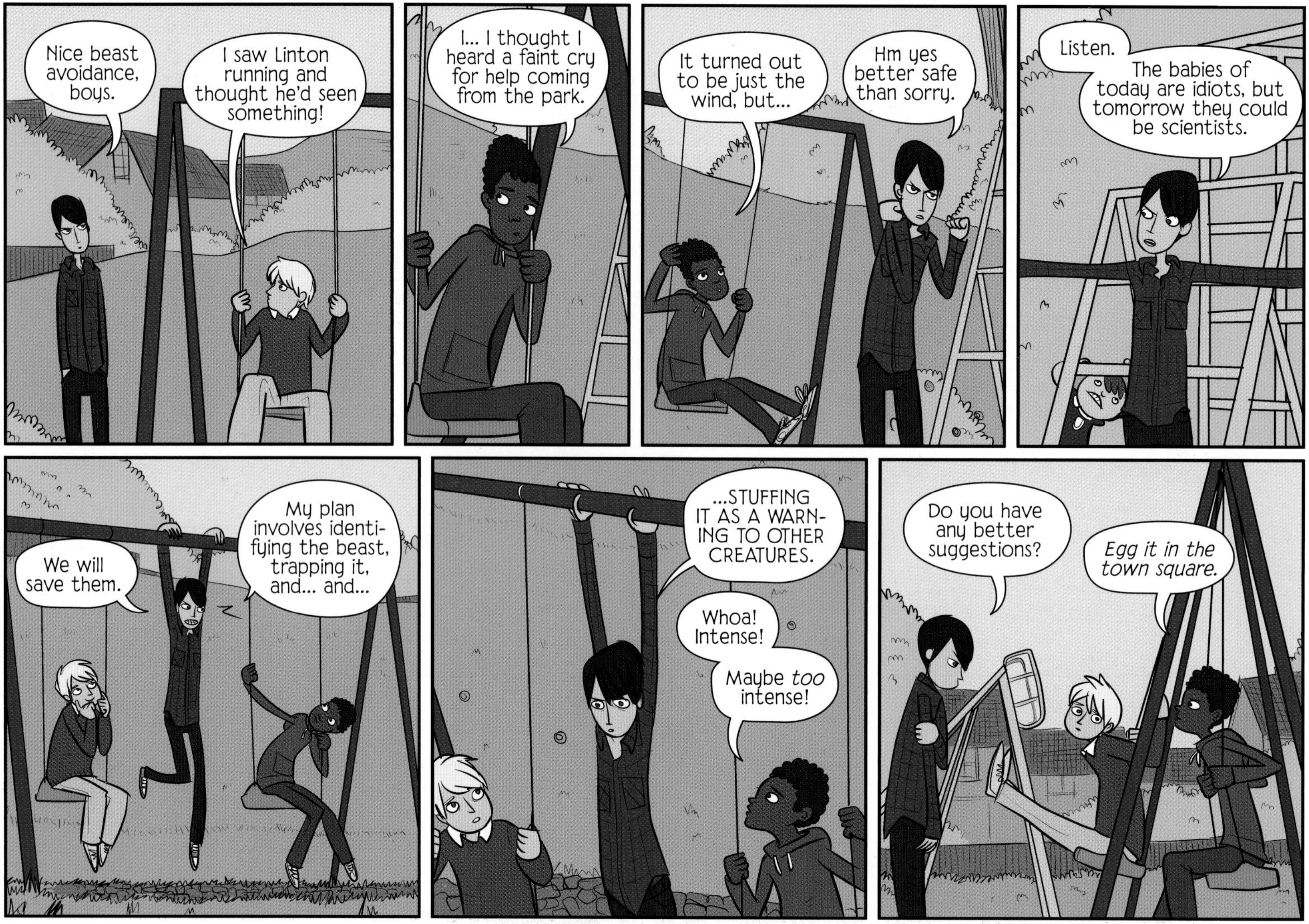
Nice beast avoidance, boys.
I saw Linton running and thought he'd seen something!
I... I thought I heard a faint cry for help coming from the park.
It turned out to be just the wind, but...
Hm yes better safe than sorry.
Listen.
The babies of today are idiots, but tomorrow they could be scientists.
We will save them.
My plan involves identifying the beast, trapping it, and... and...
...STUFFING IT AS A WARNING TO OTHER CREATURES.
Whoa! Intense!
Maybe *too* intense!
Do you have any better suggestions?
Egg it in the town square.

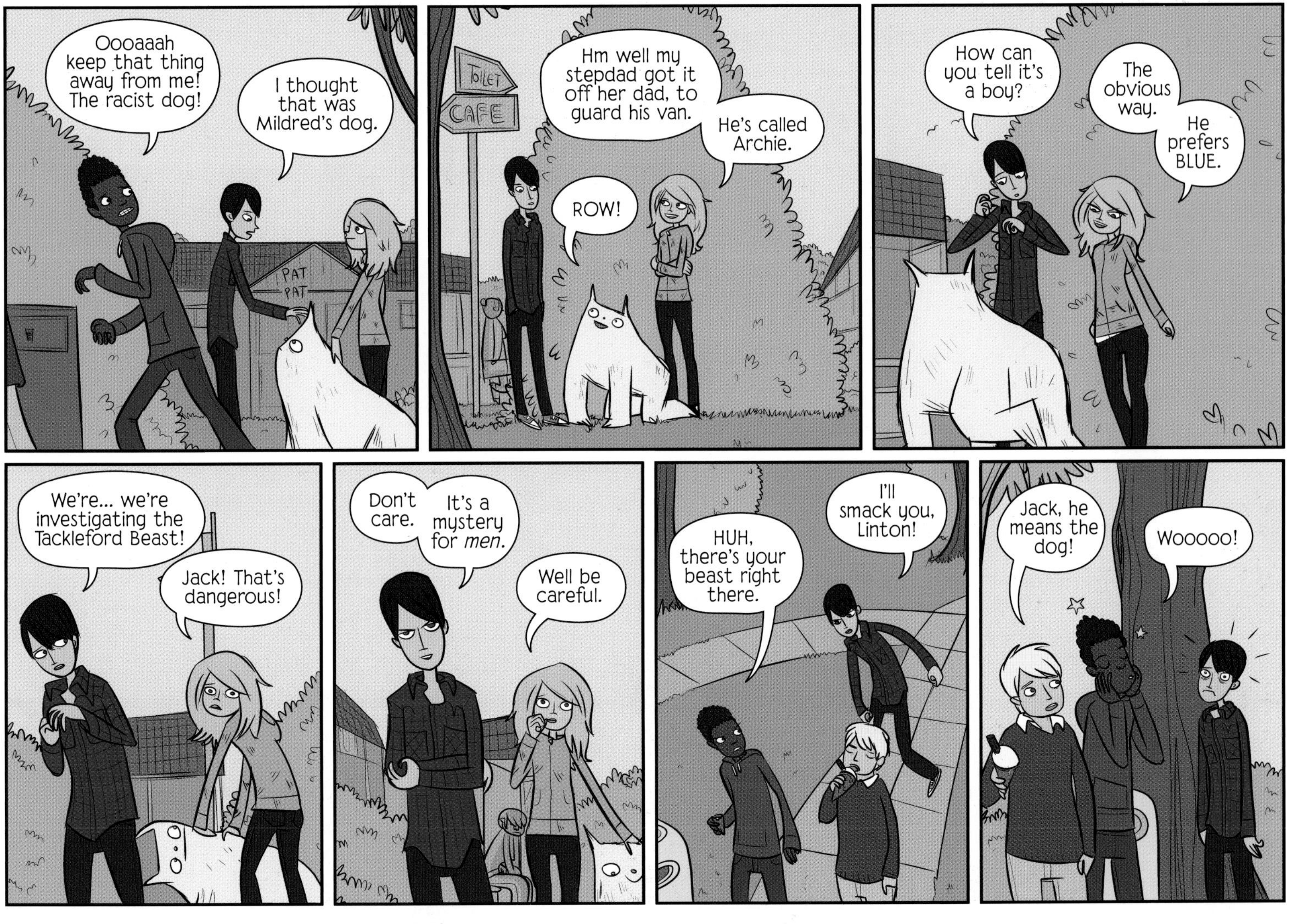
Oooaaah keep that thing away from me! The racist dog!
I thought that was Mildred's dog.
PAT PAT
TOILET
CAFE
Hm well my stepdad got it off her dad, to guard his van.
He's called Archie.
ROW!
How can you tell it's a boy?
The obvious way.
He prefers BLUE.
We're... we're investigating the Tackleford Beast!
Jack! That's dangerous!
Don't care.
It's a mystery for *men*.
Well be careful.
HUH, there's your beast right there.
I'll smack you, Linton!
Jack, he means the dog!
Wooooo!

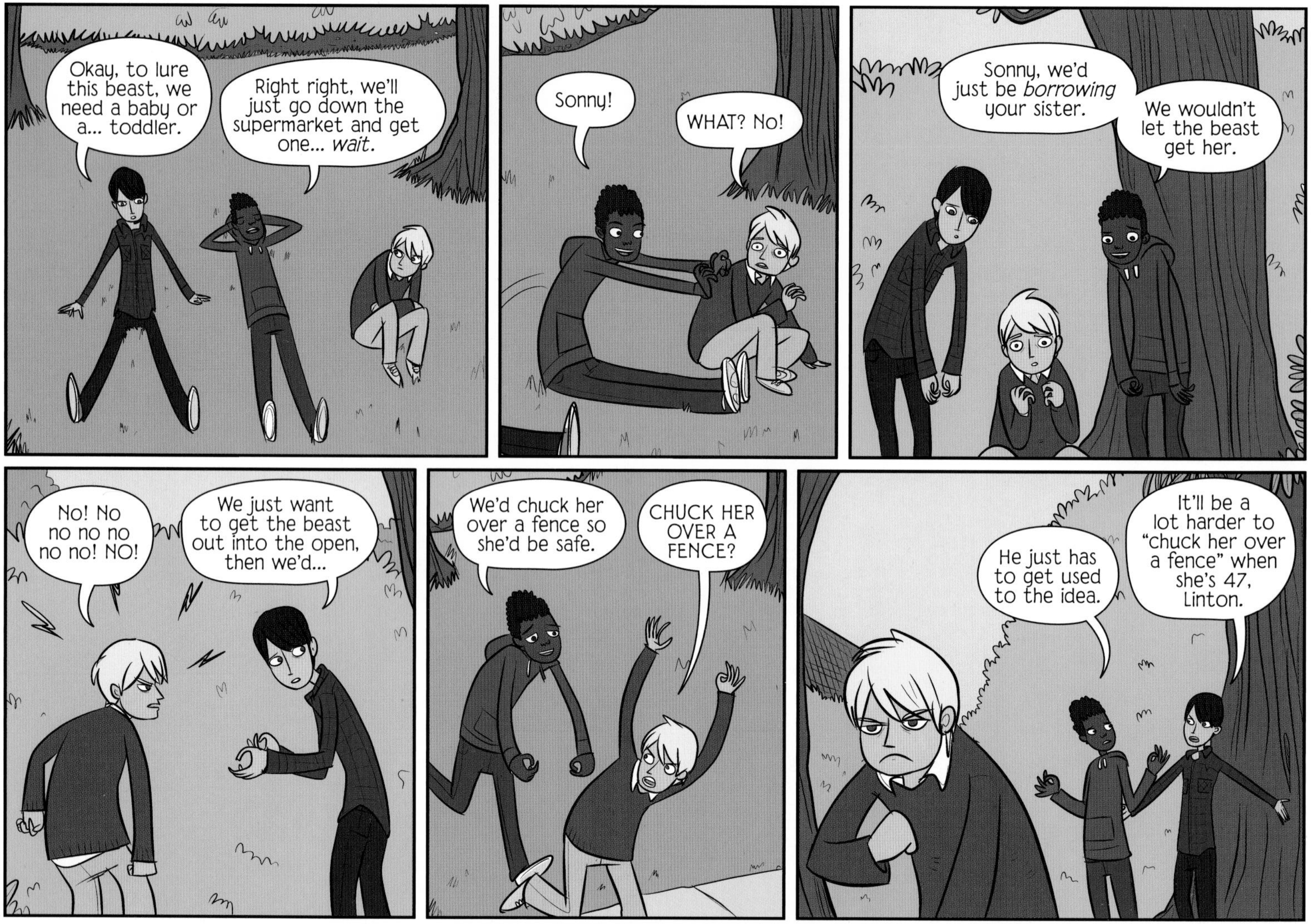
Okay, to lure this beast, we need a baby or a... toddler.
Right right, we'll just go down the supermarket and get one... *wait*.
Sonny!
WHAT? No!
Sonny, we'd just be *borrowing* your sister.
We wouldn't let the beast get her.
No! No no no no no no! NO!
We just want to get the beast out into the open, then we'd...
We'd chuck her over a fence so she'd be safe.
CHUCK HER OVER A FENCE?
He just has to get used to the idea.
It'll be a lot harder to "chuck her over a fence" when she's 47, Linton.

STOMP STOMP STOMP STOMP STOMP

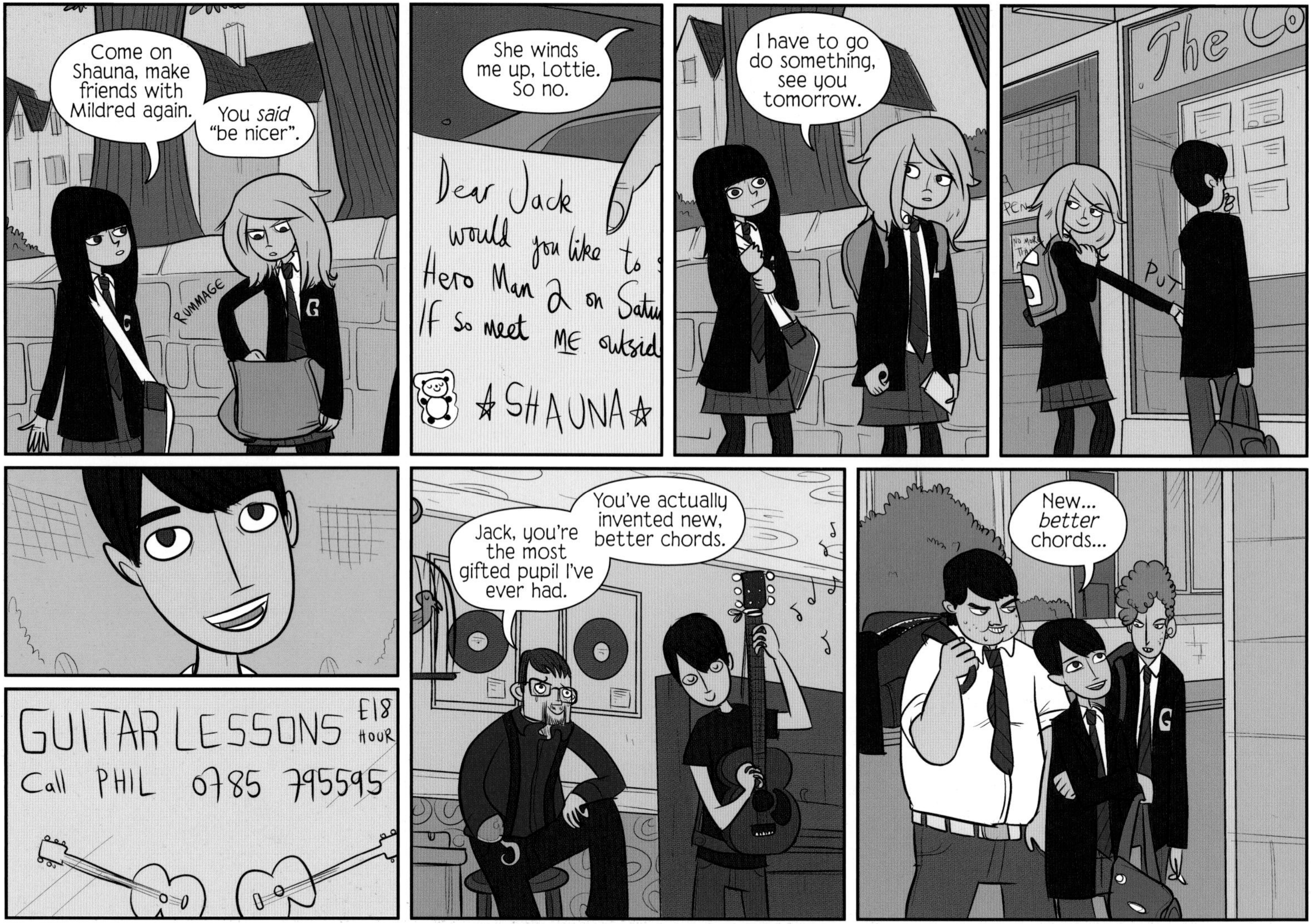
Come on Shauna, make friends with Mildred again.
You *said* "be nicer".
RUMMAGE
She winds me up, Lottie. So no.
Dear Jack
would you like to
Hero Man 2 on Satu
If so meet ME outsid
★SHAUNA★
I have to go do something, see you tomorrow.
GUITAR LESSONS £18 HOUR
Call PHIL 0785 795595
Jack, you're the most gifted pupil I've ever had.
You've actually invented new, better chords.
New... *better* chords...

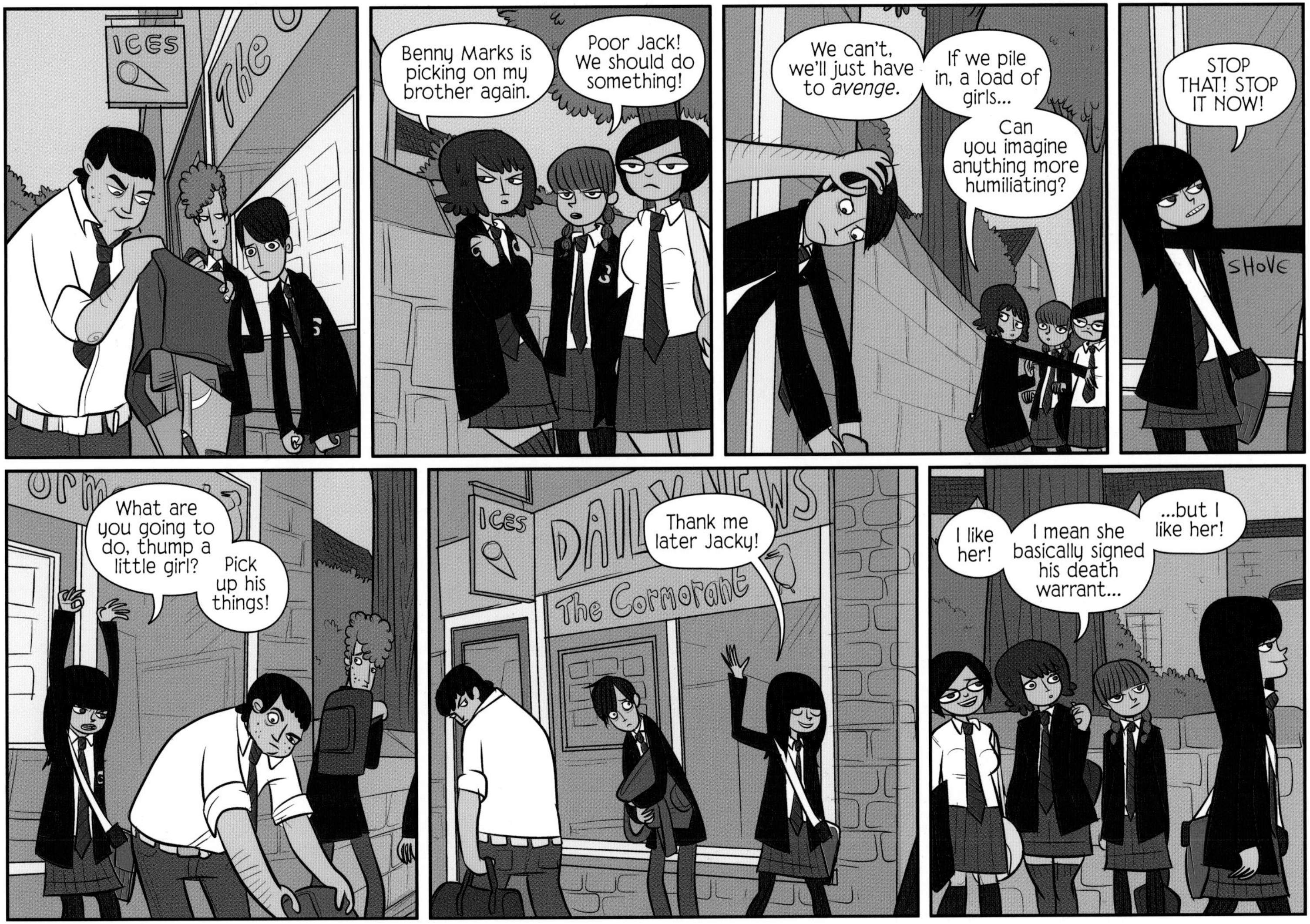
ICES
Benny Marks is picking on my brother again.
Poor Jack! We should do something!
We can't, we'll just have to *avenge*.
If we pile in, a load of girls...
Can you imagine anything more humiliating?
STOP THAT! STOP IT NOW!
SHOVE
What are you going to do, thump a little girl?
Pick up his things!
ICES
DAILY NEWS
The Cormorant
Thank me later Jacky!
I like her!
I mean she basically signed his death warrant...
...but I like her!

FFLUSSSHHH
SIT ON IT

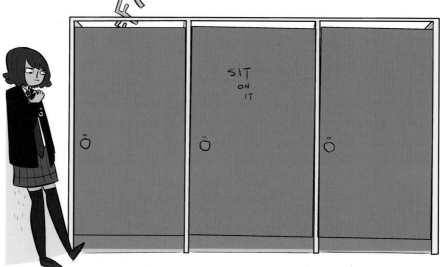

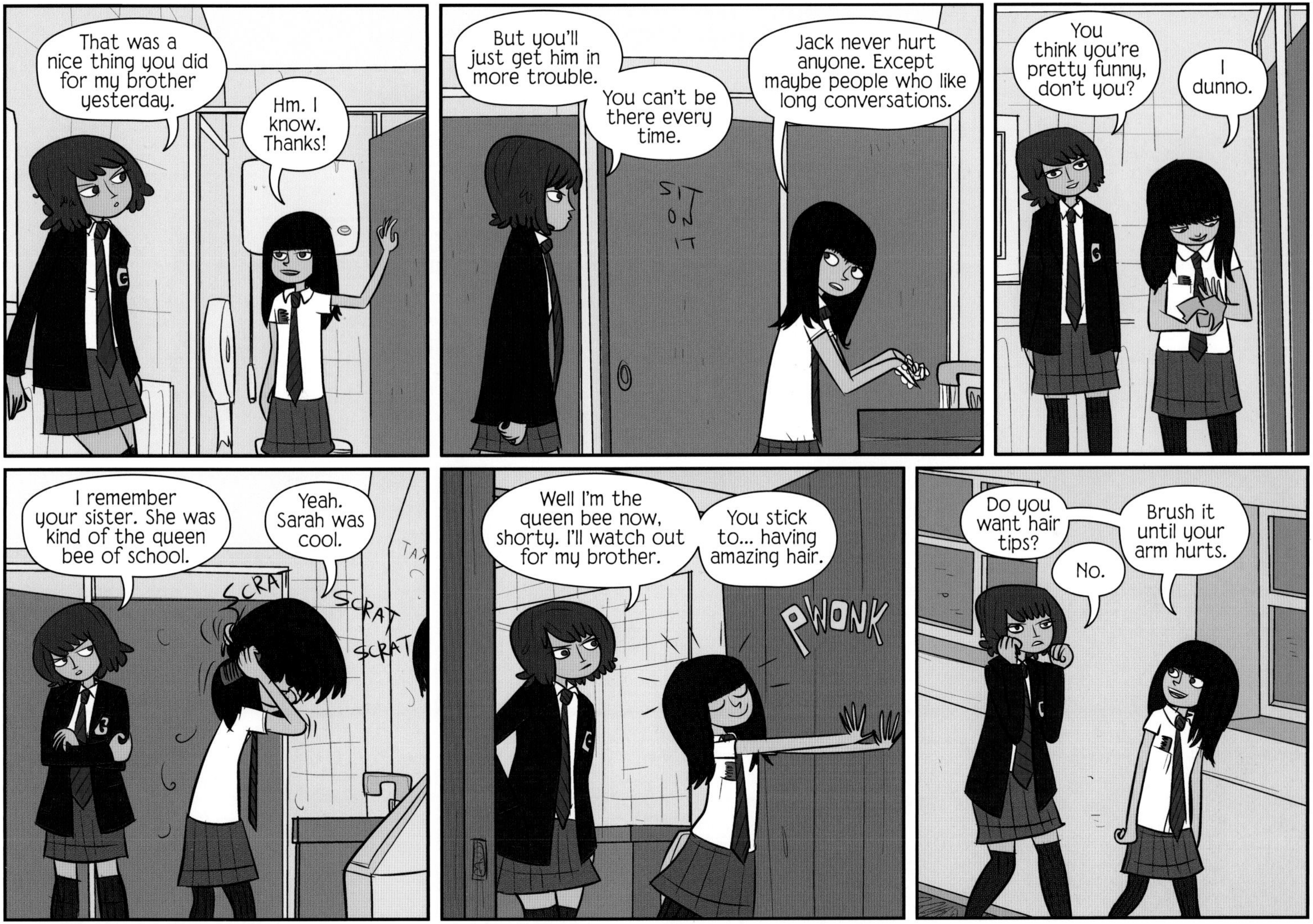
That was a nice thing you did for my brother yesterday.
Hm. I know. Thanks!
But you'll just get him in more trouble.
You can't be there every time.
SIT ON IT
Jack never hurt anyone. Except maybe people who like long conversations.
You think you're pretty funny, don't you?
I dunno.
I remember your sister. She was kind of the queen bee of school.
Yeah. Sarah was cool.
SCRAT
SCRAT
SCRAT
Well I'm the queen bee now, shorty. I'll watch out for my brother.
You stick to... having amazing hair.
PWONK
Do you want hair tips?
No.
Brush it until your arm hurts.

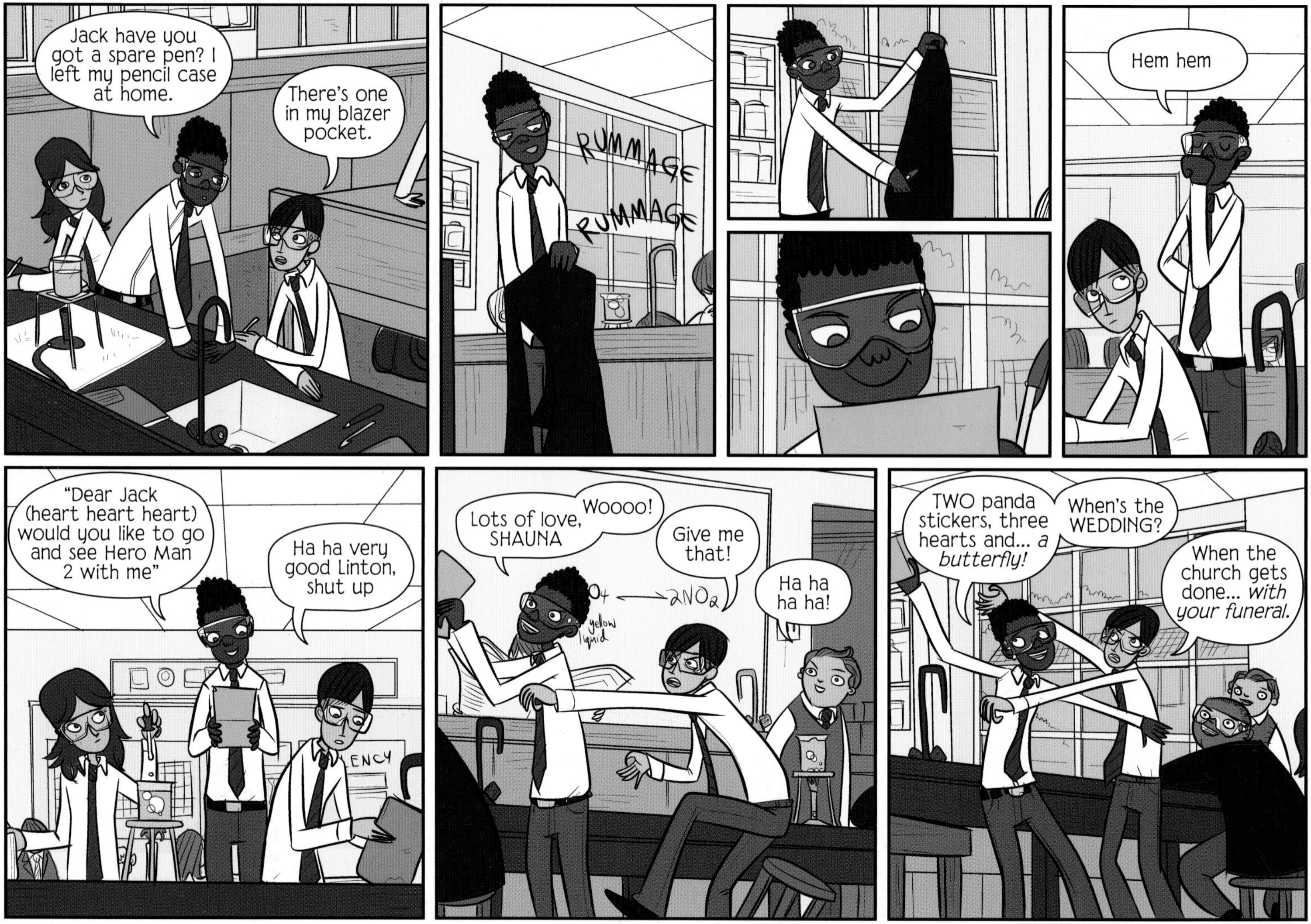
Jack have you got a spare pen? I left my pencil case at home.
There's one in my blazer pocket.
RUMMAGE
RUMMAGE
Hem hem
"Dear Jack (heart heart heart) would you like to go and see Hero Man 2 with me"
Ha ha very good Linton, shut up
Lots of love, SHAUNA
Woooo!
Give me that!
Ha ha ha ha!
TWO panda stickers, three hearts and... *a butterfly!*
When's the WEDDING?
When the church gets done... *with your funeral.*

Why, Finch?

Sir can I change from working with Linton on the river project please?

Political differences? Artistic differences? *Rise above it.*

But *sir-*

I'm already impressed by how you're taking the high ground.

It shows character. Good on you, Finch.

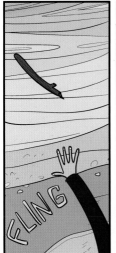

FLING

All right, start the stop-watch... NOW!

SPLOSH

PIP

15.6 seconds.

Fifteen... point six... seconds...

PIP

...heart heart kiss kiss..

...PANDA STICKER. Next!

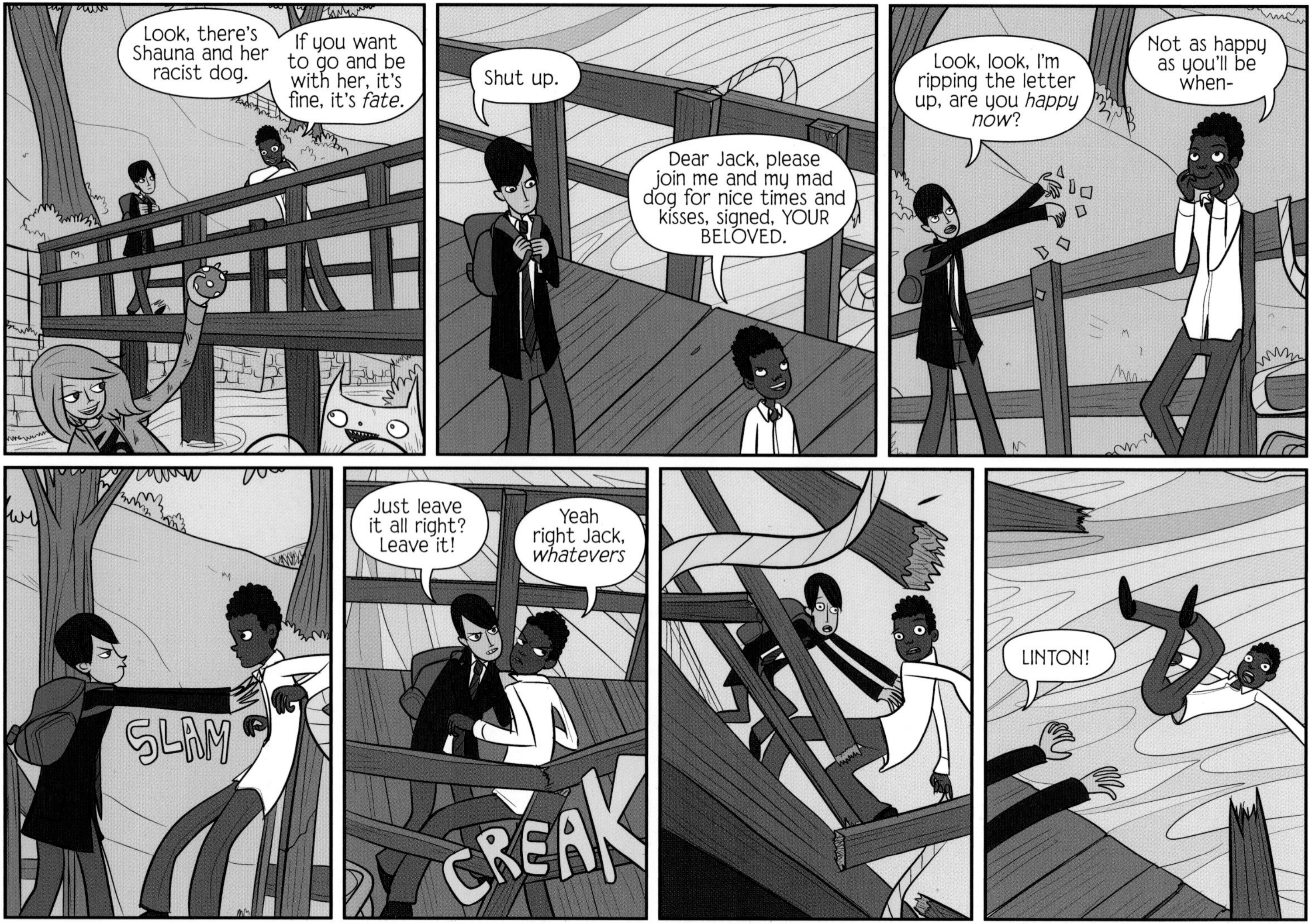
Look, there's Shauna and her racist dog.
If you want to go and be with her, it's fine, it's *fate.*
Shut up.
Dear Jack, please join me and my mad dog for nice times and kisses, signed, YOUR BELOVED.
Look, look, I'm ripping the letter up, are you *happy now*?
Not as happy as you'll be when-
SLAM
Just leave it all right? Leave it!
Yeah right Jack, *whatevers*
CREAK
LINTON!

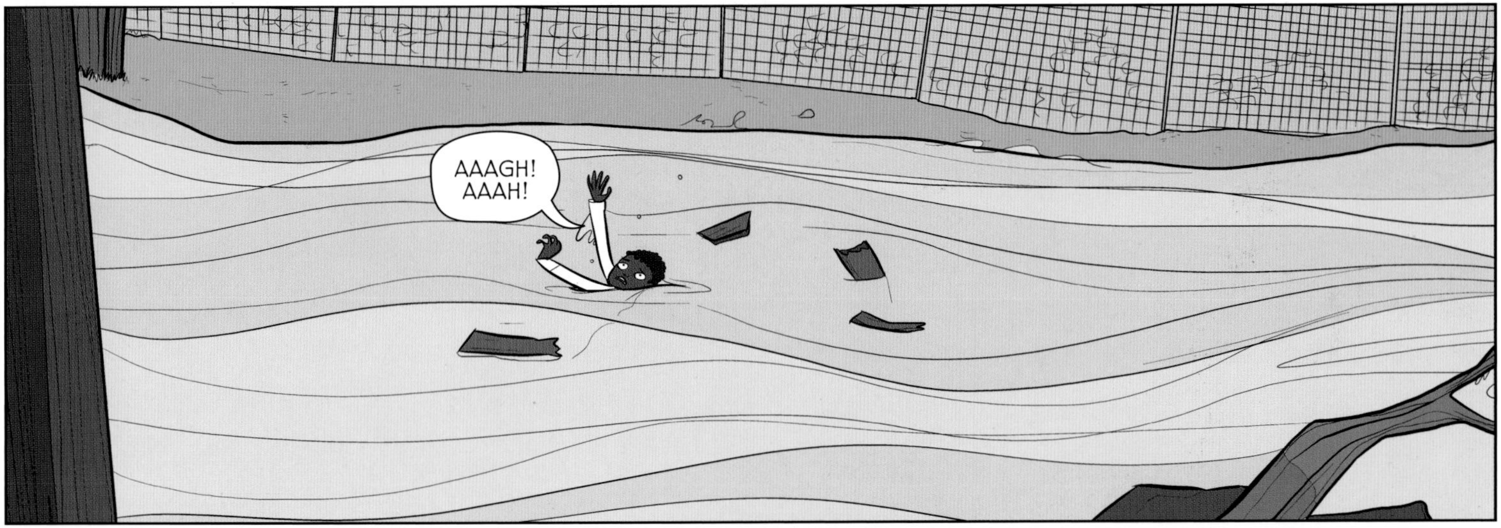
AAAGH! AAAH!

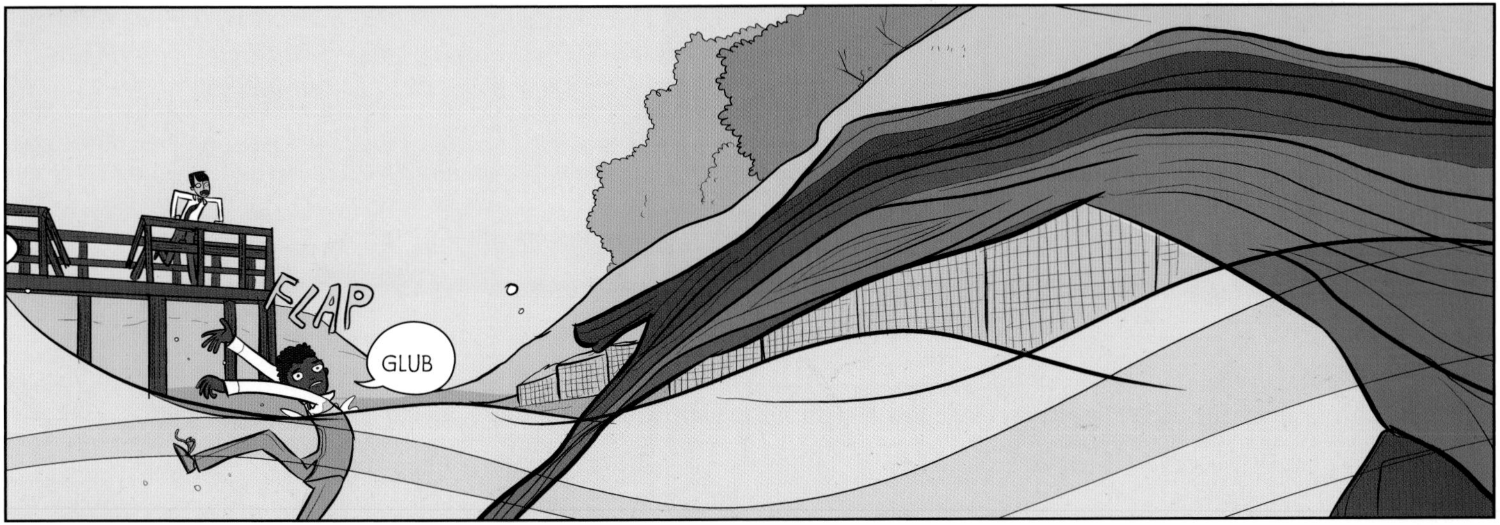
FLAP
GLUB

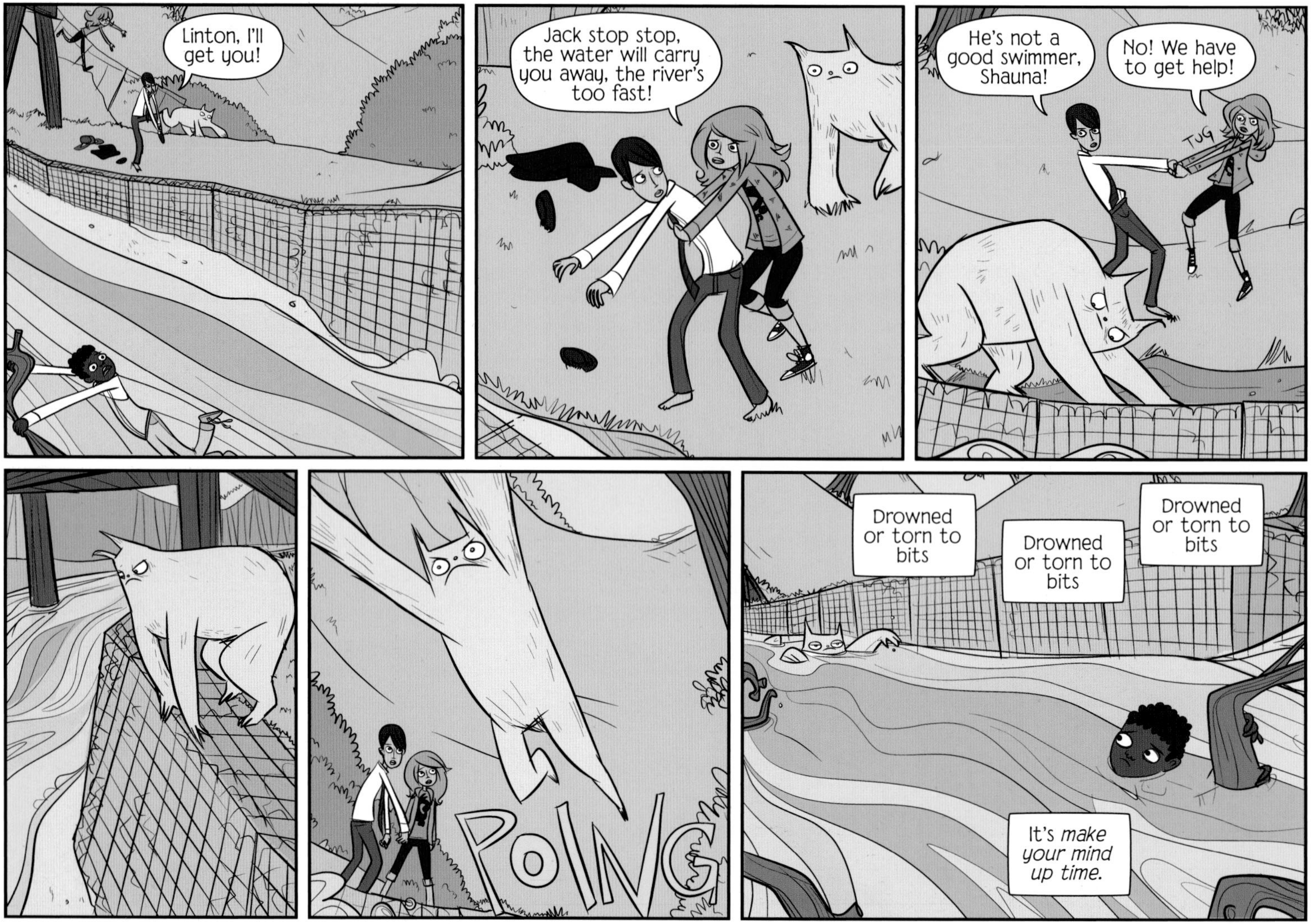
Linton, I'll get you!
Jack stop stop, the water will carry you away, the river's too fast!
He's not a good swimmer, Shauna!
No! We have to get help!
TUG
POING
Drowned or torn to bits
Drowned or torn to bits
Drowned or torn to bits
It's *make your mind up time.*

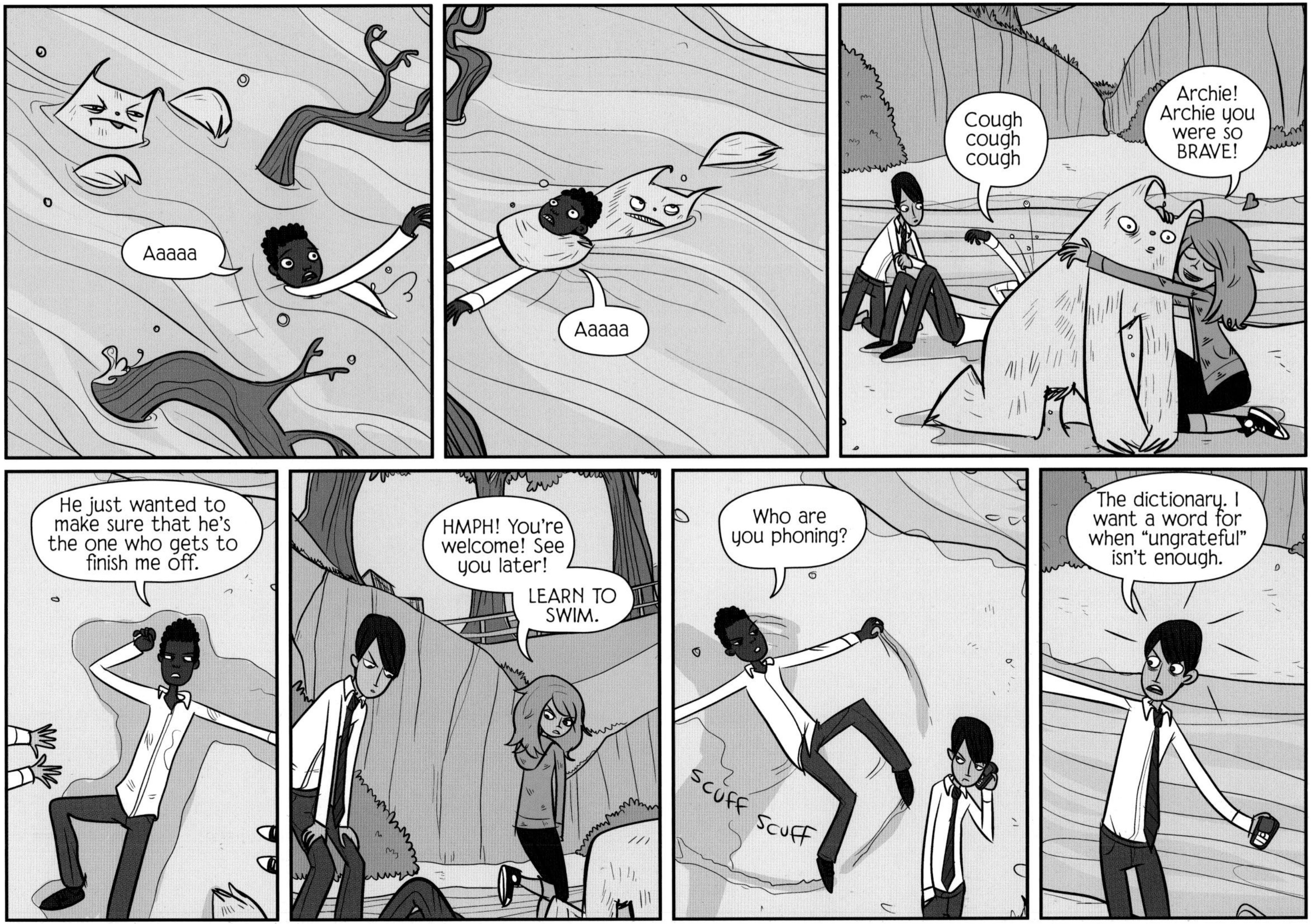
Aaaaa
Aaaaa
Cough cough cough
Archie! Archie you were so BRAVE!
He just wanted to make sure that he's the one who gets to finish me off.
HMPH! You're welcome! See you later!
LEARN TO SWIM.
Who are you phoning?
SCUFF
SCUFF
The dictionary. I want a word for when "ungrateful" isn't enough.

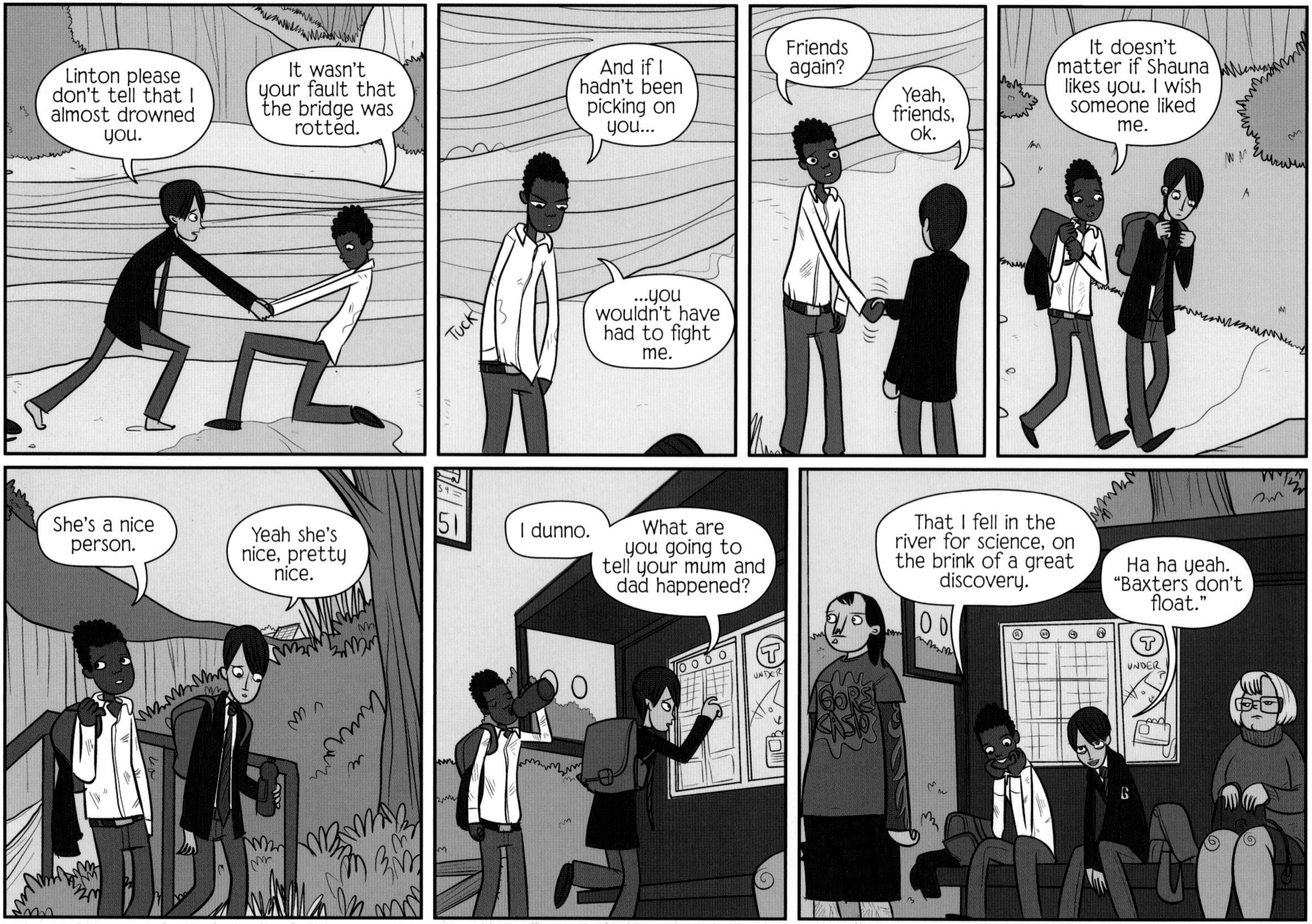
Linton please don't tell that I almost drowned you.
It wasn't your fault that the bridge was rotted.
And if I hadn't been picking on you...
TUCK
...you wouldn't have had to fight me.
Friends again?
Yeah, friends, ok.
It doesn't matter if Shauna likes you. I wish someone liked me.
She's a nice person.
Yeah she's nice, pretty nice.
I dunno.
What are you going to tell your mum and dad happened?
That I fell in the river for science, on the brink of a great discovery.
Ha ha yeah. "Baxters don't float."

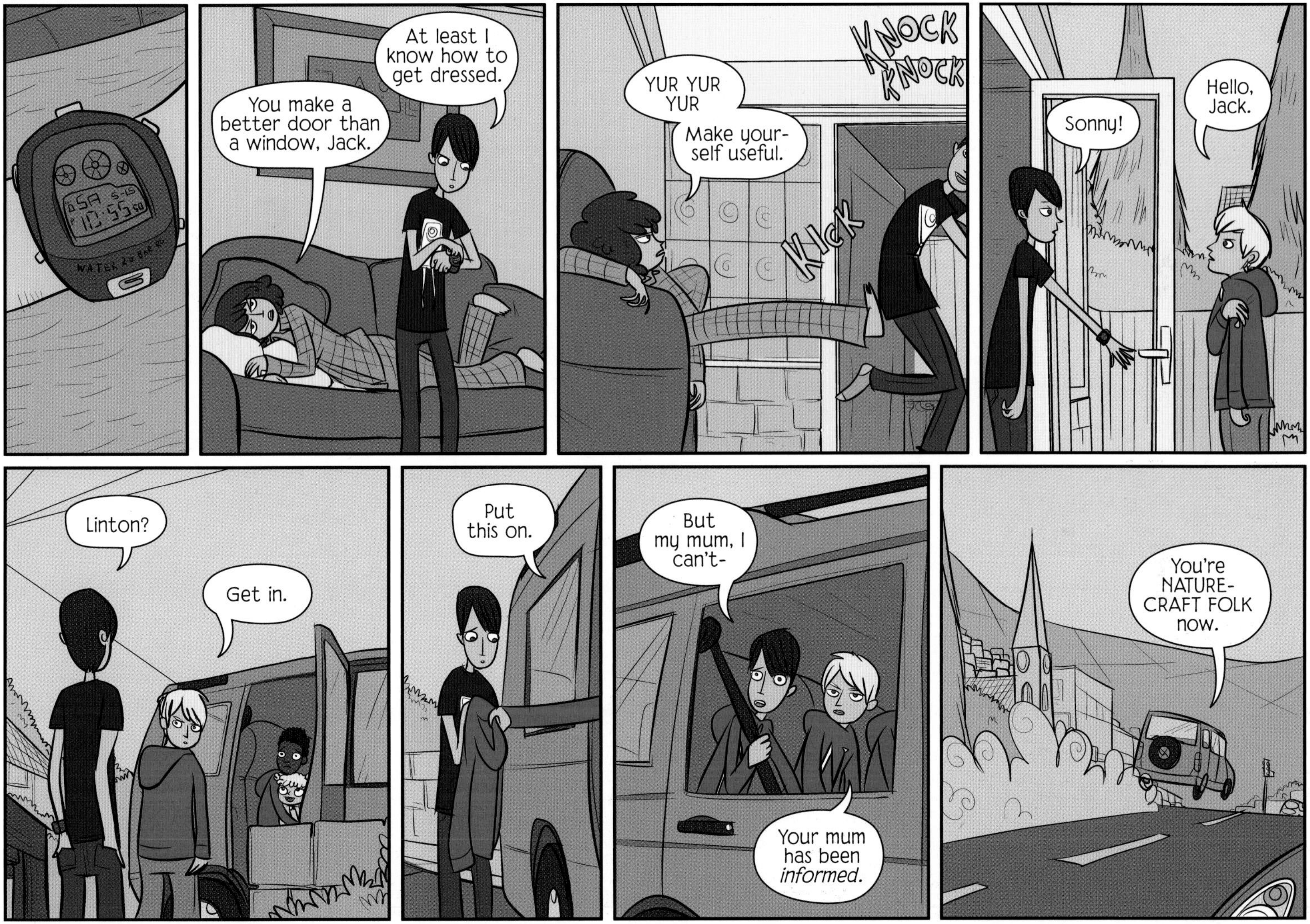

WATER 20 BAR
At least I know how to get dressed.
You make a better door than a window, Jack.
KNOCK KNOCK
YUR YUR YUR
Make yourself useful.
KICK
Sonny!
Hello, Jack.
Linton?
Get in.
Put this on.
But my mum, I can't-
Your mum has been *informed.*
You're NATURE-CRAFT FOLK now.

Bad Machinery, Volume Two

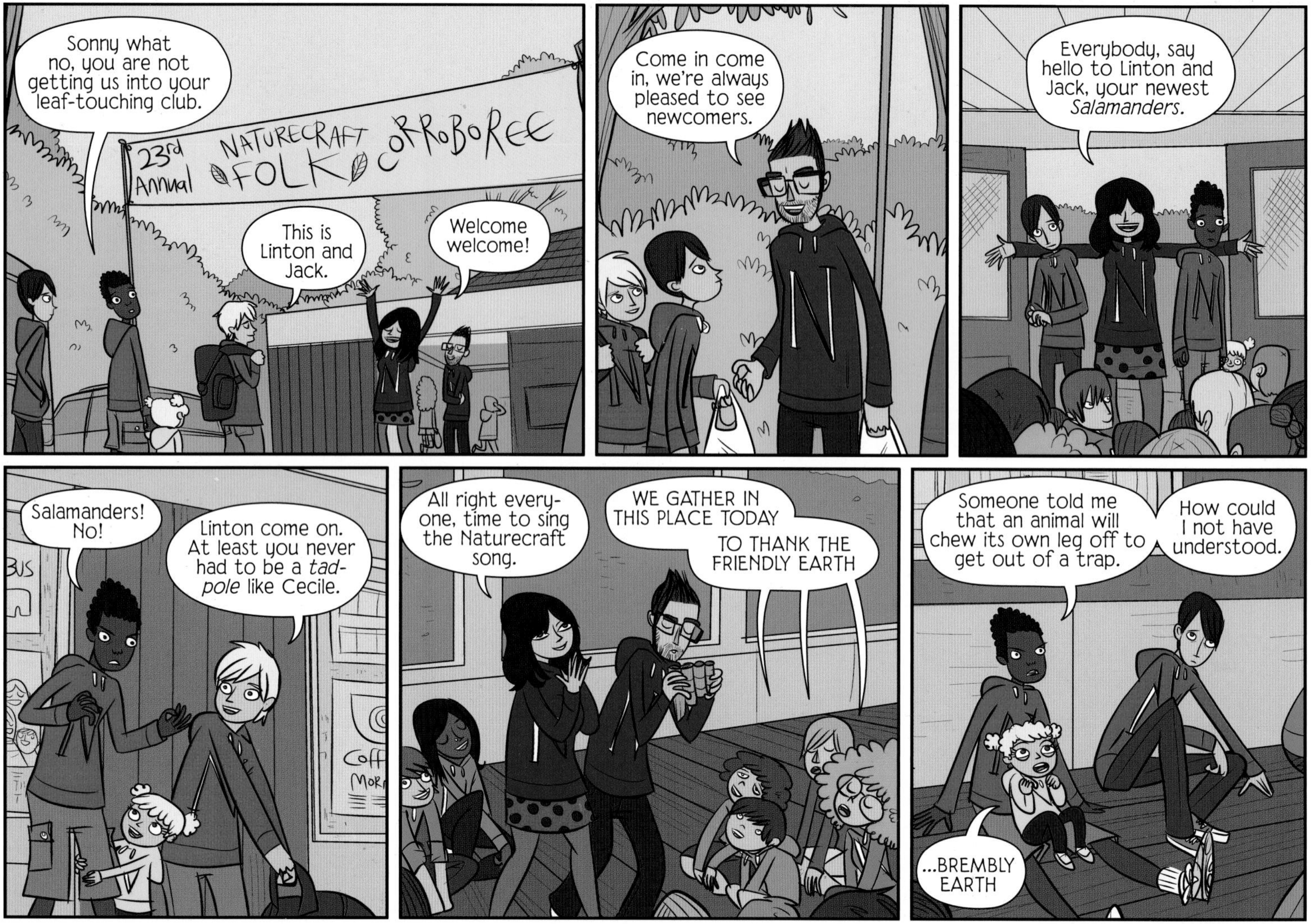
Sonny what no, you are not getting us into your leaf-touching club.
23rd Annual NATURECRAFT FOLK CORROBOREE
This is Linton and Jack.
Welcome welcome!
Come in come in, we're always pleased to see newcomers.
Everybody, say hello to Linton and Jack, your newest *Salamanders*.
Salamanders! No!
Linton come on. At least you never had to be a *tad-pole* like Cecile.
All right every-one, time to sing the Naturecraft song.
WE GATHER IN THIS PLACE TODAY
TO THANK THE FRIENDLY EARTH
Someone told me that an animal will chew its own leg off to get out of a trap.
How could I not have understood.
...BREMBLY EARTH

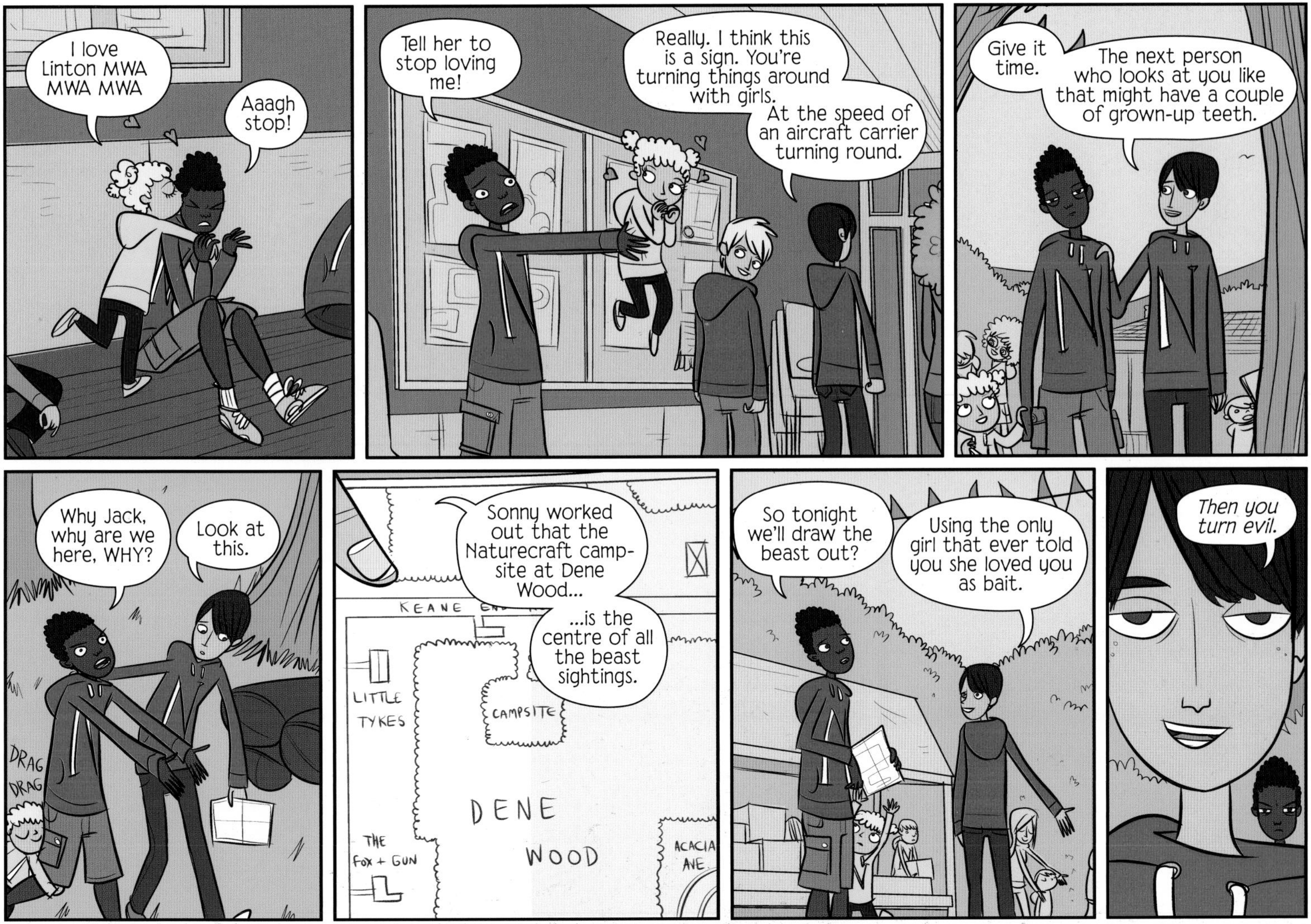
I love Linton MWA MWA MWA
Aaagh stop!
Tell her to stop loving me!
Really. I think this is a sign. You're turning things around with girls.
At the speed of an aircraft carrier turning round.
Give it time.
The next person who looks at you like that might have a couple of grown-up teeth.
Why Jack, why are we here, WHY?
Look at this.
DRAG
DRAG
Sonny worked out that the Naturecraft camp-site at Dene Wood...
...is the centre of all the beast sightings.
KEANE
LITTLE TYKES
CAMPSITE
DENE
WOOD
THE FOX + GUN
ACACIA AVE
So tonight we'll draw the beast out?
Using the only girl that ever told you she loved you as bait.
Then you turn evil.

Bad Machinery, Volume Two

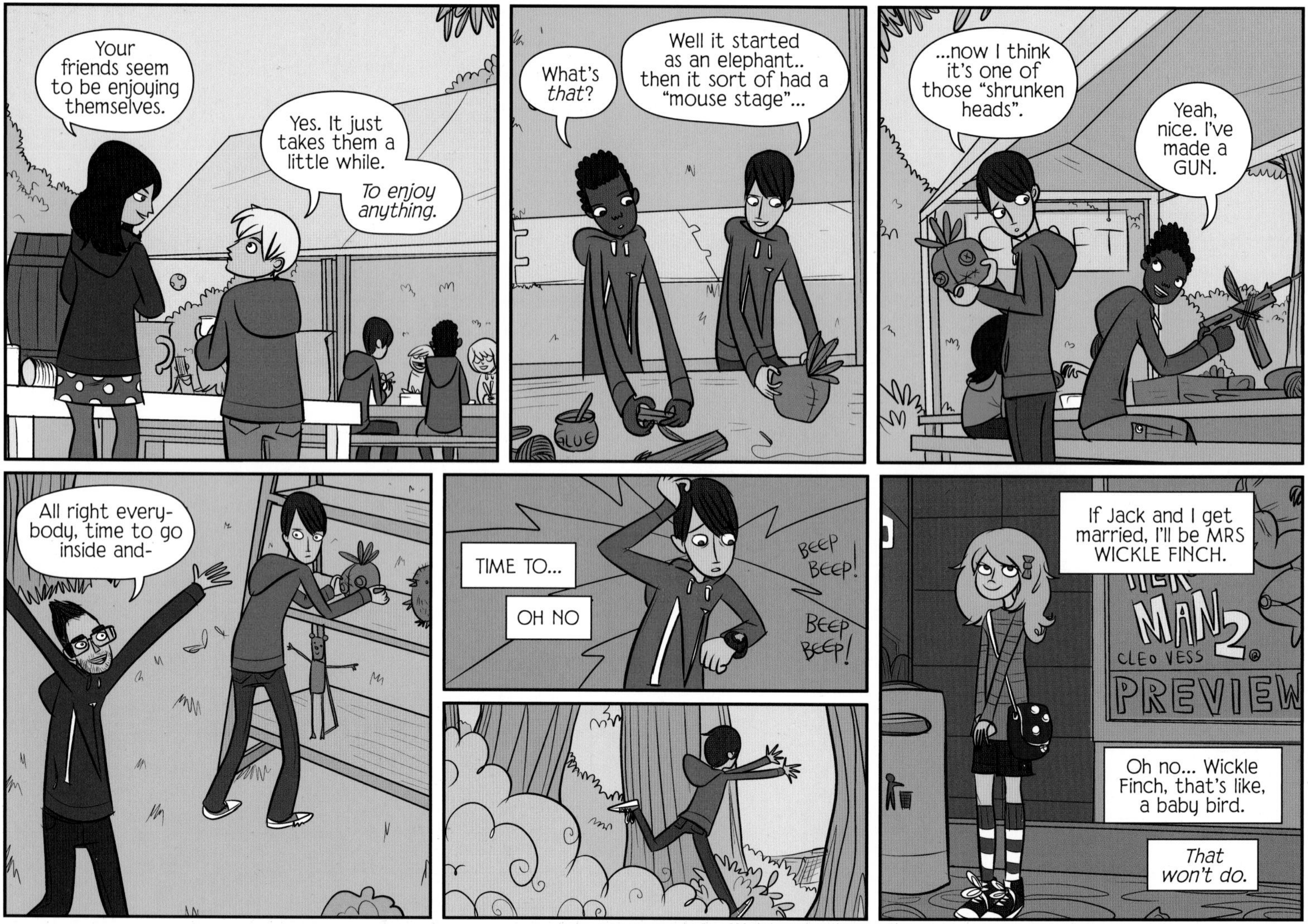
Your friends seem to be enjoying themselves.
Yes. It just takes them a little while.
To enjoy anything.
What's *that*?
Well it started as an elephant.. then it sort of had a "mouse stage"...
...now I think it's one of those "shrunken heads".
Yeah, nice. I've made a GUN.
GLUE
All right every-body, time to go inside and-
TIME TO...
OH NO
BEEP BEEP!
BEEP BEEP!
If Jack and I get married, I'll be MRS WICKLE FINCH.
MAN 2
CLEO VESS
PREVIEW
Oh no... Wickle Finch, that's like, a baby bird.
That won't do.

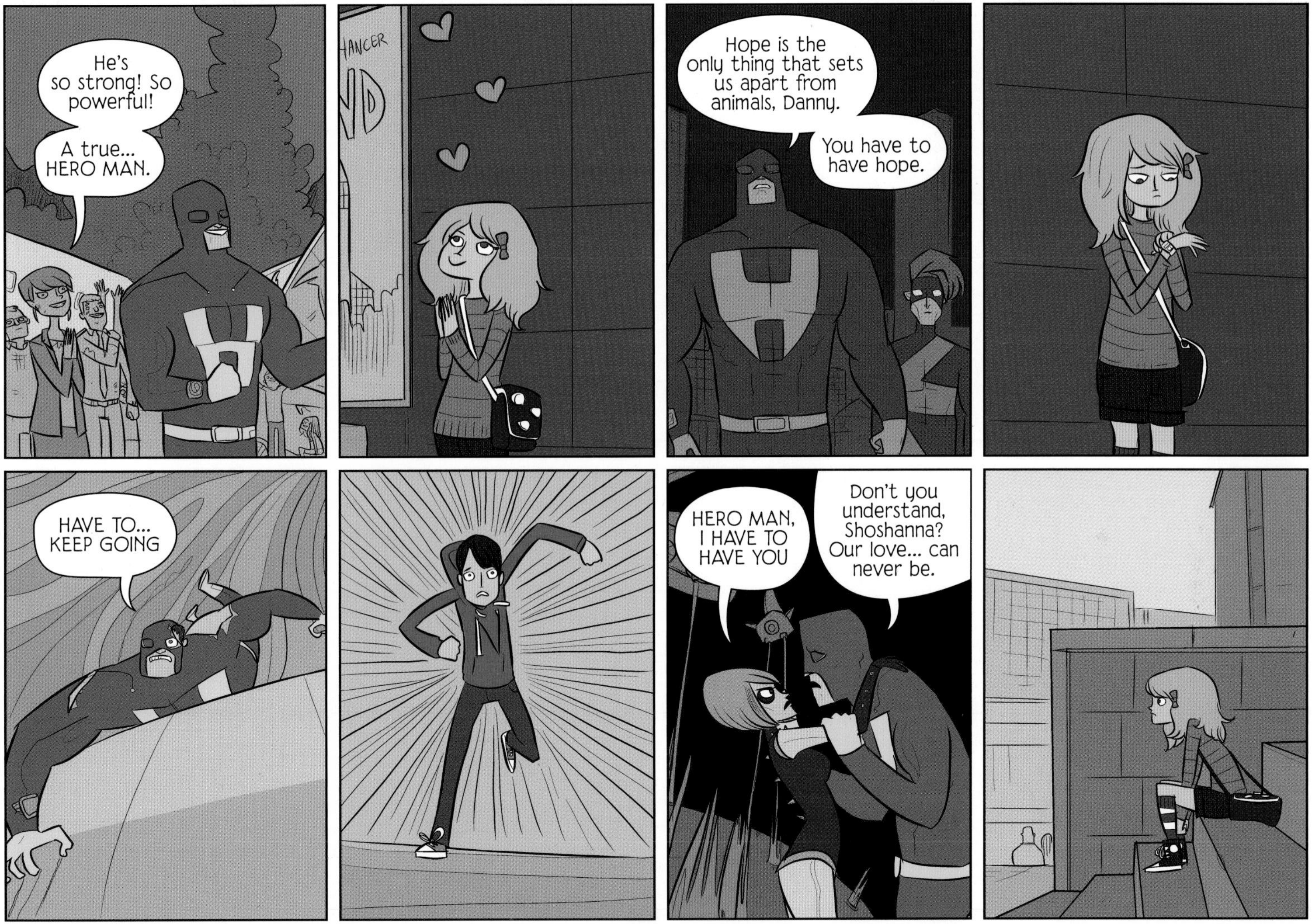
He's so strong! So powerful!
A true... HERO MAN.
Hope is the only thing that sets us apart from animals, Danny.
You have to have hope.
HAVE TO... KEEP GOING
HERO MAN, I HAVE TO HAVE YOU
Don't you understand, Shoshanna? Our love... can never be.

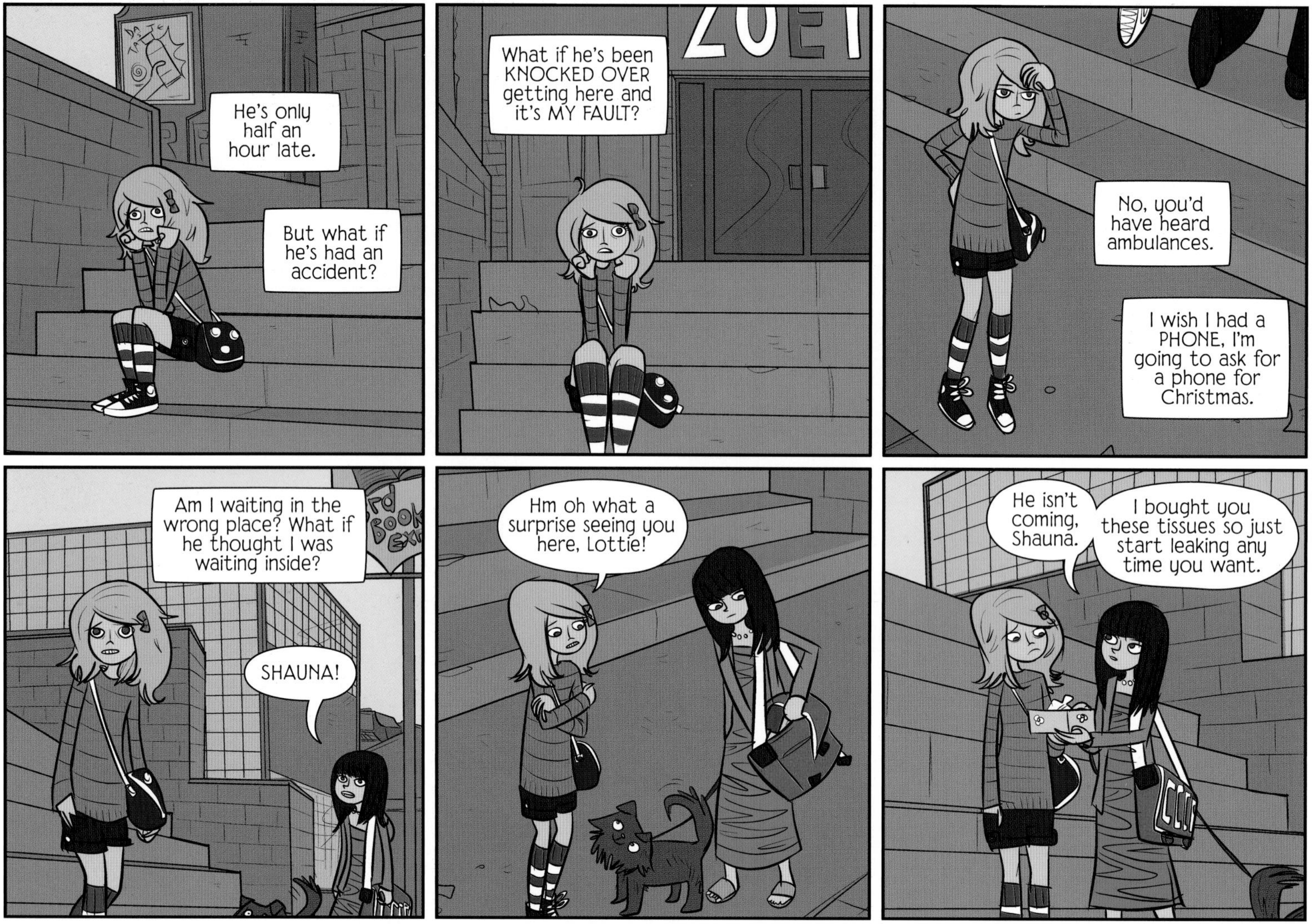
He's only half an hour late.
But what if he's had an accident?
What if he's been KNOCKED OVER getting here and it's MY FAULT?
No, you'd have heard ambulances.
I wish I had a PHONE, I'm going to ask for a phone for Christmas.
Am I waiting in the wrong place? What if he thought I was waiting inside?
SHAUNA!
Hm oh what a surprise seeing you here, Lottie!
He isn't coming, Shauna.
I bought you these tissues so just start leaking any time you want.

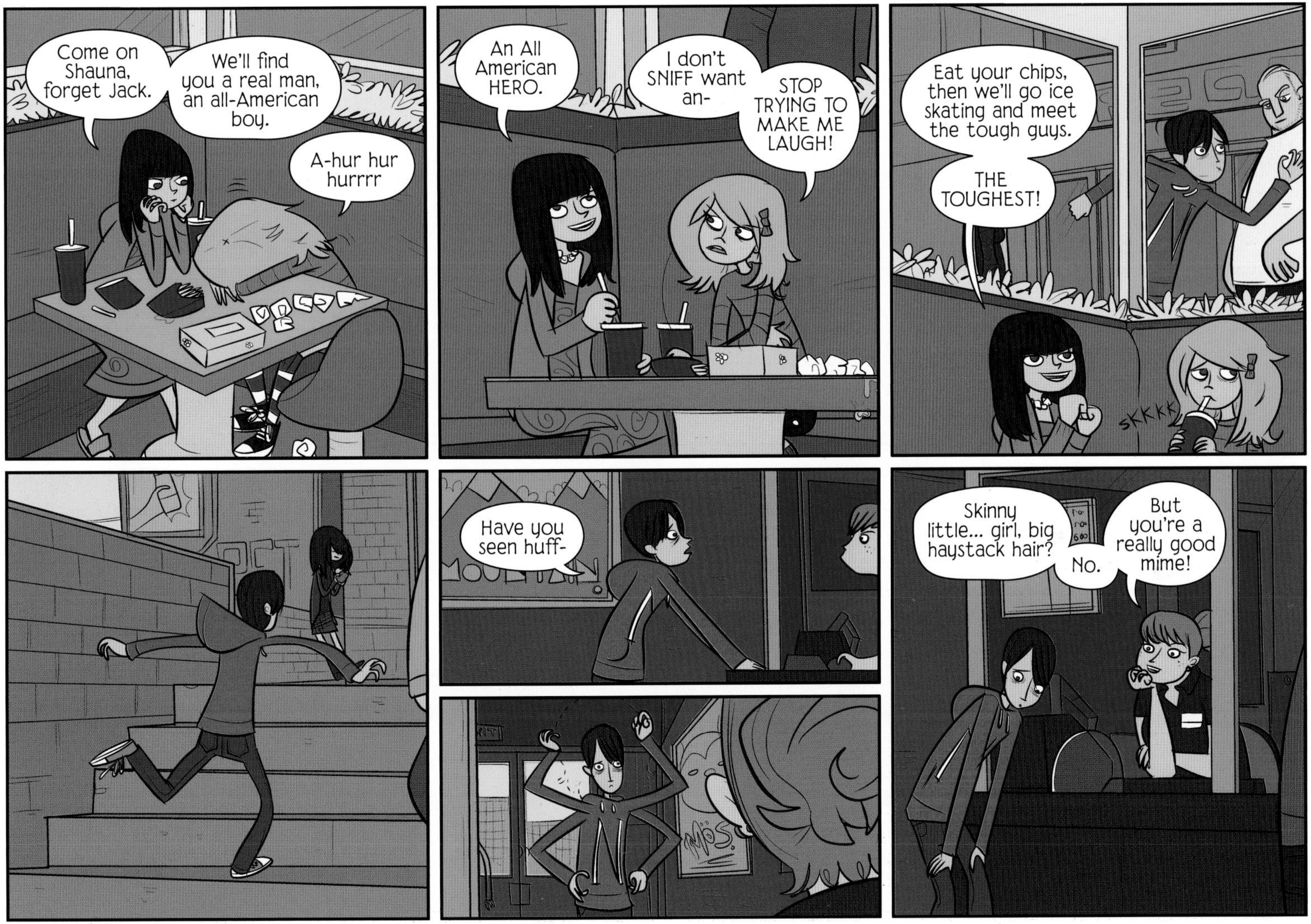

Come on Shauna, forget Jack.
We'll find you a real man, an all-American boy.
A-hur hur hurrrr
An All American HERO.
I don't SNIFF want an-
STOP TRYING TO MAKE ME LAUGH!
Eat your chips, then we'll go ice skating and meet the tough guys.
THE TOUGHEST!
SKKKK
Have you seen huff-
Skinny little... girl, big haystack hair?
No.
But you're a really good mime!

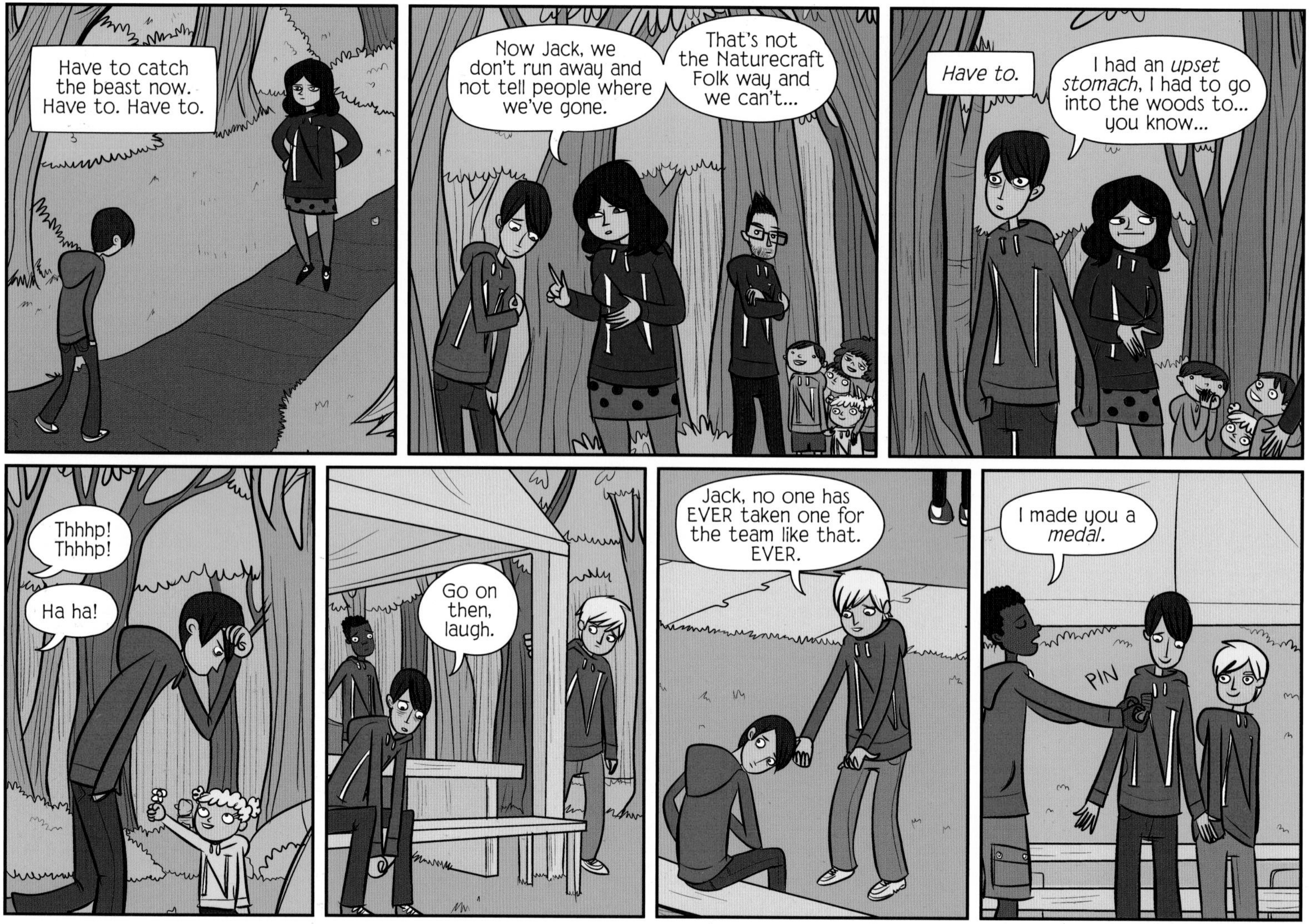
Have to catch the beast now. Have to. Have to.
Now Jack, we don't run away and not tell people where we've gone.
That's not the Naturecraft Folk way and we can't...
Have to.
I had an *upset stomach*, I had to go into the woods to... you know...
Thhhp! Thhhp!
Ha ha!
Go on then, laugh.
Jack, no one has EVER taken one for the team like that. EVER.
I made you a *medal*.
PIN

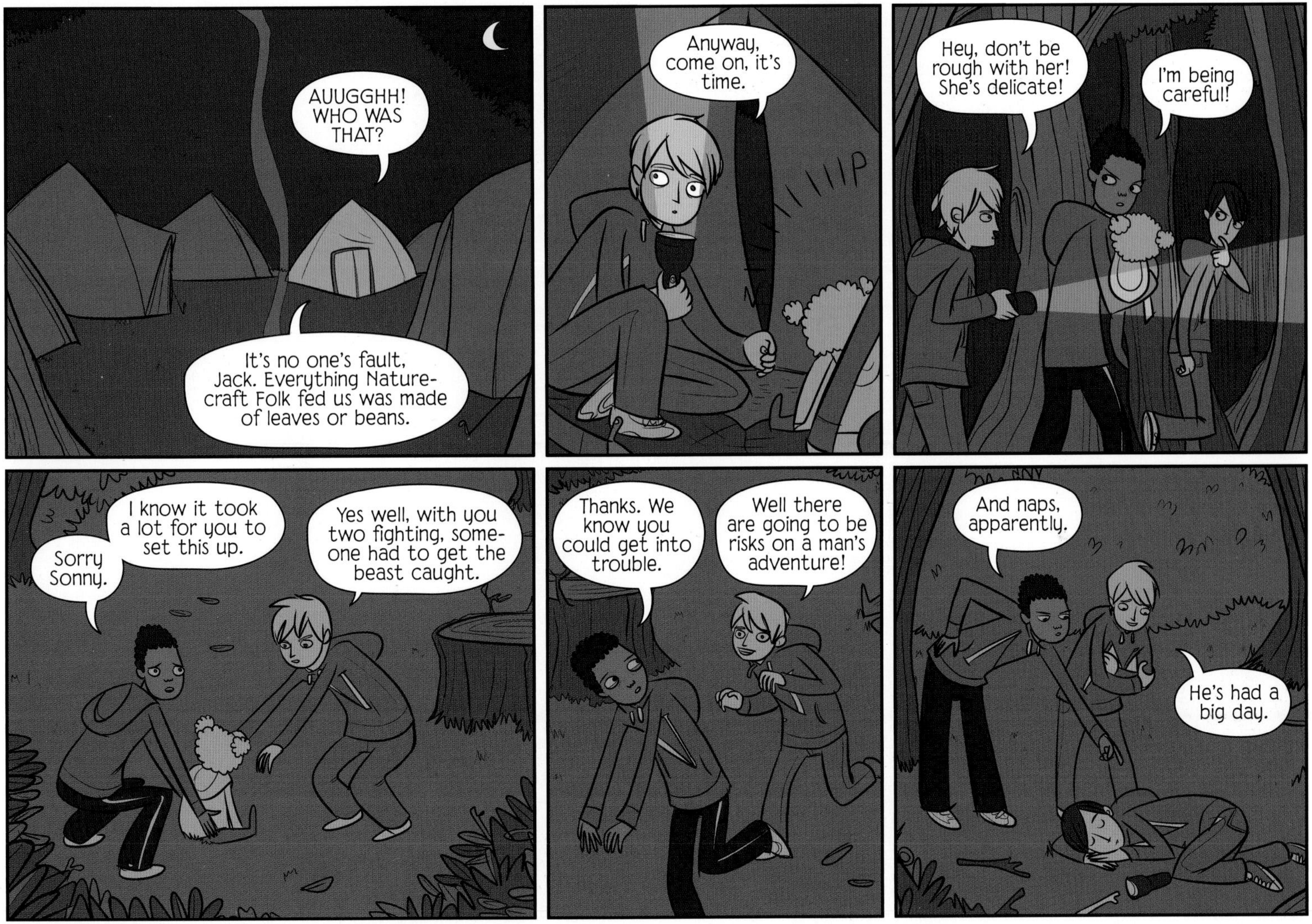
AUUGGHH! WHO WAS THAT?
It's no one's fault, Jack. Everything Nature-craft Folk fed us was made of leaves or beans.
Anyway, come on, it's time.
Hey, don't be rough with her! She's delicate!
I'm being careful!
Sorry Sonny.
I know it took a lot for you to set this up.
Yes well, with you two fighting, some-one had to get the beast caught.
Thanks. We know you could get into trouble.
Well there are going to be risks on a man's adventure!
And naps, apparently.
He's had a big day.

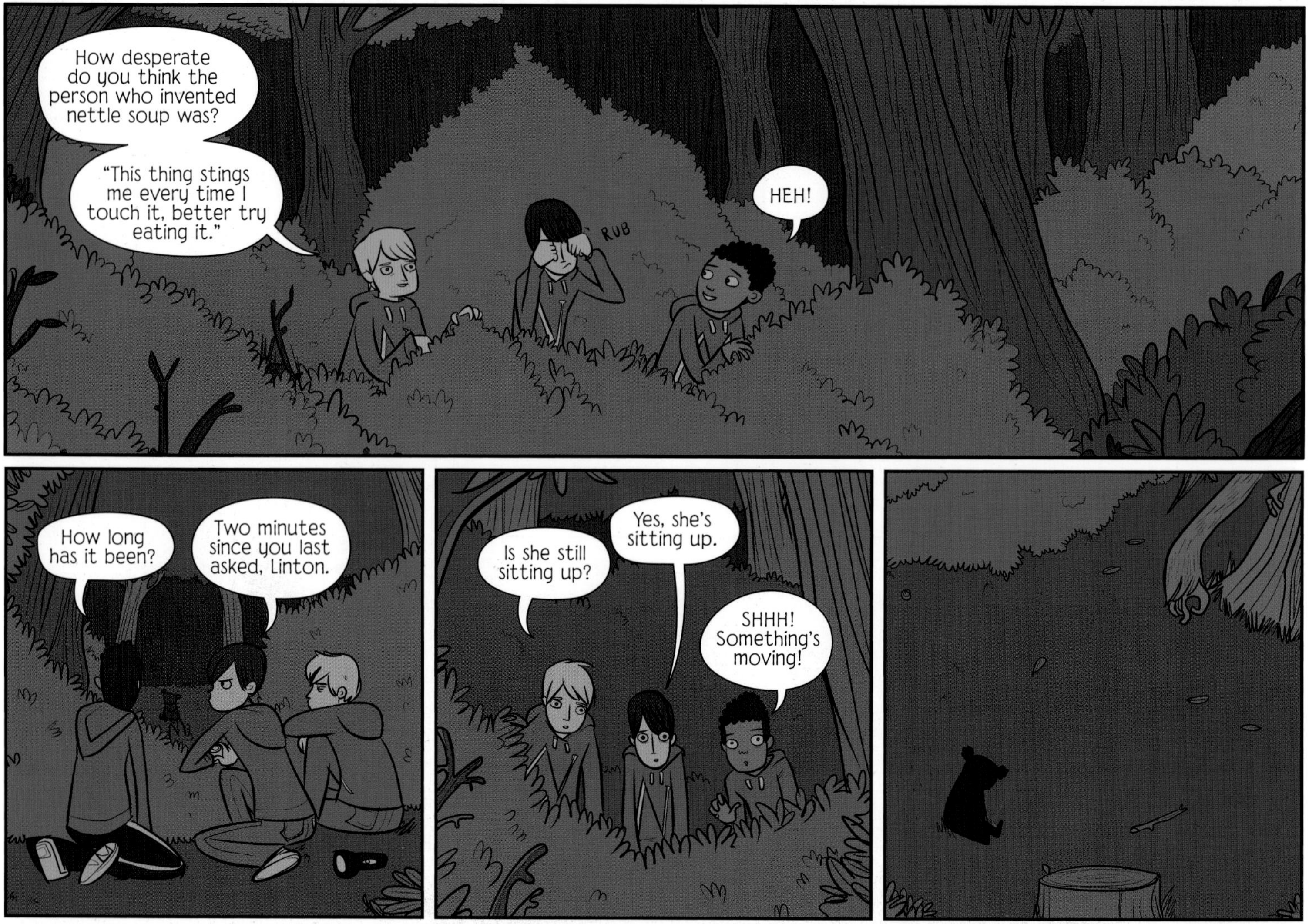
How desperate do you think the person who invented nettle soup was?
"This thing stings me every time I touch it, better try eating it."
RUB
HEH!
How long has it been?
Two minutes since you last asked, Linton.
Is she still sitting up?
Yes, she's sitting up.
SHHH! Something's moving!

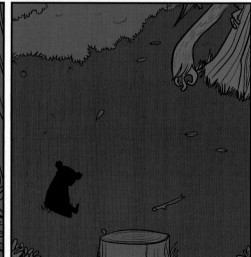

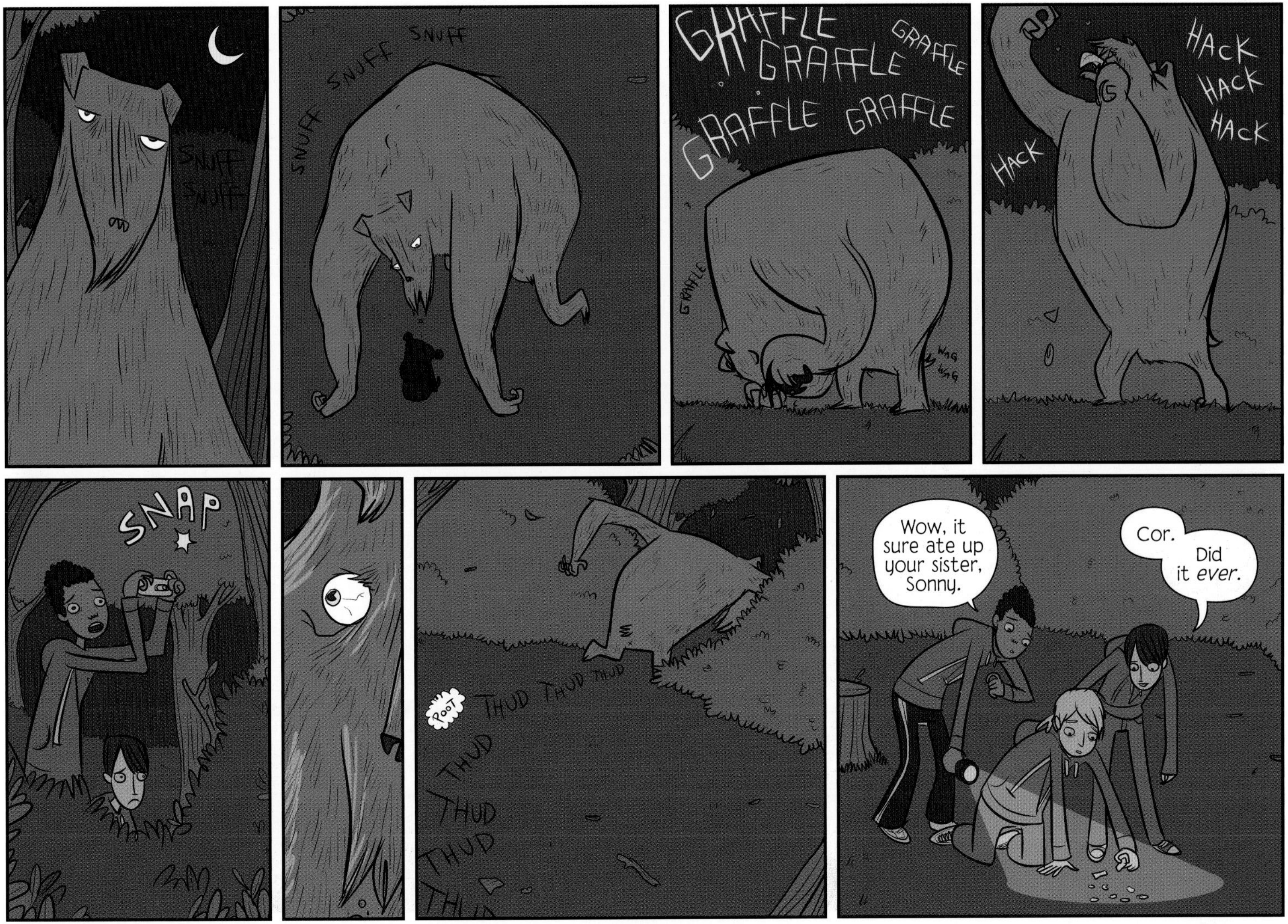
SNUFF
SNUFF
SNUFF
SNUFF
SNUFF
SNUFF
GRAFFLE
GRAFFLE
GRAFFLE
GRAFFLE
GRAFFLE
GRAFFLE
WAG
WAG
HACK
HACK
HACK
HACK
SNAP
POOT
THUD THUD THUD
THUD
THUD
THUD
Wow, it sure ate up your sister, Sonny.
Cor.
Did it *ever*.

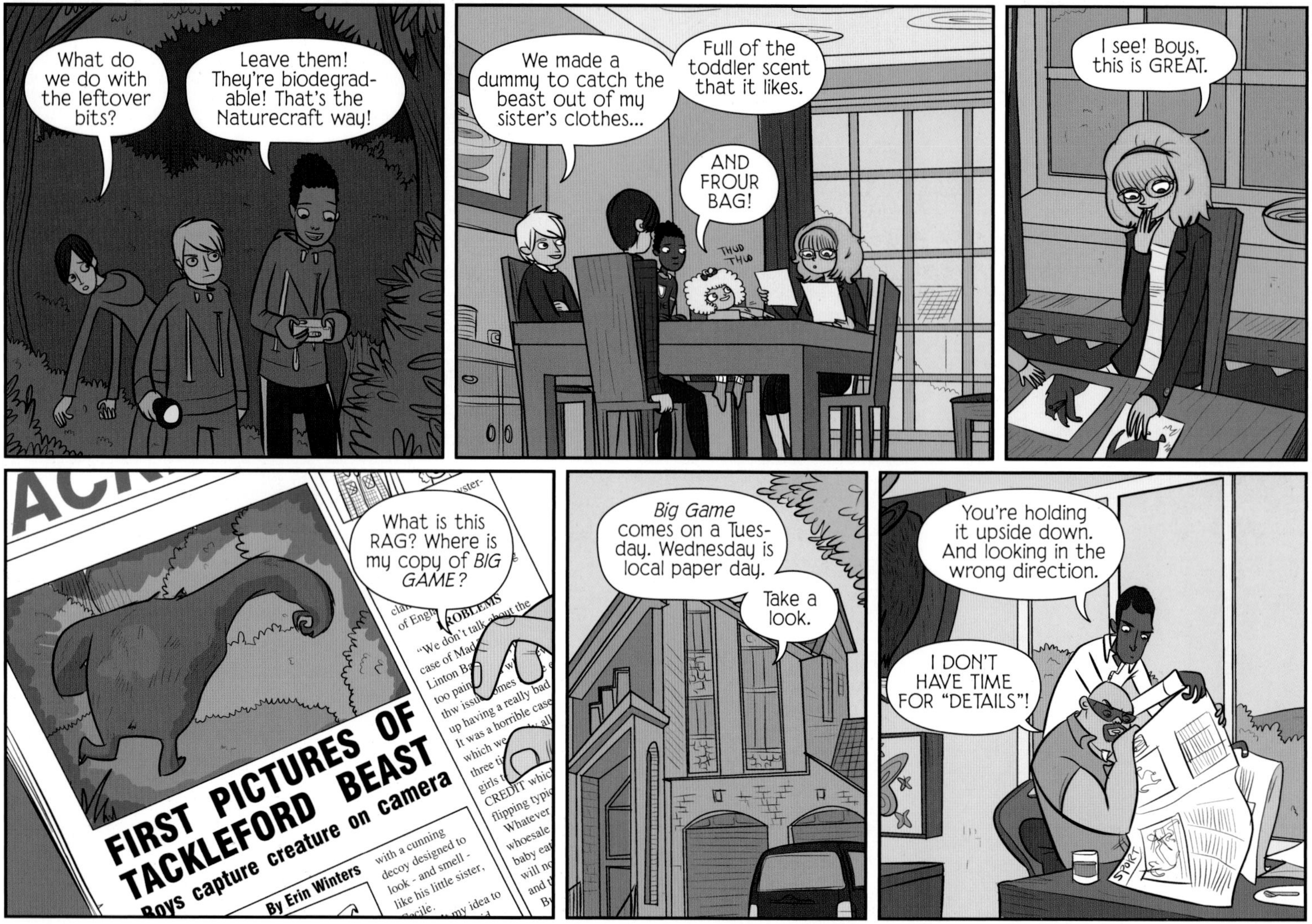
What do we do with the leftover bits?
Leave them! They're biodegradable! That's the Naturecraft way!
We made a dummy to catch the beast out of my sister's clothes...
Full of the toddler scent that it likes.
AND FROUR BAG!
THUD THUD
I see! Boys, this is GREAT.
What is this RAG? Where is my copy of *BIG GAME?*
FIRST PICTURES OF TACKLEFORD BEAST
Boys capture creature on camera
By Erin Winters
with a cunning decoy designed to look - and smell - like his little sister,
Big Game comes on a Tuesday. Wednesday is local paper day.
Take a look.
You're holding it upside down. And looking in the wrong direction.
I DON'T HAVE TIME FOR "DETAILS"!
SPORT

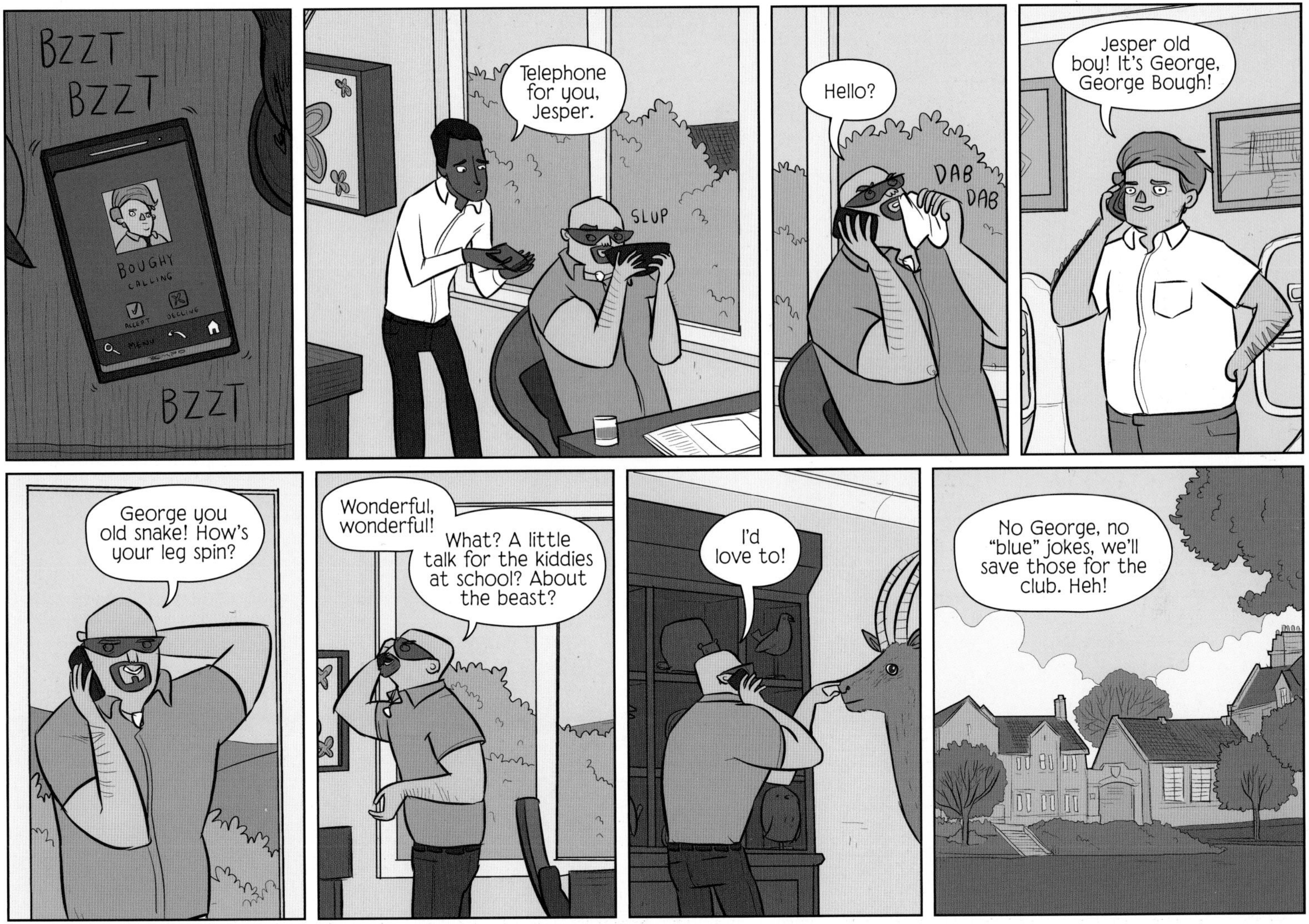
BZZT
BZZT
BOUGHY
CALLING
ACCEPT
DECLINE
MENU
BZZT
Telephone for you, Jesper.
SLUP
Hello?
DAB
DAB
Jesper old boy! It's George, George Bough!
George you old snake! How's your leg spin?
Wonderful, wonderful!
What? A little talk for the kiddies at school? About the beast?
I'd love to!
No George, no "blue" jokes, we'll save those for the club. Heh!

Bad Machinery, Volume Two

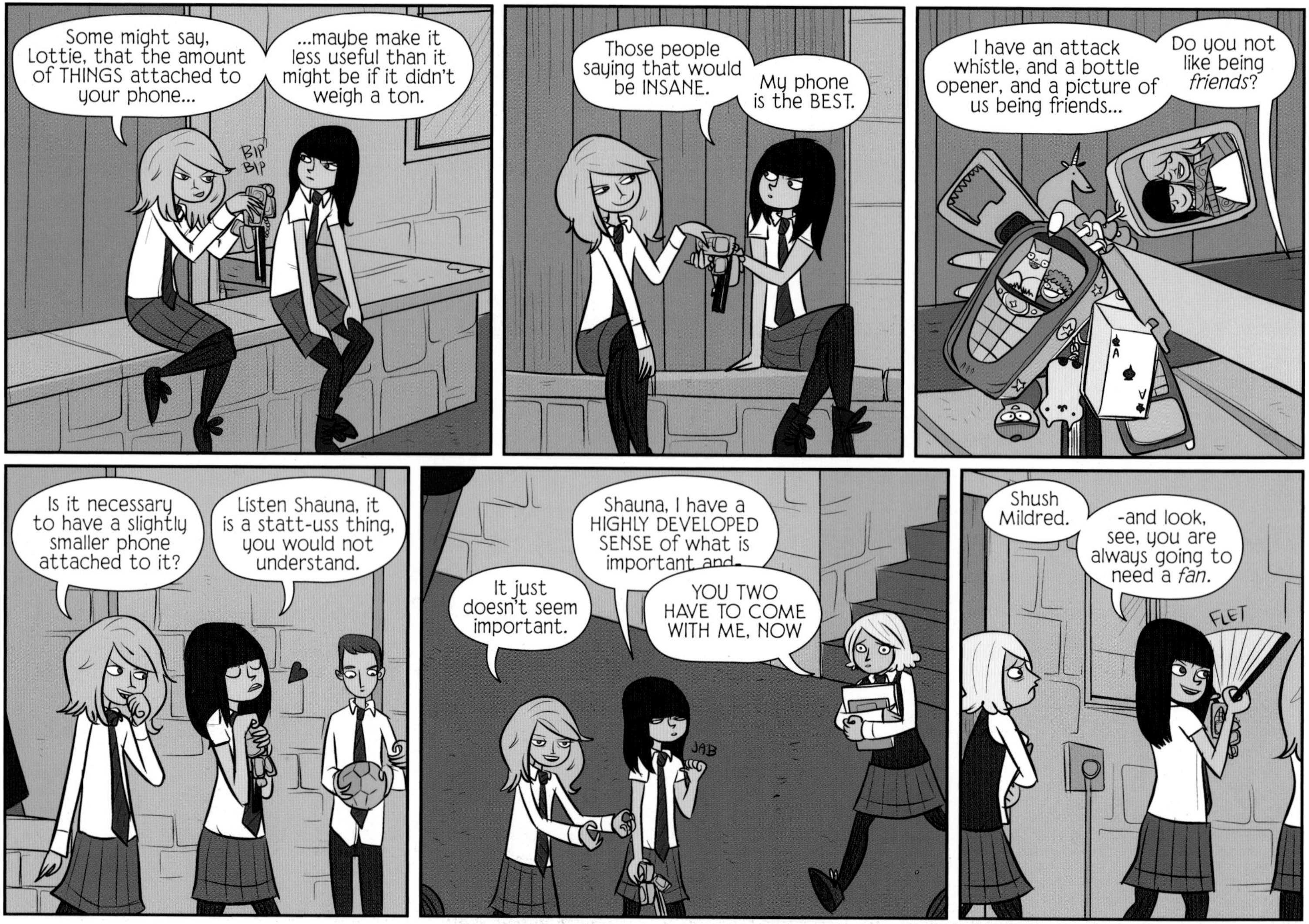

Some might say, Lottie, that the amount of THINGS attached to your phone...
...maybe make it less useful than it might be if it didn't weigh a ton.
BIP BIP
Those people saying that would be INSANE.
My phone is the BEST.
I have an attack whistle, and a bottle opener, and a picture of us being friends...
Do you not like being *friends*?
Is it necessary to have a slightly smaller phone attached to it?
Listen Shauna, it is a statt-uss thing, you would not understand.
It just doesn't seem important.
Shauna, I have a HIGHLY DEVELOPED SENSE of what is important and-
YOU TWO HAVE TO COME WITH ME, NOW
JAB
Shush Mildred.
-and look, see, you are always going to need a *fan*.
FLET

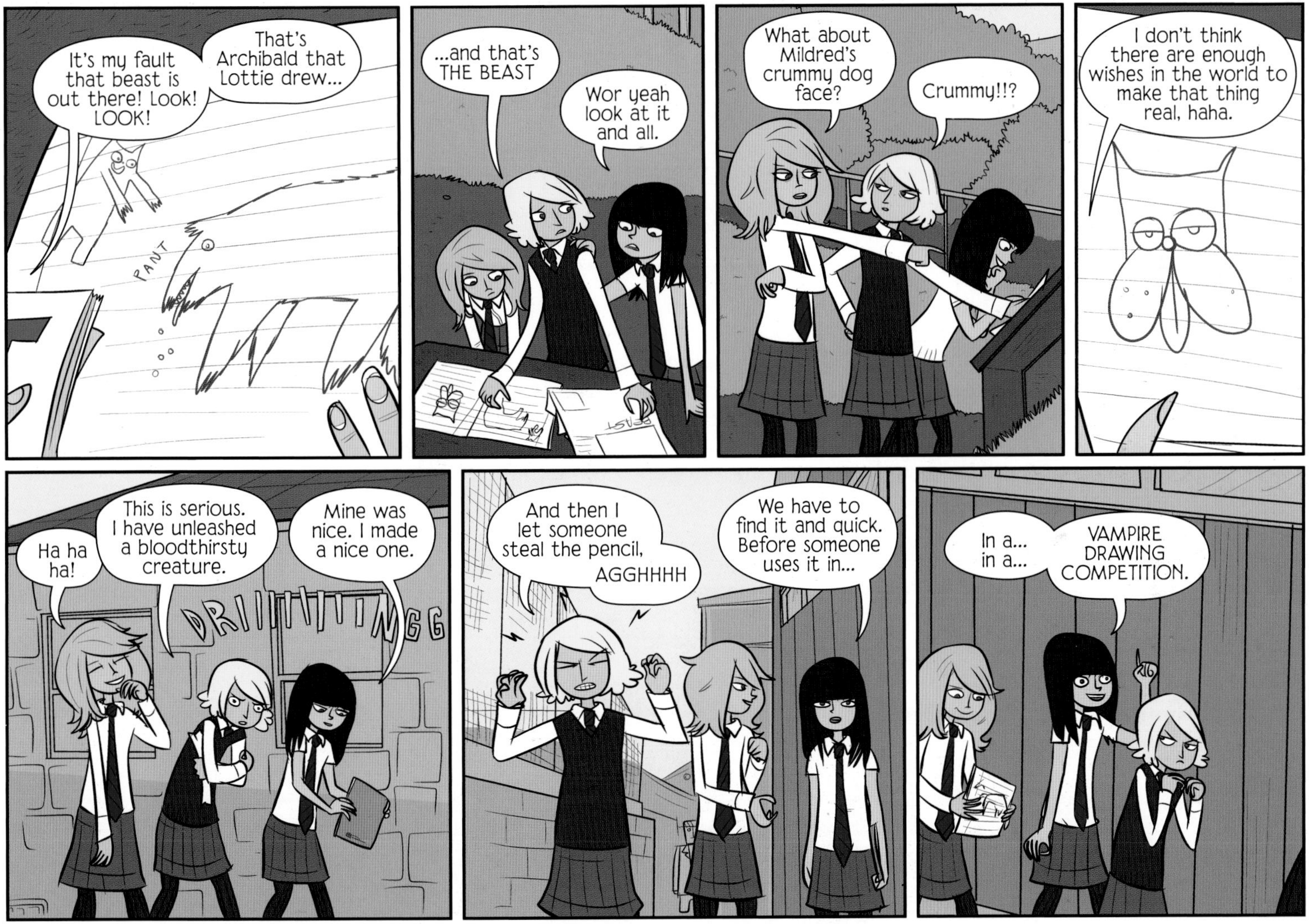

It's my fault that beast is out there! Look! LOOK!
That's Archibald that Lottie drew...
PANT
...and that's THE BEAST
Wor yeah look at it and all.
What about Mildred's crummy dog face?
Crummy!!?
I don't think there are enough wishes in the world to make that thing real, haha.
Ha ha ha!
This is serious. I have unleashed a bloodthirsty creature.
Mine was nice. I made a nice one.
DRIIIIIIIINGG
And then I let someone steal the pencil,
AGGHHHH
We have to find it and quick. Before someone uses it in...
In a... in a...
VAMPIRE DRAWING COMPETITION.

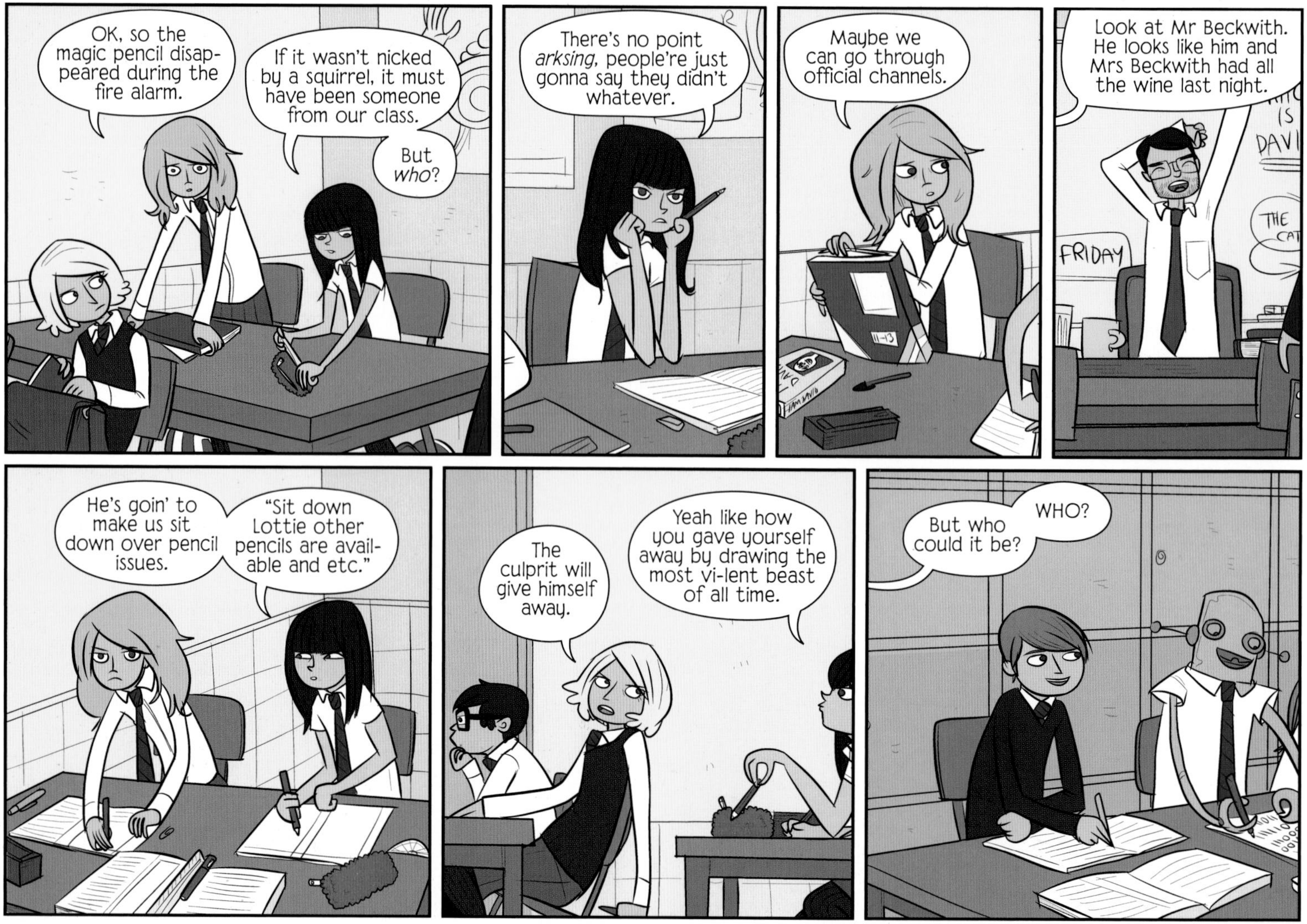
OK, so the magic pencil disappeared during the fire alarm.
If it wasn't nicked by a squirrel, it must have been someone from our class.
But *who*?
There's no point *arksing*, people're just gonna say they didn't whatever.
Maybe we can go through official channels.
Look at Mr Beckwith. He looks like him and Mrs Beckwith had all the wine last night.
FRIDAY
He's goin' to make us sit down over pencil issues.
"Sit down Lottie other pencils are available and etc."
The culprit will give himself away.
Yeah like how you gave yourself away by drawing the most vi-lent beast of all time.
But who could it be?
WHO?

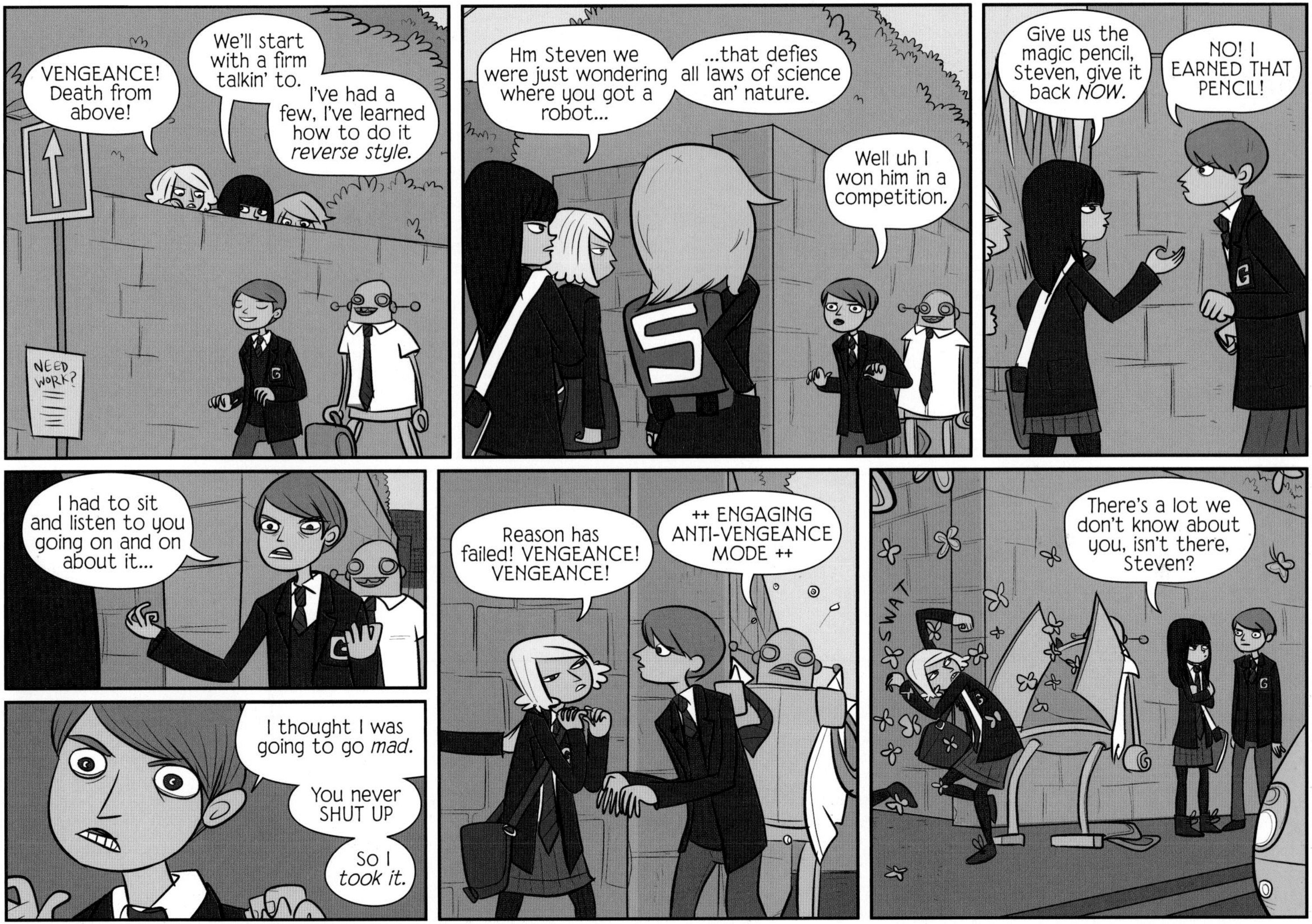
VENGEANCE! Death from above!
We'll start with a firm talkin' to.
I've had a few, I've learned how to do it *reverse style.*
NEED WORK?
Hm Steven we were just wondering where you got a robot...
...that defies all laws of science an' nature.
Well uh I won him in a competition.
Give us the magic pencil, Steven, give it back *NOW.*
NO! I EARNED THAT PENCIL!
I had to sit and listen to you going on and on about it...
I thought I was going to go *mad.*
You never SHUT UP
So I *took it.*
Reason has failed! VENGEANCE! VENGEANCE!
++ ENGAGING ANTI-VENGEANCE MODE ++
SWAT
There's a lot we don't know about you, isn't there, Steven?

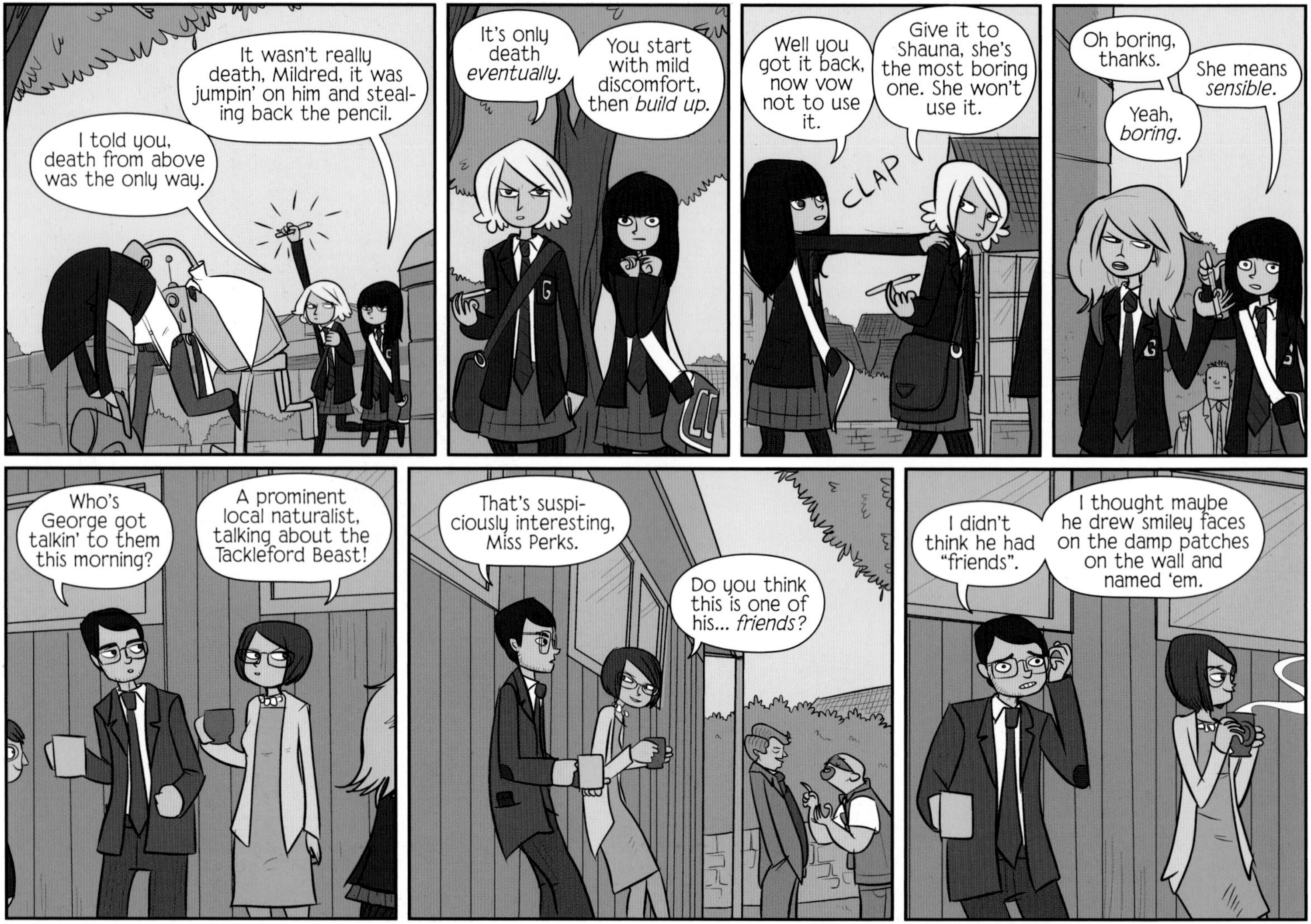
It wasn't really death, Mildred, it was jumpin' on him and stealing back the pencil.
I told you, death from above was the only way.
It's only death *eventually.*
You start with mild discomfort, then *build up.*
Well you got it back, now vow not to use it.
Give it to Shauna, she's the most boring one. She won't use it.
CLAP
Oh boring, thanks.
She means *sensible.*
Yeah, *boring.*
Who's George got talkin' to them this morning?
A prominent local naturalist, talking about the Tackleford Beast!
That's suspiciously interesting, Miss Perks.
Do you think this is one of his... *friends?*
I didn't think he had "friends".
I thought maybe he drew smiley faces on the damp patches on the wall and named 'em.

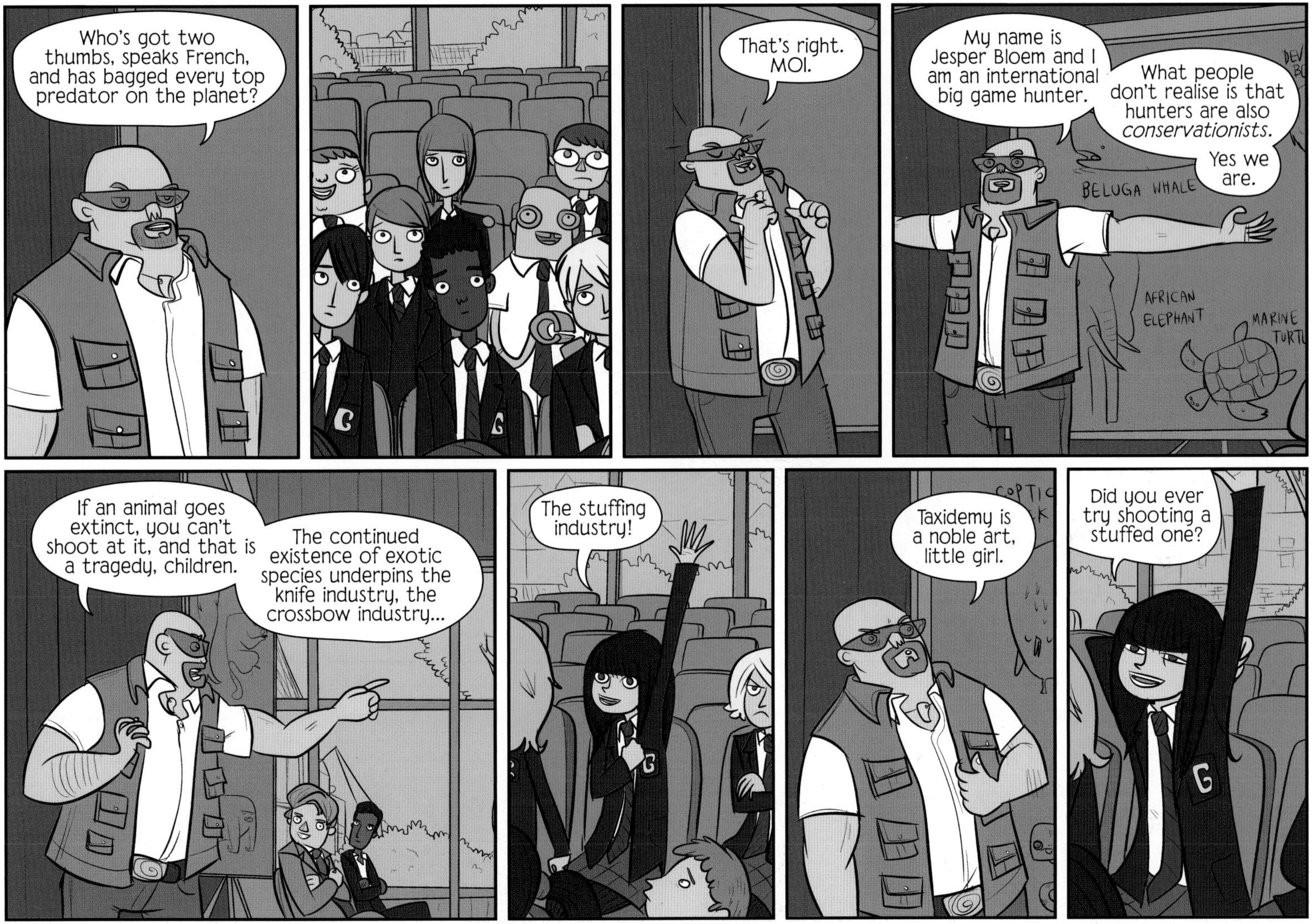

Who's got two thumbs, speaks French, and has bagged every top predator on the planet?
That's right. MOI.
My name is Jesper Bloem and I am an international big game hunter.
What people don't realise is that hunters are also *conservationists.*
Yes we are.
BELUGA WHALE
AFRICAN ELEPHANT
If an animal goes extinct, you can't shoot at it, and that is a tragedy, children.
The continued existence of exotic species underpins the knife industry, the crossbow industry...
The stuffing industry!
Taxidemy is a noble art, little girl.
Did you ever try shooting a stuffed one?

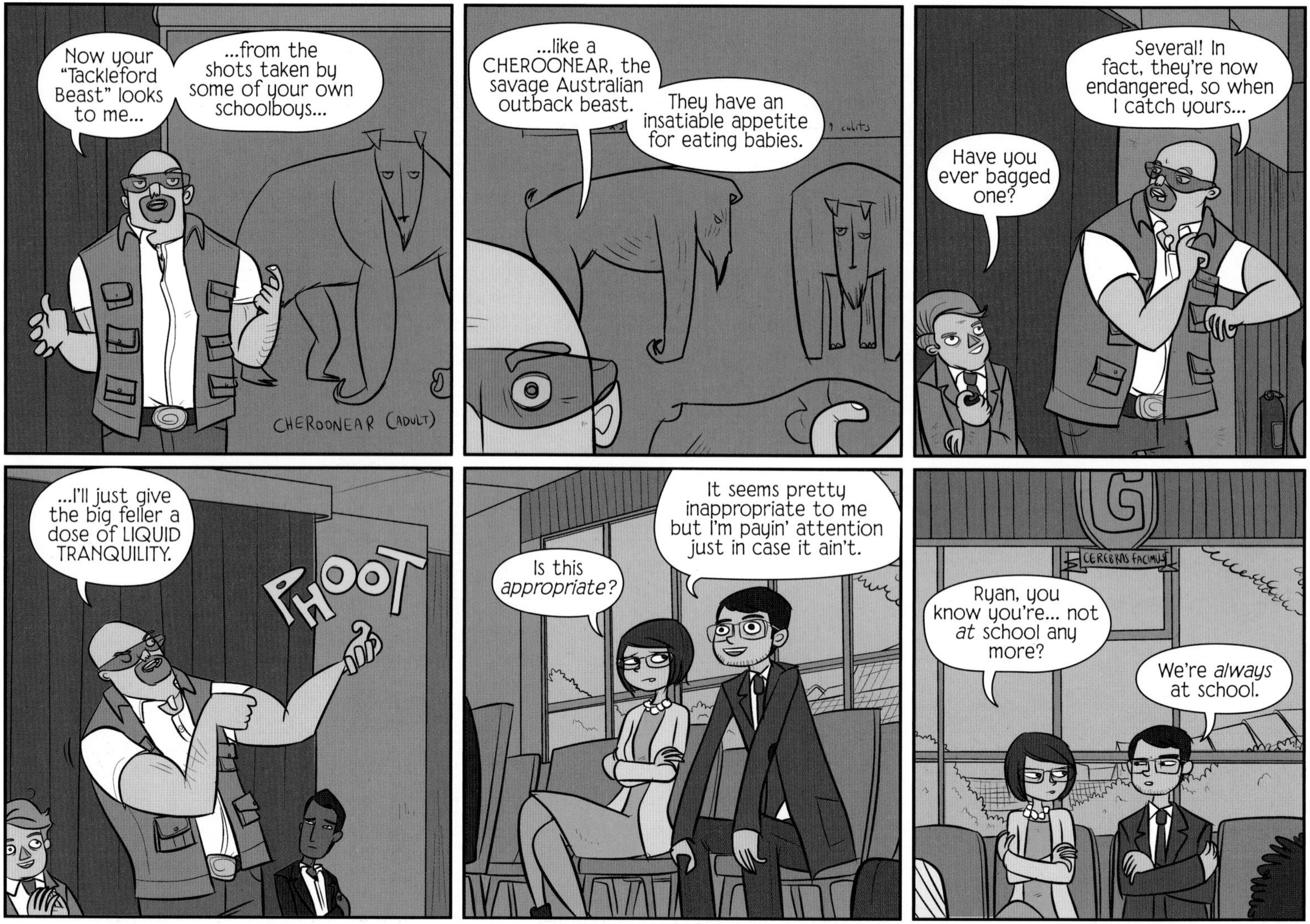
Now your "Tackleford Beast" looks to me...
...from the shots taken by some of your own schoolboys...
CHEROONEAR (ADULT)
...like a CHEROONEAR, the savage Australian outback beast.
They have an insatiable appetite for eating babies.
Have you ever bagged one?
Several! In fact, they're now endangered, so when I catch yours...
...I'll just give the big feller a dose of LIQUID TRANQUILITY.
PHOOT
Is this *appropriate?*
It seems pretty inappropriate to me but I'm payin' attention just in case it ain't.
Ryan, you know you're... not *at* school any more?
We're *always* at school.

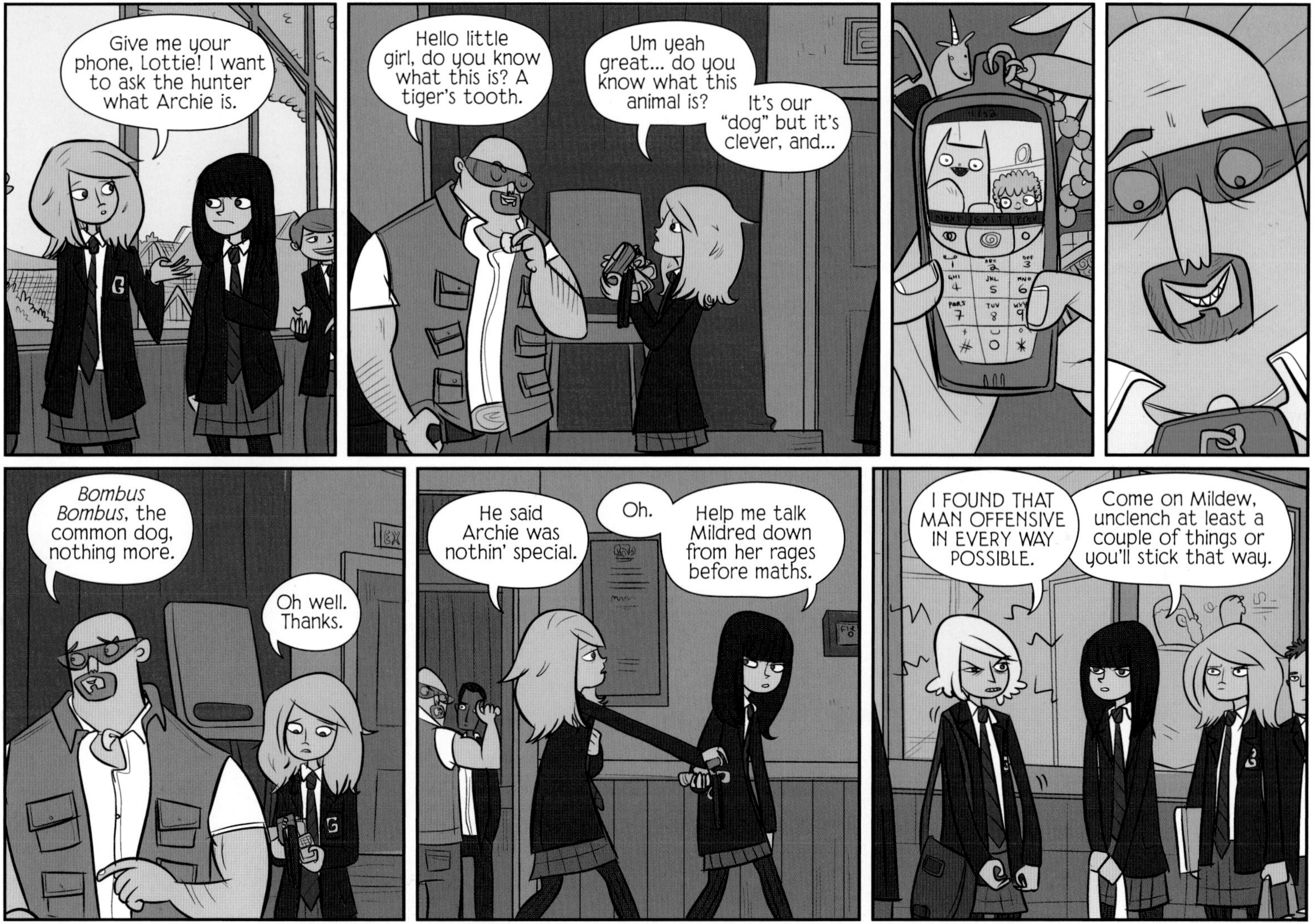
Give me your phone, Lottie! I want to ask the hunter what Archie is.
Hello little girl, do you know what this is? A tiger's tooth.
Um yeah great... do you know what this animal is?
It's our "dog" but it's clever, and...
Bombus Bombus, the common dog, nothing more.
Oh well. Thanks.
He said Archie was nothin' special.
Oh.
Help me talk Mildred down from her rages before maths.
I FOUND THAT MAN OFFENSIVE IN EVERY WAY POSSIBLE.
Come on Mildew, unclench at least a couple of things or you'll stick that way.

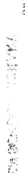

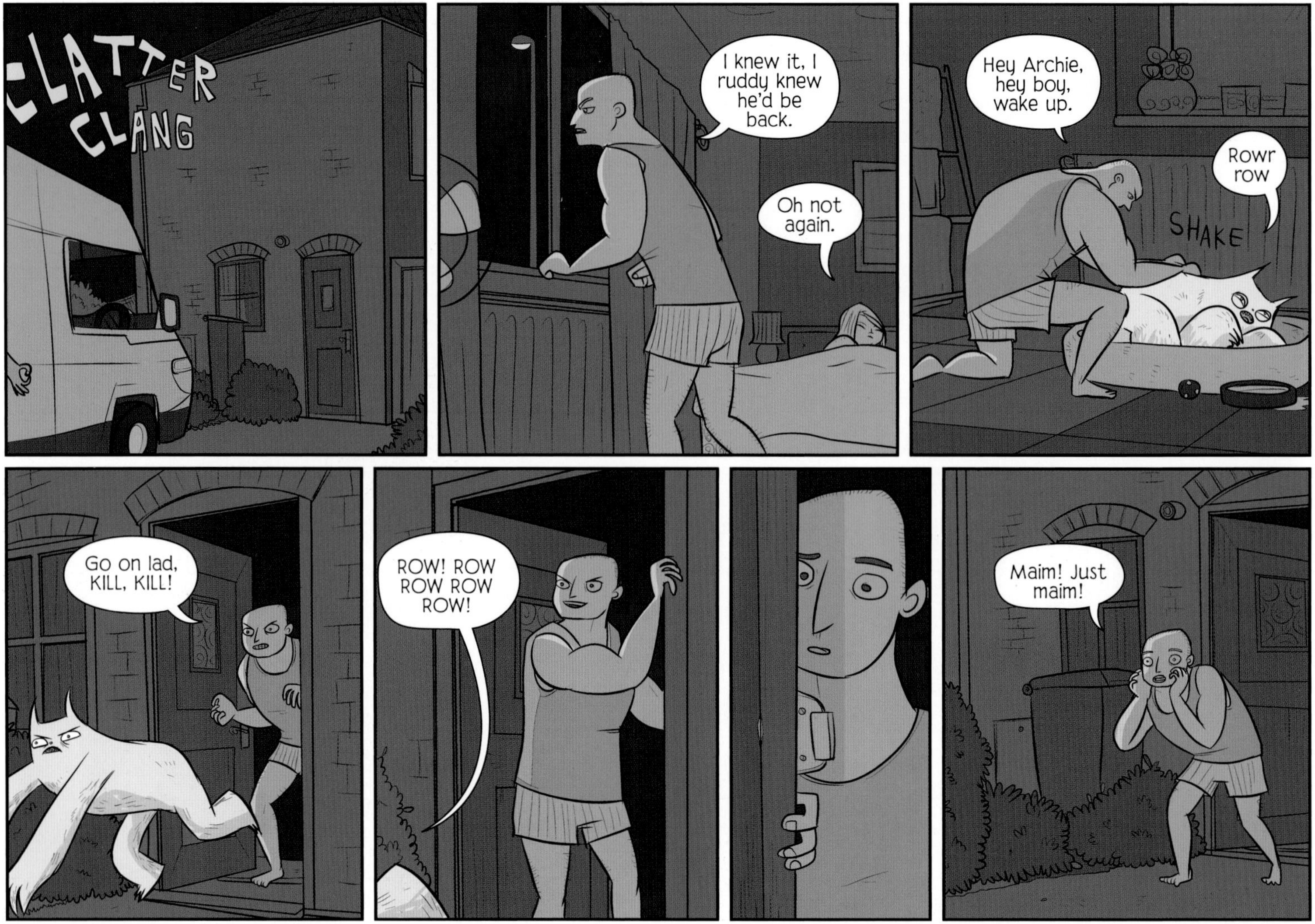
CLATTER
CLANG
I knew it, I ruddy knew he'd be back.
Oh not again.
Hey Archie, hey boy, wake up.
Rowr row
SHAKE
Go on lad, KILL, KILL!
ROW! ROW ROW ROW ROW!
Maim! Just maim!

ROW! ROW ROW ROW ROW!

PHOOT

Dan! Dan they took him! They took *Archibald*!

Don't be daft, he went mad, he'll have chased them off.

Archie?

Where... where did he go?

THEY TOOK HIM!

Shauna, no one's going to stick around to get bitten.

She doesn't make things up, love.

I'll go and look.

These men took him, they stole him!

Calm down love, you'll make yourself sick.

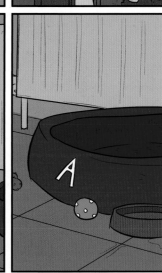

A

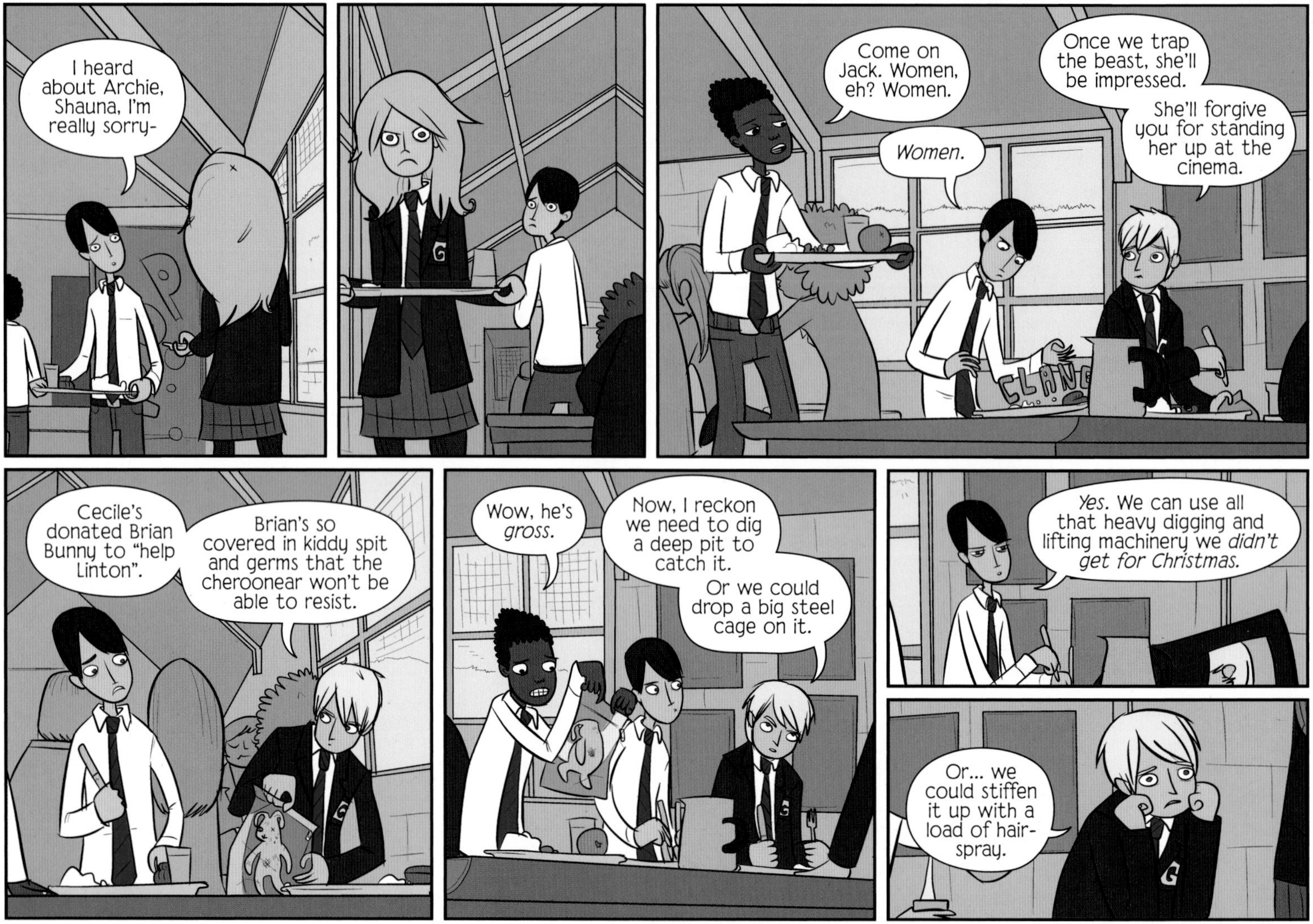
I heard about Archie, Shauna, I'm really sorry-
Come on Jack. Women, eh? Women.
Women.
Once we trap the beast, she'll be impressed.
She'll forgive you for standing her up at the cinema.
CLANG
Cecile's donated Brian Bunny to "help Linton".
Brian's so covered in kiddy spit and germs that the cheroonear won't be able to resist.
Wow, he's *gross.*
Now, I reckon we need to dig a deep pit to catch it.
Or we could drop a big steel cage on it.
Yes. We can use all that heavy digging and lifting machinery we *didn't get for Christmas.*
Or... we could stiffen it up with a load of hair-spray.

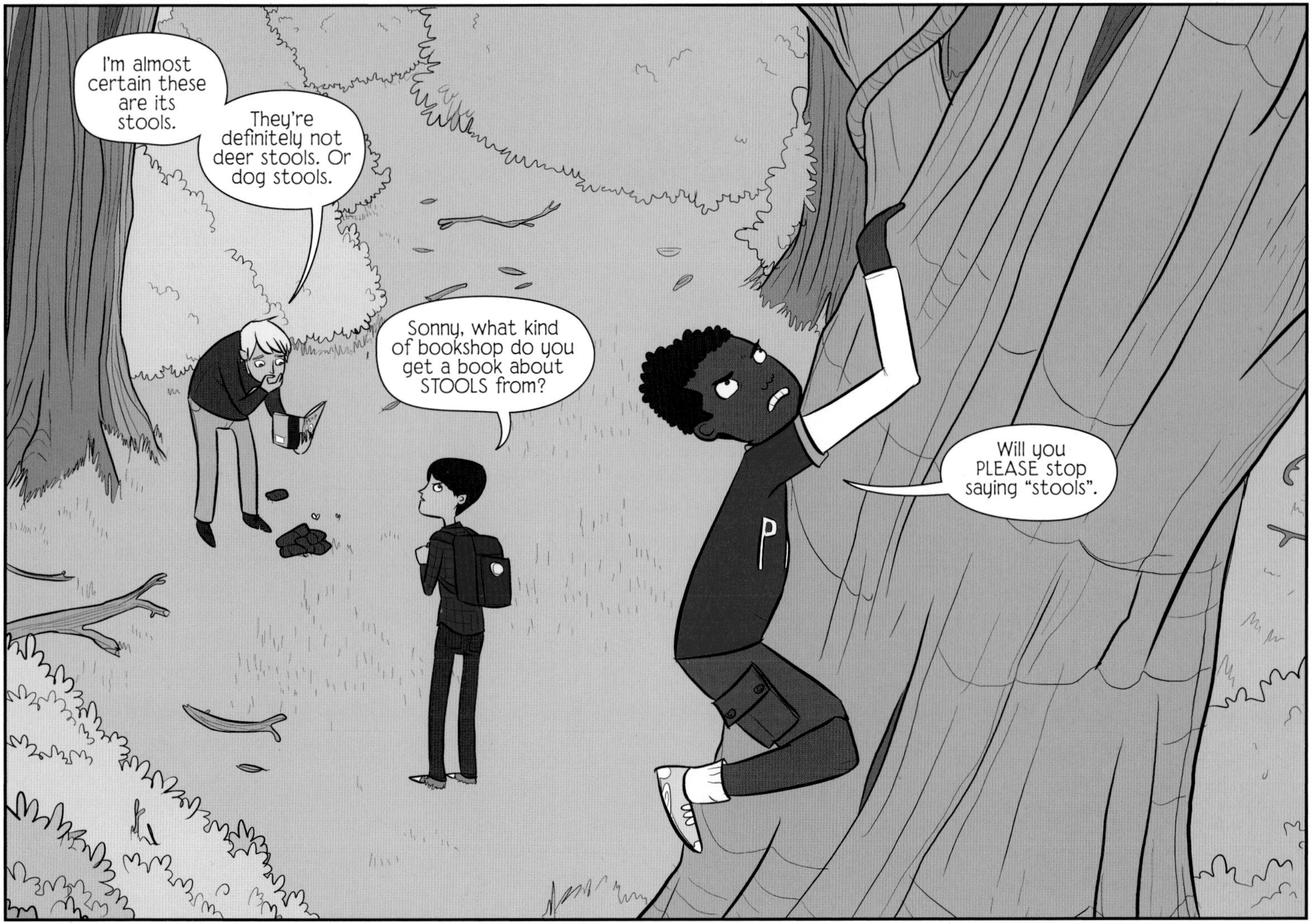
I'm almost certain these are its stools.
They're definitely not deer stools. Or dog stools.
Sonny, what kind of bookshop do you get a book about STOOLS from?
Will you PLEASE stop saying "stools".

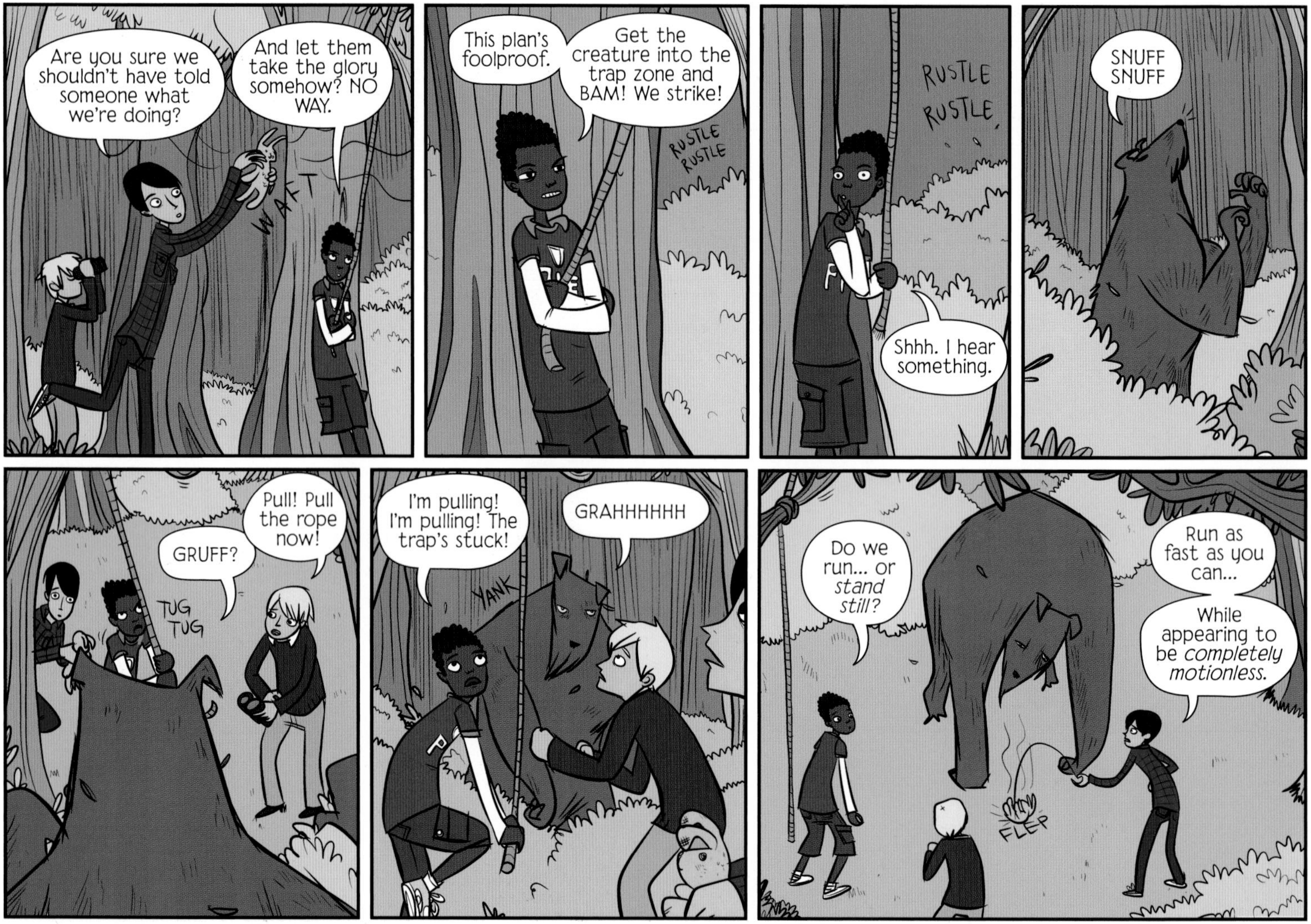
Are you sure we shouldn't have told someone what we're doing?
And let them take the glory somehow? NO WAY.
WAFT
This plan's foolproof.
Get the creature into the trap zone and BAM! We strike!
RUSTLE RUSTLE
RUSTLE RUSTLE
Shhh. I hear something.
SNUFF SNUFF
GRUFF?
Pull! Pull the rope now!
TUG TUG
I'm pulling! I'm pulling! The trap's stuck!
GRAHHHHHH
YANK
Do we run... or *stand still?*
Run as fast as you can...
While appearing to be *completely motionless.*
FLEP

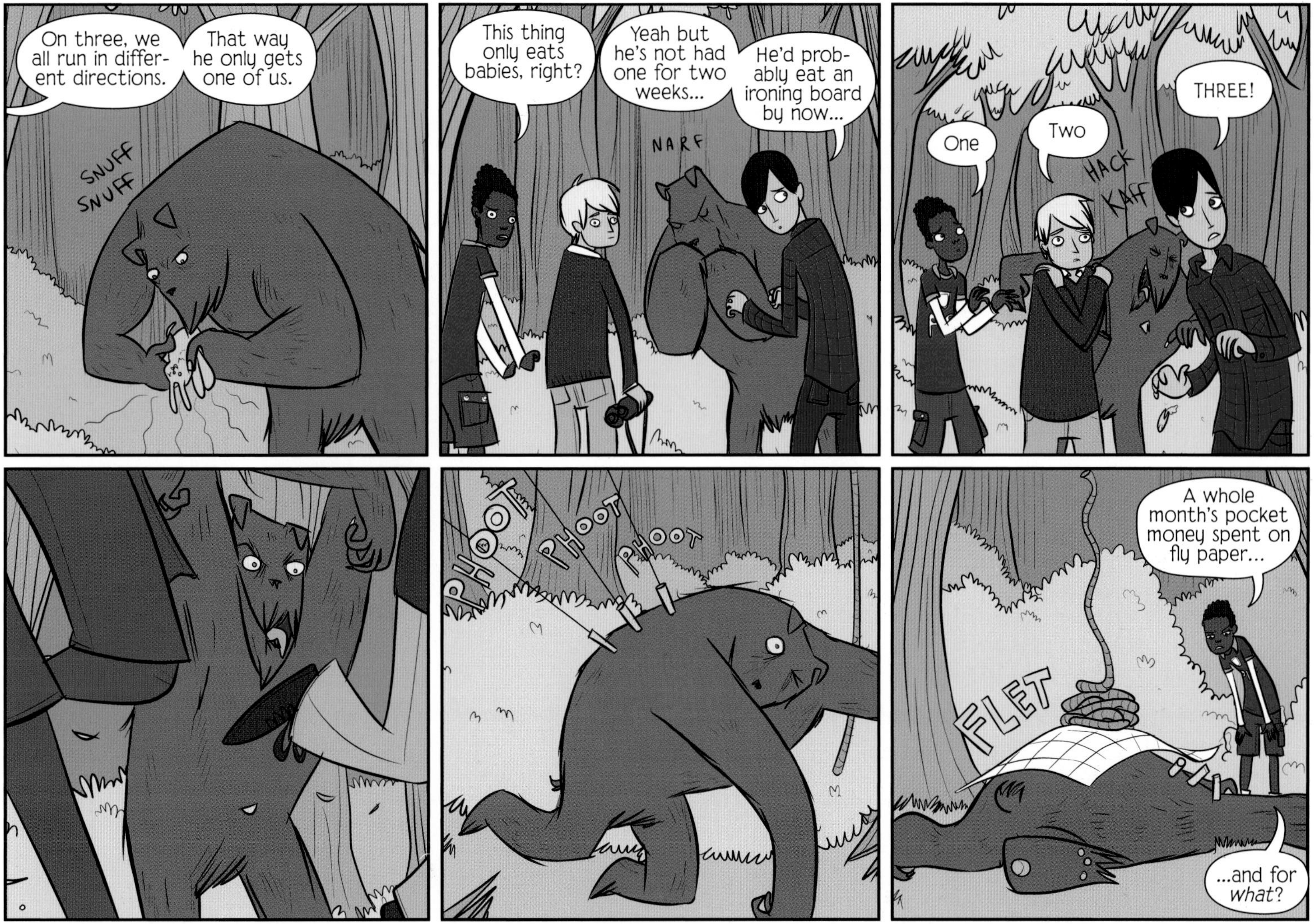
On three, we all run in differ-ent directions.
That way he only gets one of us.
SNUFF SNUFF
This thing only eats babies, right?
Yeah but he's not had one for two weeks...
He'd prob-ably eat an ironing board by now...
NARF
One
Two
HACK KAFF
THREE!
PHOOT
PHOOT
PHOOT
A whole month's pocket money spent on fly paper...
FLET
...and for *what*?

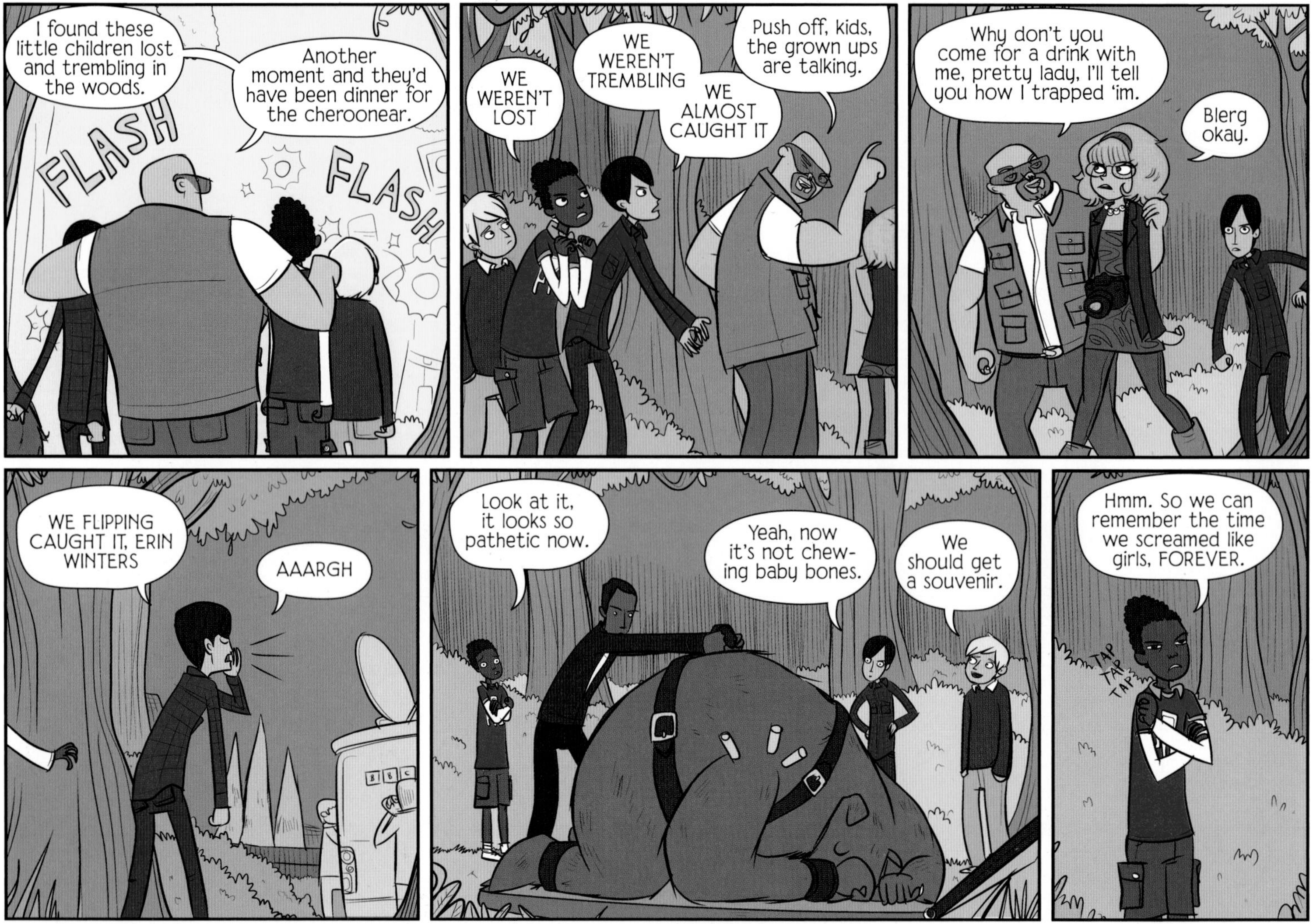
I found these little children lost and trembling in the woods.
Another moment and they'd have been dinner for the cheroonear.
FLASH
FLASH
WE WEREN'T LOST
WE WEREN'T TREMBLING
WE ALMOST CAUGHT IT
Push off, kids, the grown ups are talking.
Why don't you come for a drink with me, pretty lady, I'll tell you how I trapped 'im.
Blerg okay.
WE FLIPPING CAUGHT IT, ERIN WINTERS
AAARGH
Look at it, it looks so pathetic now.
Yeah, now it's not chewing baby bones.
We should get a souvenir.
Hmm. So we can remember the time we screamed like girls, FOREVER.
TAP TAP TAP

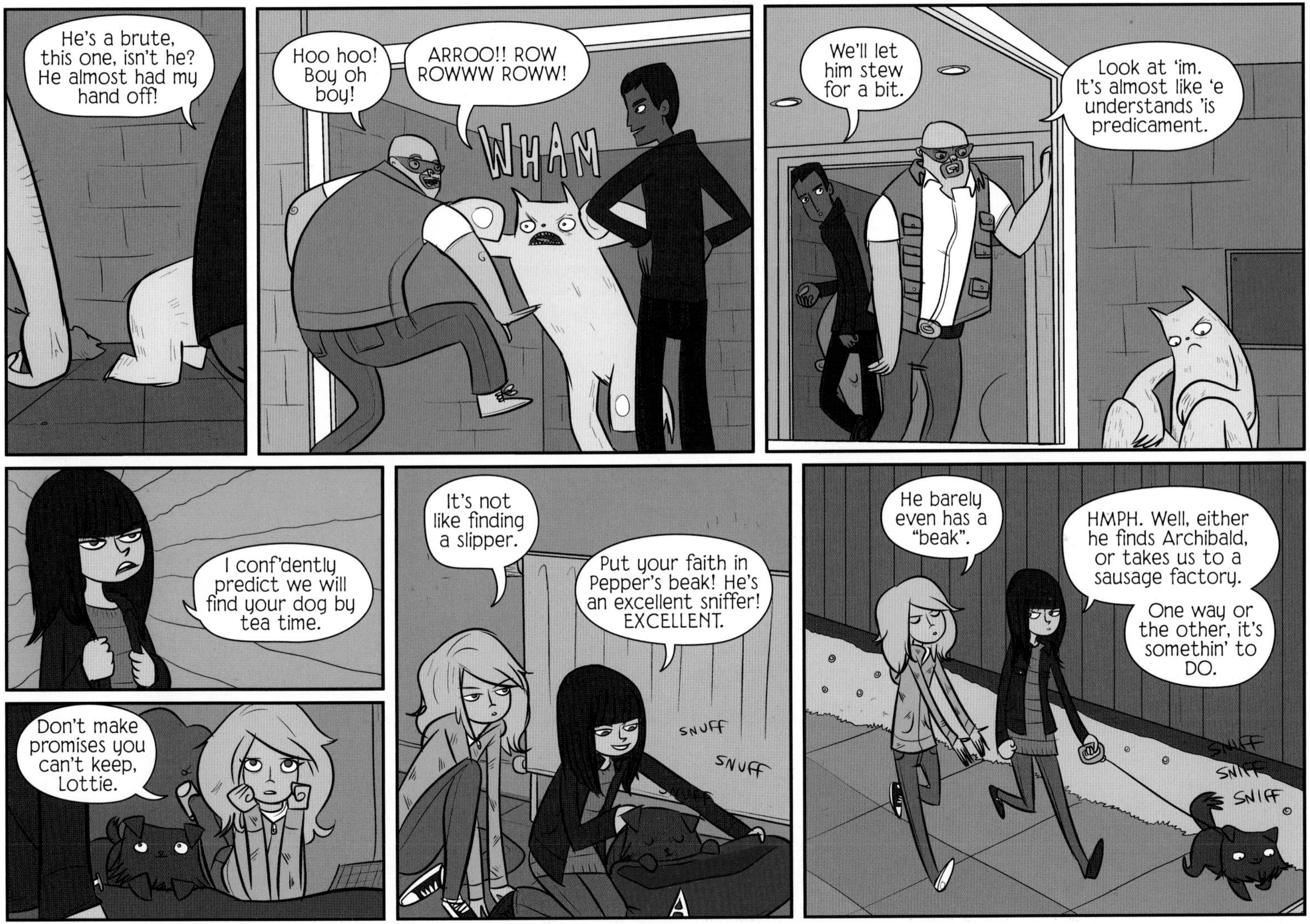
He's a brute, this one, isn't he? He almost had my hand off!
Hoo hoo! Boy oh boy!
ARROO!! ROW ROWWW ROWW!
WHAM
We'll let him stew for a bit.
Look at 'im. It's almost like 'e understands 'is predicament.
I conf'dently predict we will find your dog by tea time.
Don't make promises you can't keep, Lottie.
It's not like finding a slipper.
Put your faith in Pepper's beak! He's an excellent sniffer! EXCELLENT.
SNUFF
SNUFF
He barely even has a "beak".
HMPH. Well, either he finds Archibald, or takes us to a sausage factory.
One way or the other, it's somethin' to DO.
SNIFF
SNIFF
SNIFF

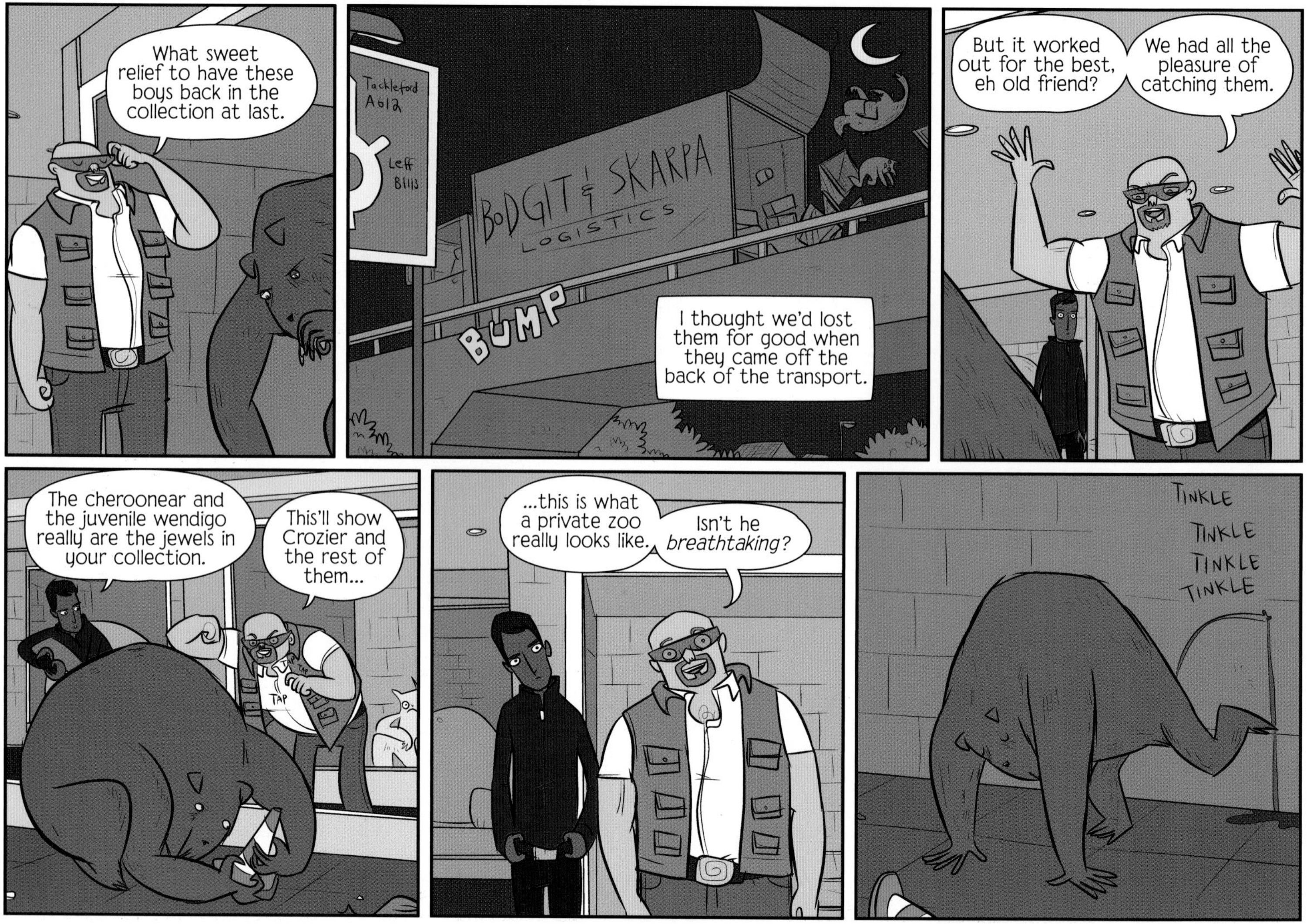
What sweet relief to have these boys back in the collection at last.
Tackleford A612
Leff B1113
BODGIT & SKARPA LOGISTICS
BUMP
I thought we'd lost them for good when they came off the back of the transport.
But it worked out for the best, eh old friend?
We had all the pleasure of catching them.
The cheroonear and the juvenile wendigo really are the jewels in your collection.
This'll show Crozier and the rest of them...
TAP TAP
TAP
...this is what a private zoo really looks like.
Isn't he *breathtaking?*
TINKLE
TINKLE
TINKLE
TINKLE

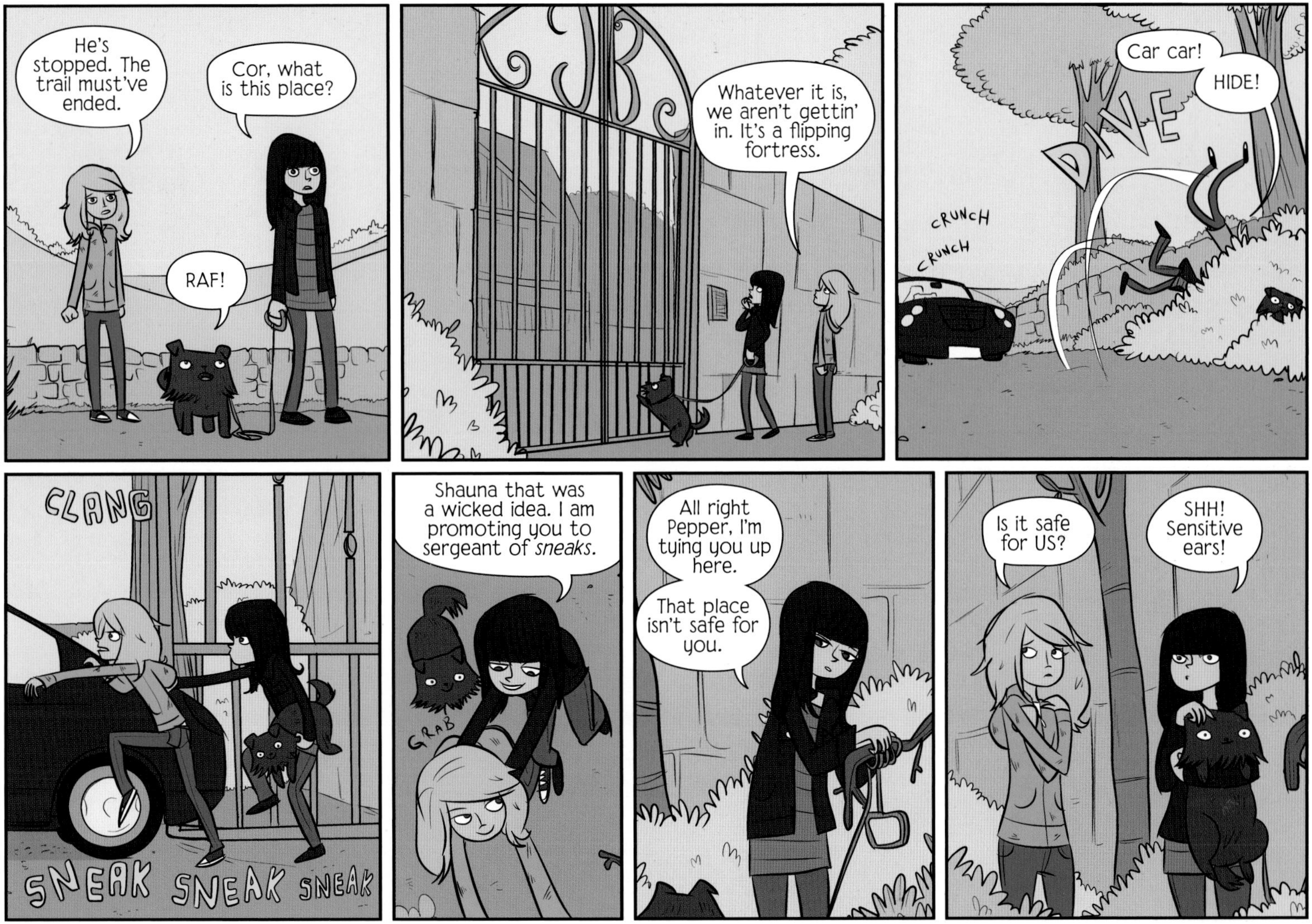

He's stopped. The trail must've ended.
Cor, what is this place?
RAF!
Whatever it is, we aren't gettin' in. It's a flipping fortress.
Car car!
HIDE!
DIVE
CRUNCH
CRUNCH
CLANG
SNEAK SNEAK SNEAK
Shauna that was a wicked idea. I am promoting you to sergeant of *sneaks.*
GRAB
All right Pepper, I'm tying you up here.
That place isn't safe for you.
Is it safe for US?
SHH! Sensitive ears!

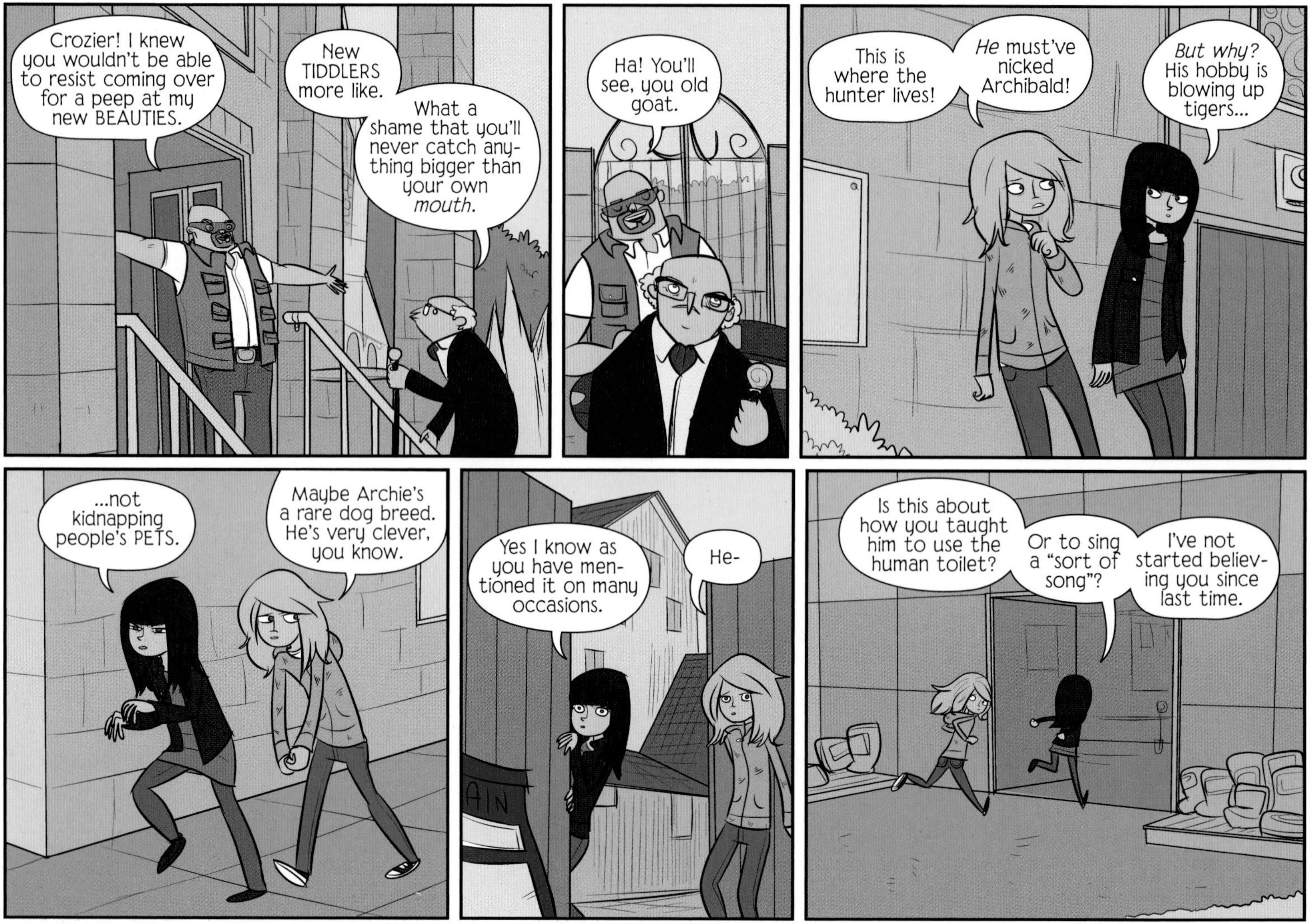
Crozier! I knew you wouldn't be able to resist coming over for a peep at my new BEAUTIES.
New TIDDLERS more like.
What a shame that you'll never catch anything bigger than your own *mouth*.
Ha! You'll see, you old goat.
This is where the hunter lives!
He must've nicked Archibald!
But why? His hobby is blowing up tigers...
...not kidnapping people's PETS.
Maybe Archie's a rare dog breed. He's very clever, you know.
Yes I know as you have mentioned it on many occasions.
He-
Is this about how you taught him to use the human toilet?
Or to sing a "sort of song"?
I've not started believing you since last time.

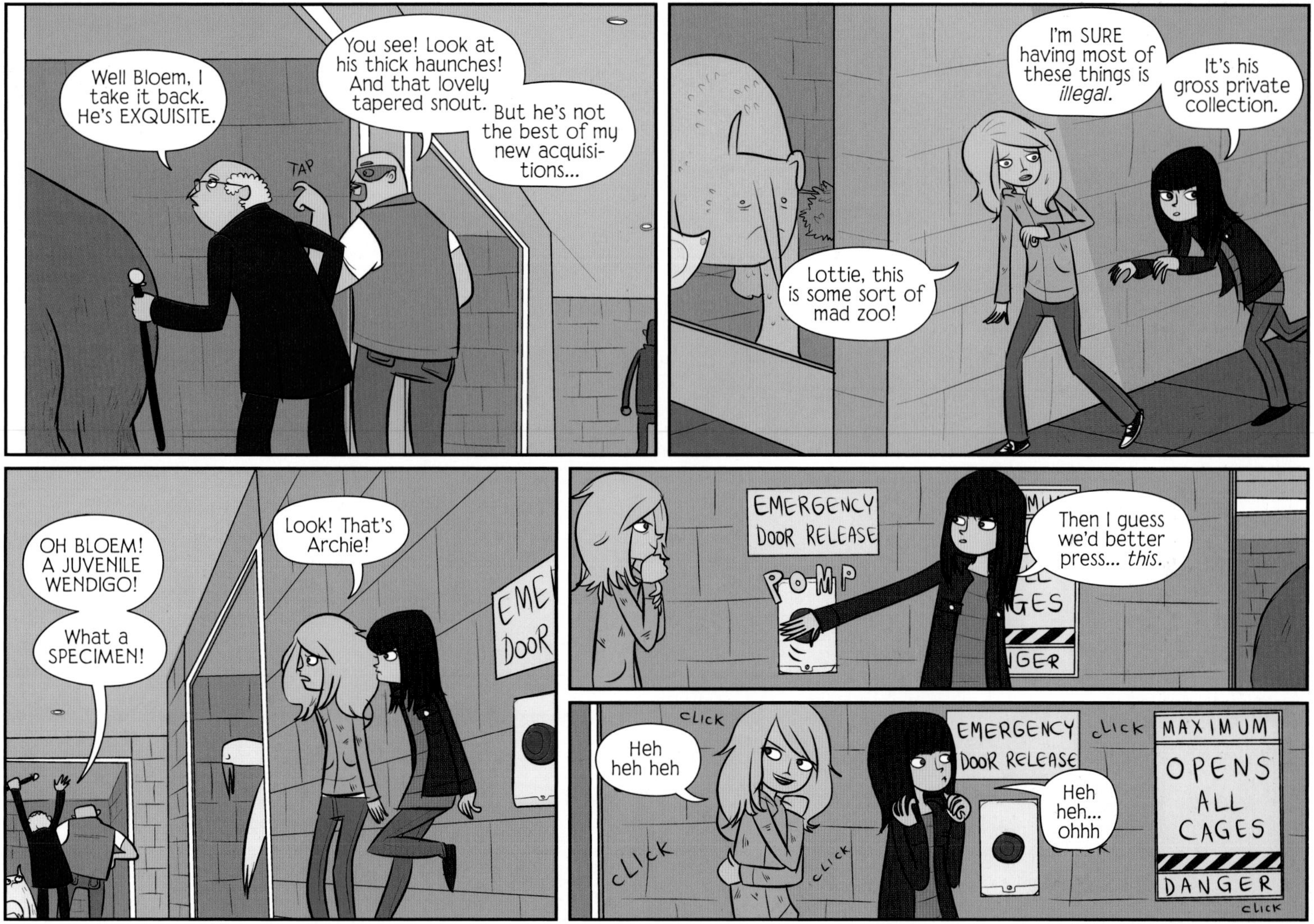
Well Bloem, I take it back. He's EXQUISITE.
TAP
You see! Look at his thick haunches! And that lovely tapered snout.
But he's not the best of my new acquisitions...
Lottie, this is some sort of mad zoo!
I'm SURE having most of these things is *illegal*.
It's his gross private collection.
OH BLOEM! A JUVENILE WENDIGO!
What a SPECIMEN!
Look! That's Archie!
EME
DOOR
EMERGENCY DOOR RELEASE
POMP
Then I guess we'd better press... *this*.
GES
GER
CLICK
Heh heh heh
EMERGENCY DOOR RELEASE
CLICK
MAXIMUM
OPENS ALL CAGES
DANGER
Heh heh... ohhh
CLICK
CLICK
CLICK

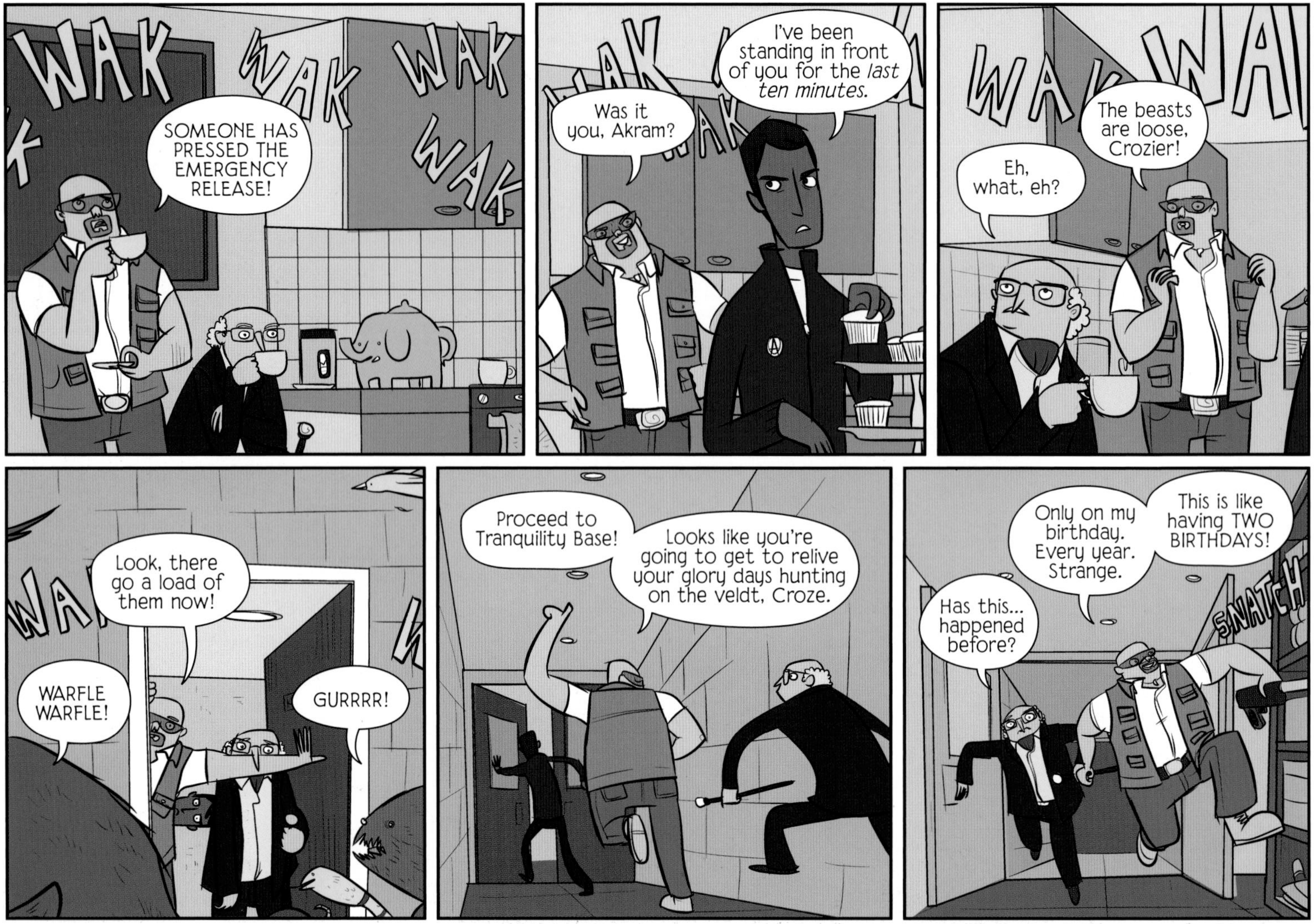
WAK
WAK
WAK
WAK
WAK
SOMEONE HAS PRESSED THE EMERGENCY RELEASE!
Was it you, Akram?
I've been standing in front of you for the *last ten minutes.*
The beasts are loose, Crozier!
Eh, what, eh?
Look, there go a load of them now!
WARFLE WARFLE!
GURRRR!
Proceed to Tranquility Base!
Looks like you're going to get to relive your glory days hunting on the veldt, Croze.
Has this... happened before?
Only on my birthday. Every year. Strange.
This is like having TWO BIRTHDAYS!
SNATCH

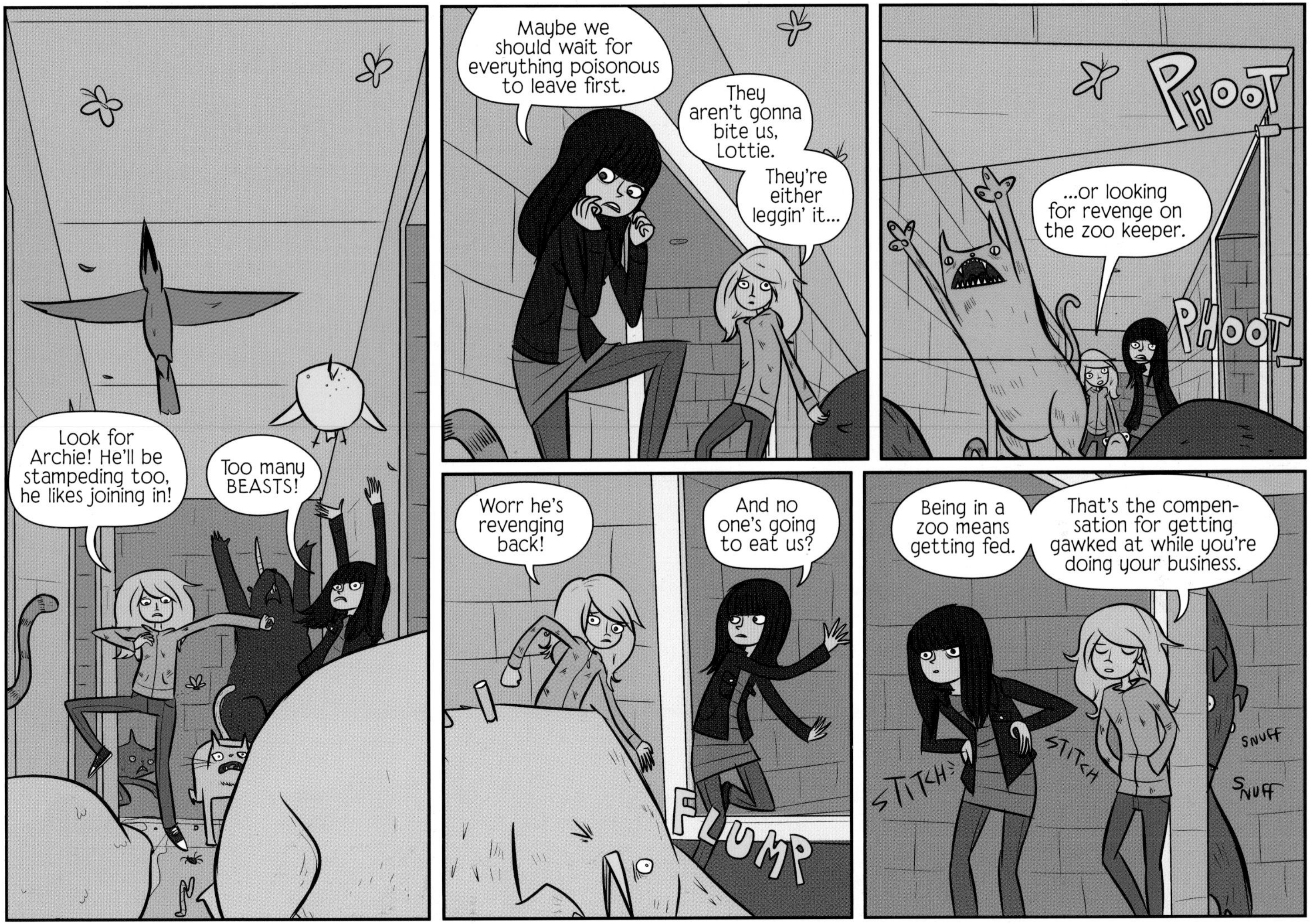
Look for Archie! He'll be stampeding too, he likes joining in!
Too many BEASTS!
Maybe we should wait for everything poisonous to leave first.
They aren't gonna bite us, Lottie.
They're either leggin' it...
PHOOT
...or looking for revenge on the zoo keeper.
PHOOT
Worr he's revenging back!
And no one's going to eat us?
FLUMP
Being in a zoo means getting fed.
That's the compen-sation for getting gawked at while you're doing your business.
STITCH
STITCH
SNUFF
SNUFF

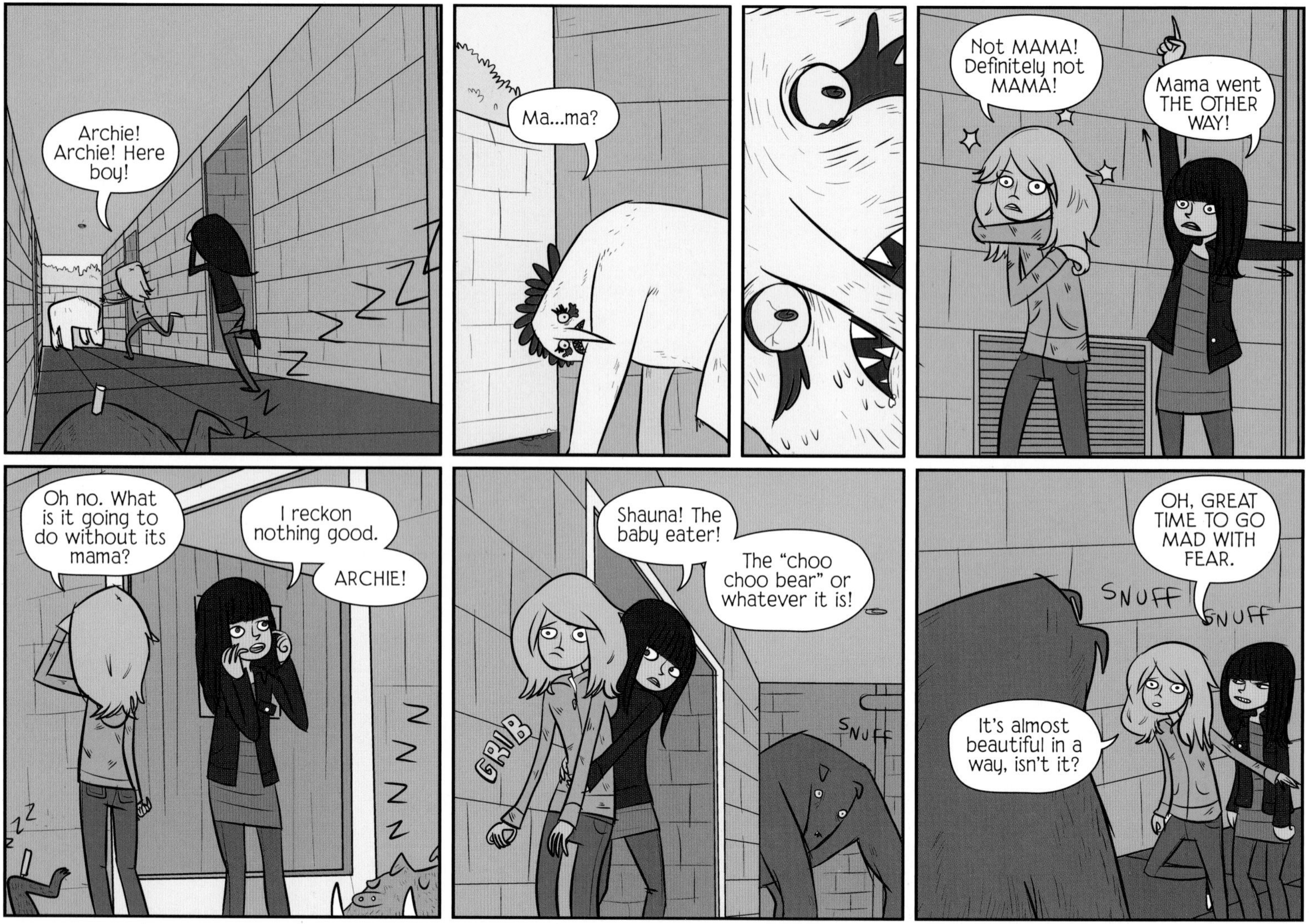
Archie! Archie! Here boy!
Ma...ma?
Not MAMA! Definitely not MAMA!
Mama went THE OTHER WAY!
Oh no. What is it going to do without its mama?
I reckon nothing good.
ARCHIE!
Shauna! The baby eater!
The "choo choo bear" or whatever it is!
GRIB
SNUFF
OH, GREAT TIME TO GO MAD WITH FEAR.
SNUFF
SNUFF
It's almost beautiful in a way, isn't it?

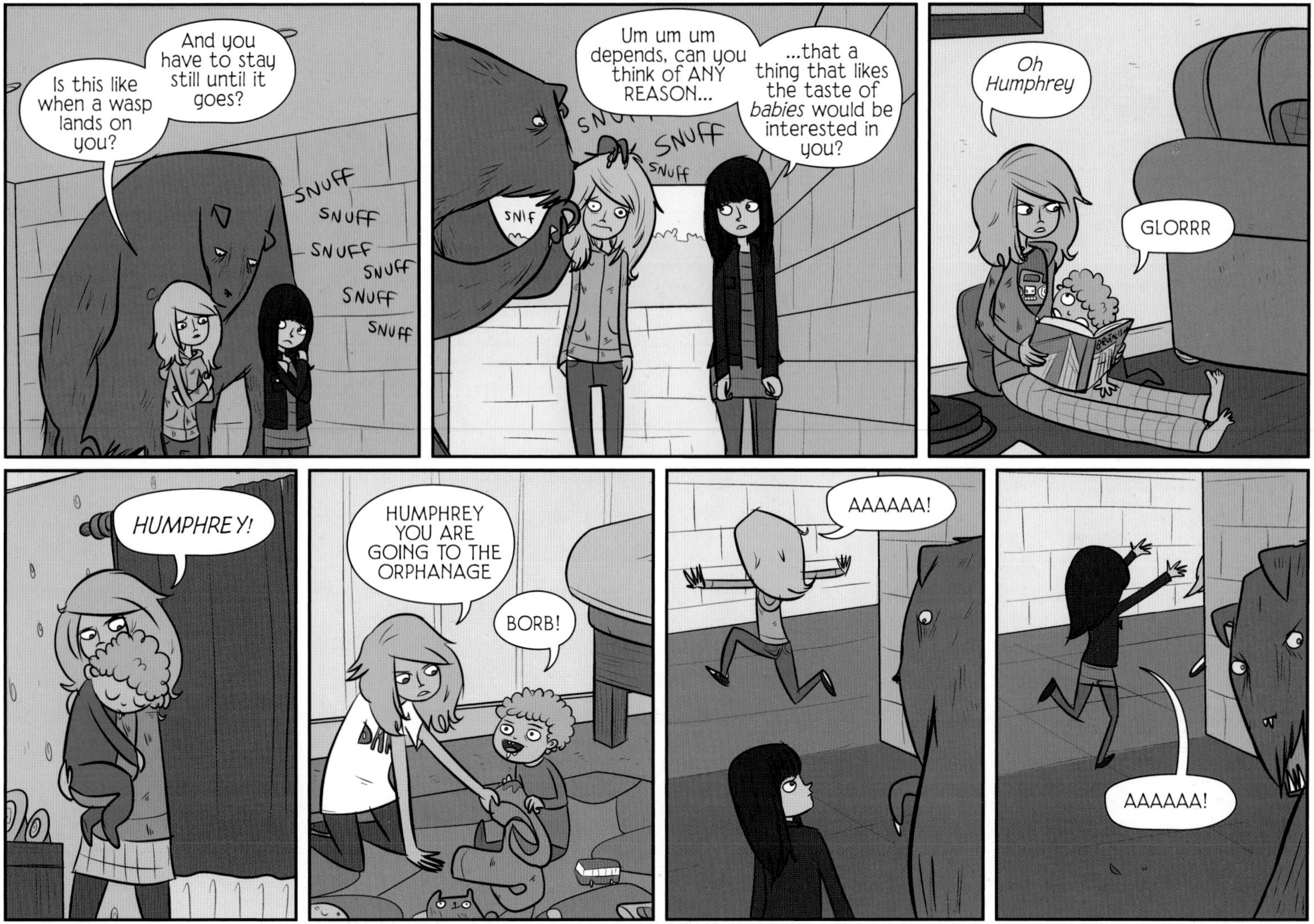

Is this like when a wasp lands on you?
And you have to stay still until it goes?
SNUFF
SNUFF
SNUFF
SNUFF
SNUFF
SNUFF
Um um um depends, can you think of ANY REASON...
...that a thing that likes the taste of *babies* would be interested in you?
SNUFF
SNUFF
SNIF
Oh Humphrey
GLORRR
HUMPHREY!
HUMPHREY YOU ARE GOING TO THE ORPHANAGE
BORB!
AAAAAA!
AAAAAA!

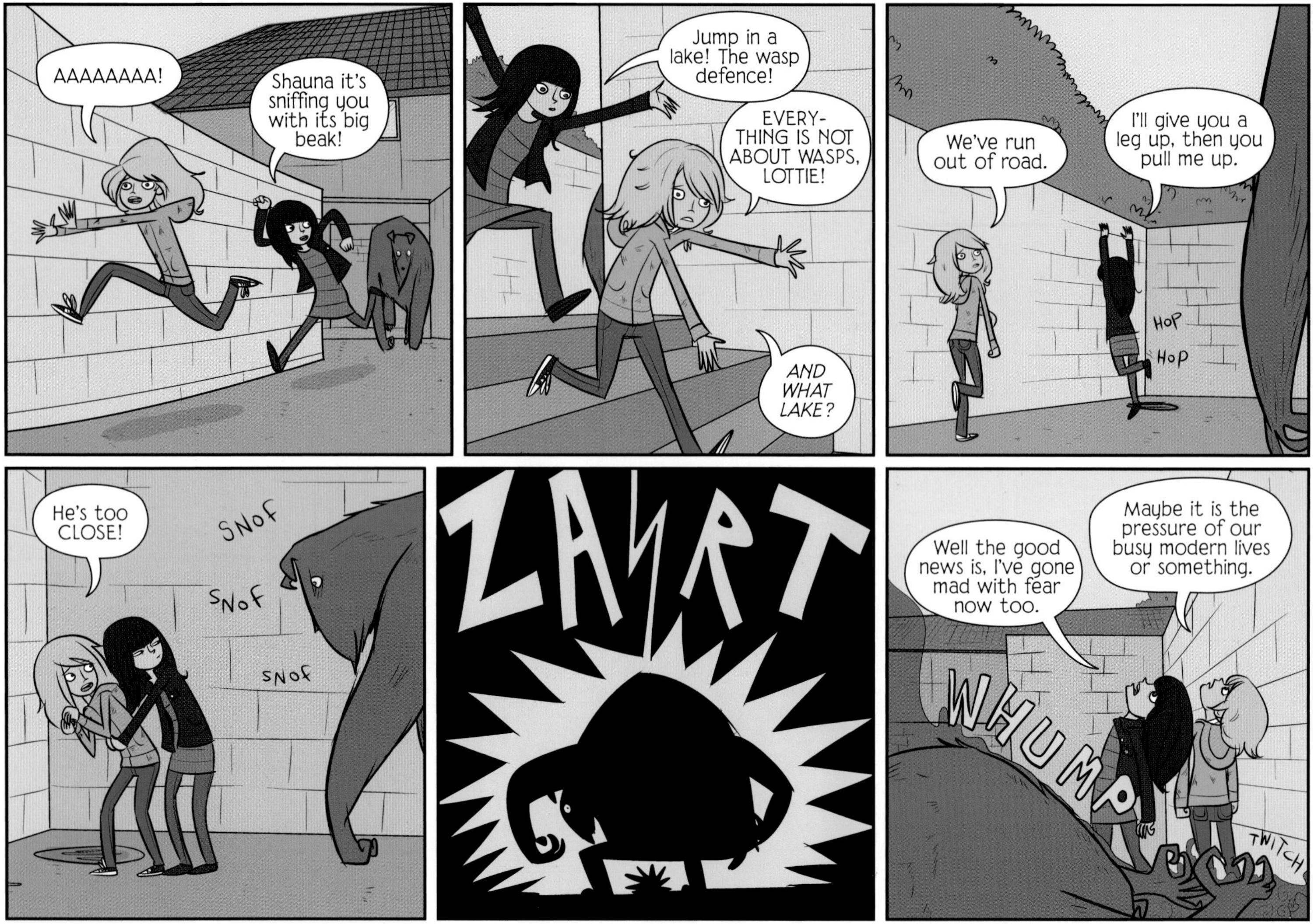
AAAAAAAA!
Shauna it's sniffing you with its big beak!
Jump in a lake! The wasp defence!
EVERY-THING IS NOT ABOUT WASPS, LOTTIE!
AND WHAT LAKE?
We've run out of road.
I'll give you a leg up, then you pull me up.
HOP
HOP
He's too CLOSE!
SNOF
SNOF
SNOF
ZAЯRT
WHUMP
Well the good news is, I've gone mad with fear now too.
Maybe it is the pressure of our busy modern lives or something.
TWITCH

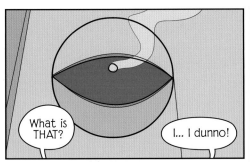

What is THAT?

I... I dunno!

It would be easier to tell if I could fit it all in my eyes at once!

WEIRD

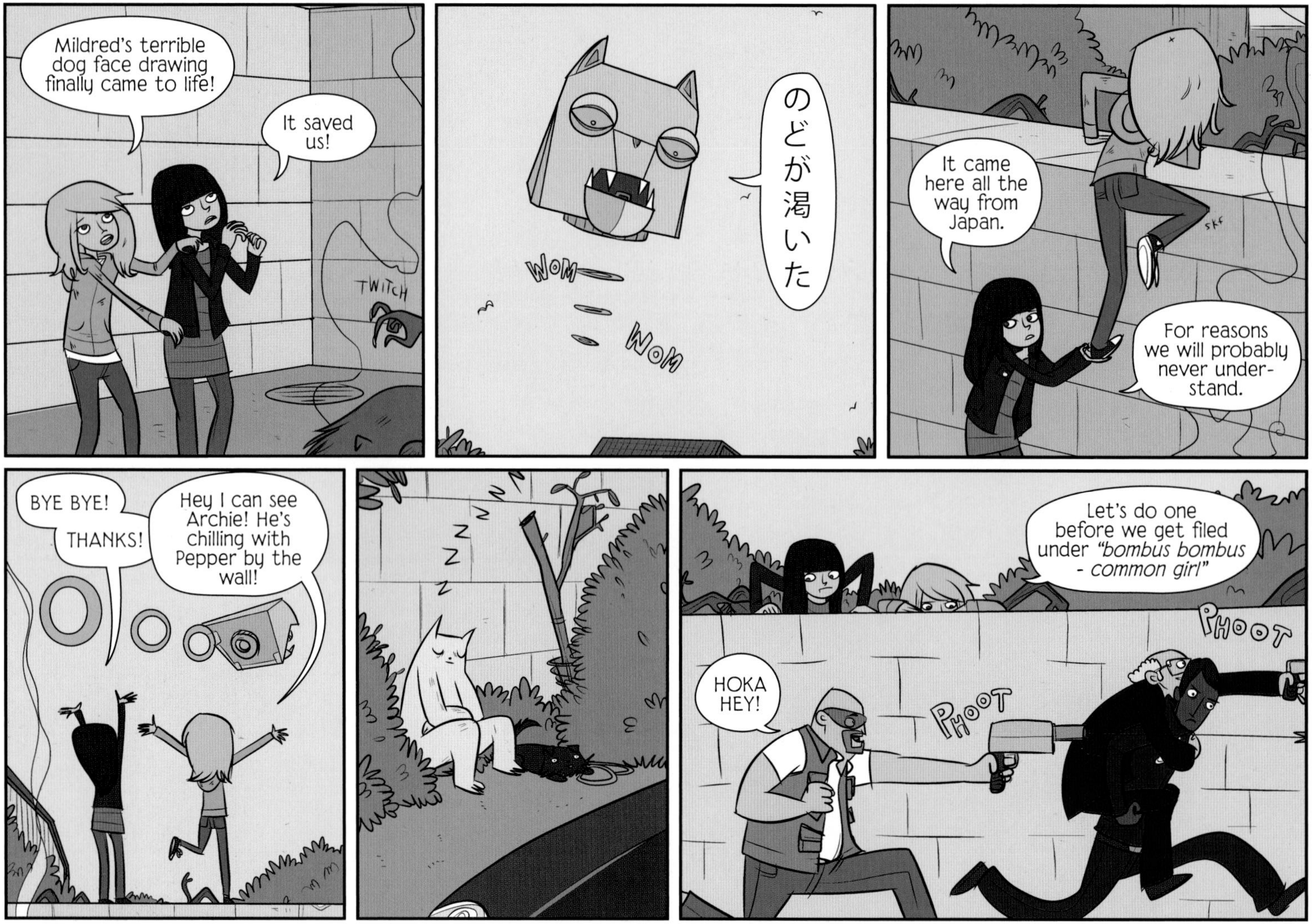
Mildred's terrible dog face drawing finally came to life!
It saved us!
TWITCH
WOM
WOM
のどが渇いた
It came here all the way from Japan.
For reasons we will probably never under-stand.
BYE BYE!
THANKS!
Hey I can see Archie! He's chilling with Pepper by the wall!
Z Z Z Z Z Z
Let's do one before we get filed under *"bombus bombus - common girl"*
PHOOT
HOKA HEY!
PHOOT

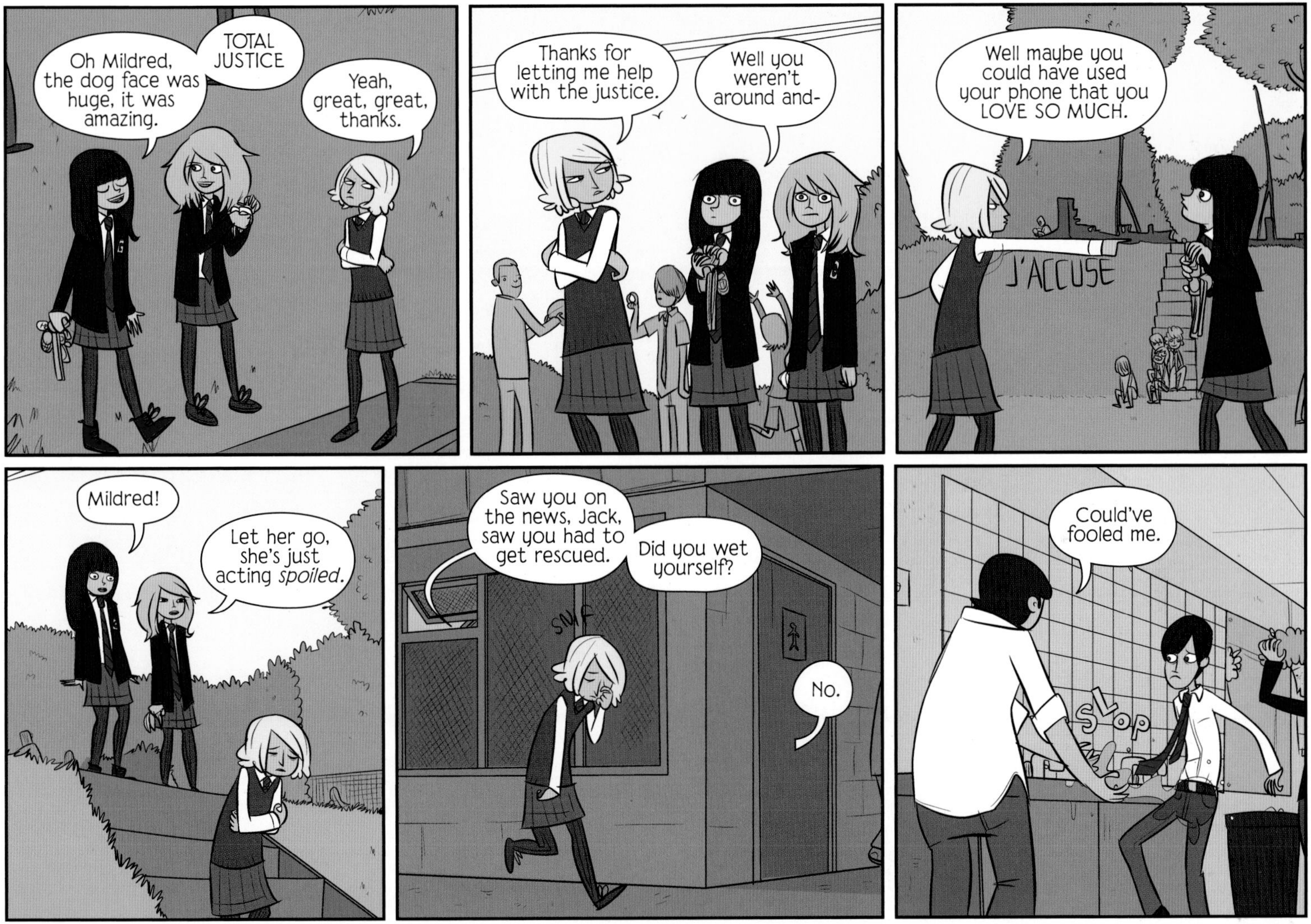
Oh Mildred, the dog face was huge, it was amazing.
TOTAL JUSTICE
Yeah, great, great, thanks.
Thanks for letting me help with the justice.
Well you weren't around and-
Well maybe you could have used your phone that you LOVE SO MUCH.
J'ACCUSE
Mildred!
Let her go, she's just acting *spoiled*.
Saw you on the news, Jack, saw you had to get rescued.
Did you wet yourself?
SNIF
No.
Could've fooled me.
SLOP

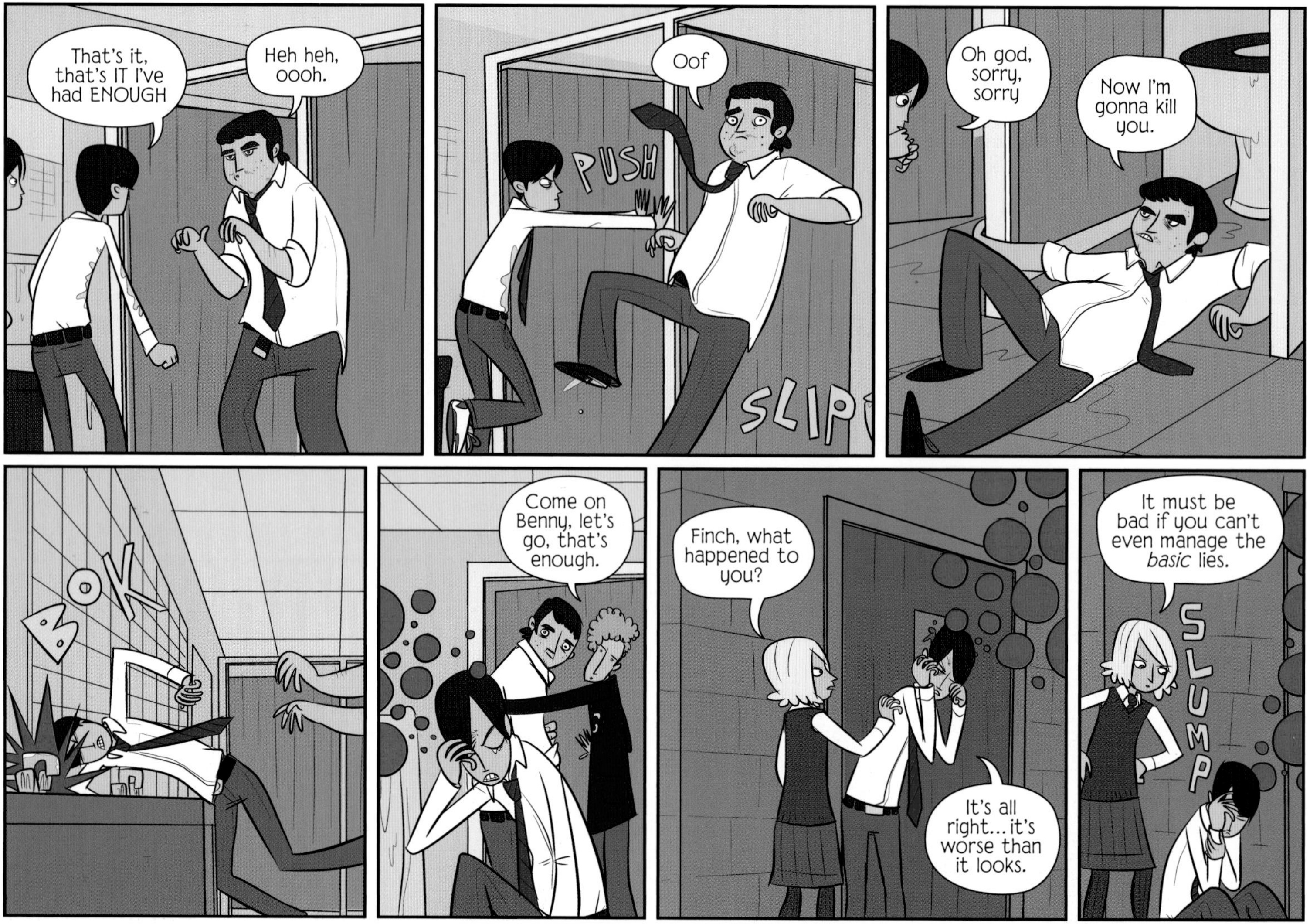
That's it, that's IT I've had ENOUGH
Heh heh, oooh.
Oof
PUSH
SLIP
Oh god, sorry, sorry
Now I'm gonna kill you.
BOK
Come on Benny, let's go, that's enough.
Finch, what happened to you?
It's all right... it's worse than it looks.
It must be bad if you can't even manage the *basic* lies.
SLUMP

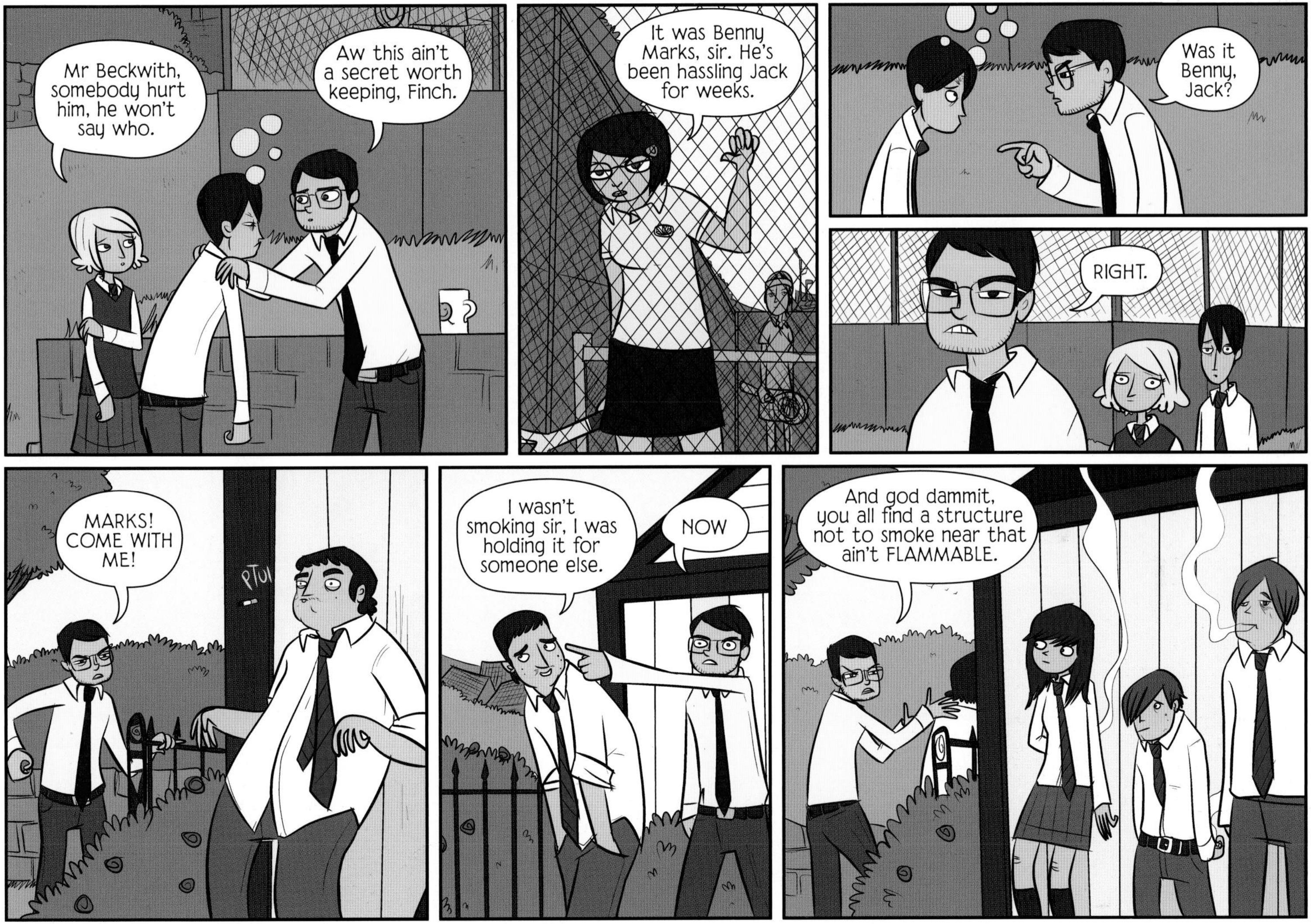
Mr Beckwith, somebody hurt him, he won't say who.
Aw this ain't a secret worth keeping, Finch.
It was Benny Marks, sir. He's been hassling Jack for weeks.
Was it Benny, Jack?
RIGHT.
MARKS! COME WITH ME!
PTUI
I wasn't smoking sir, I was holding it for someone else.
NOW
And god dammit, you all find a structure not to smoke near that ain't FLAMMABLE.

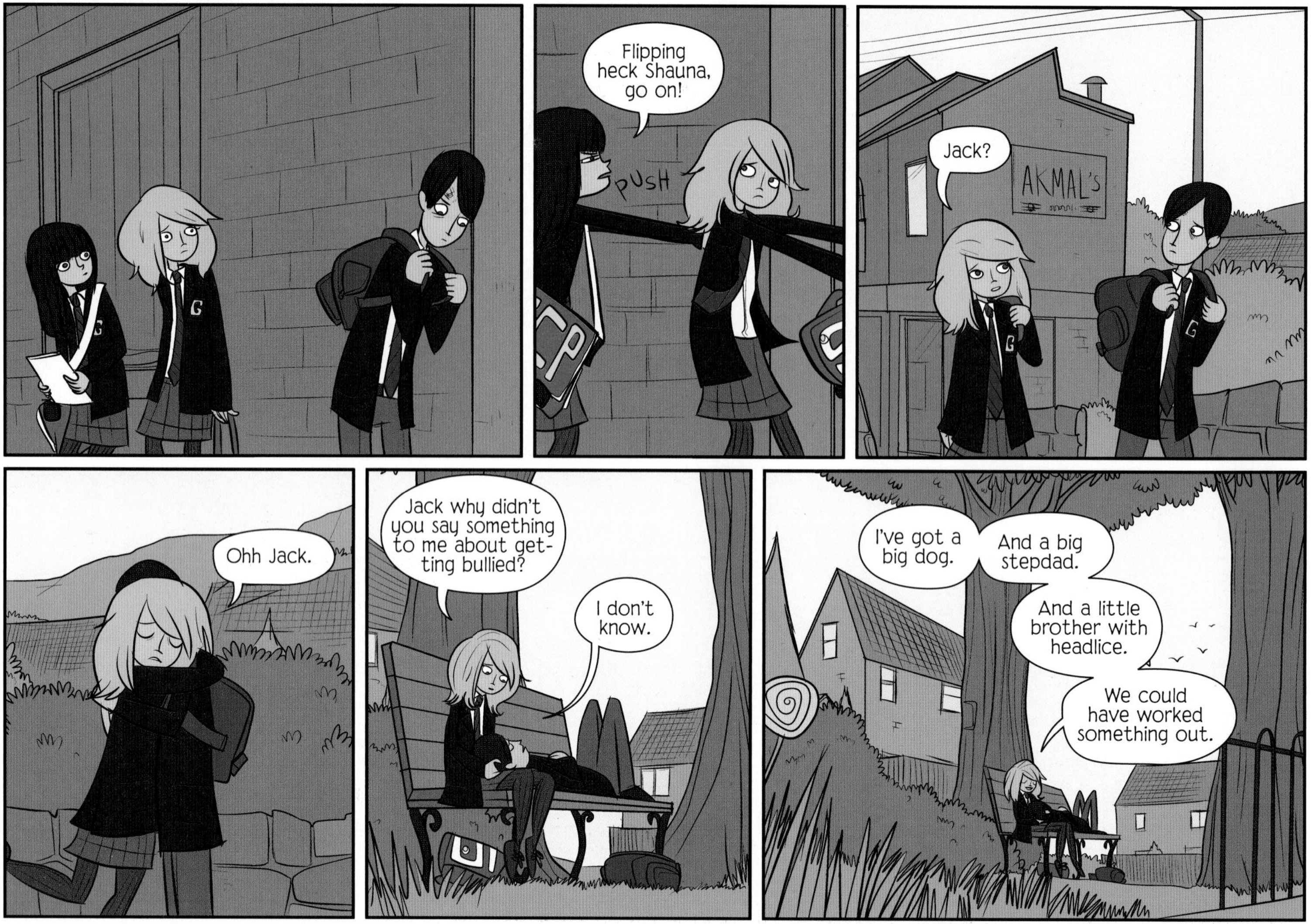

Flipping heck Shauna, go on!
PUSH
Jack?
AKMAL'S
Ohh Jack.
Jack why didn't you say something to me about get-ting bullied?
I don't know.
I've got a big dog.
And a big stepdad.
And a little brother with headlice.
We could have worked something out.

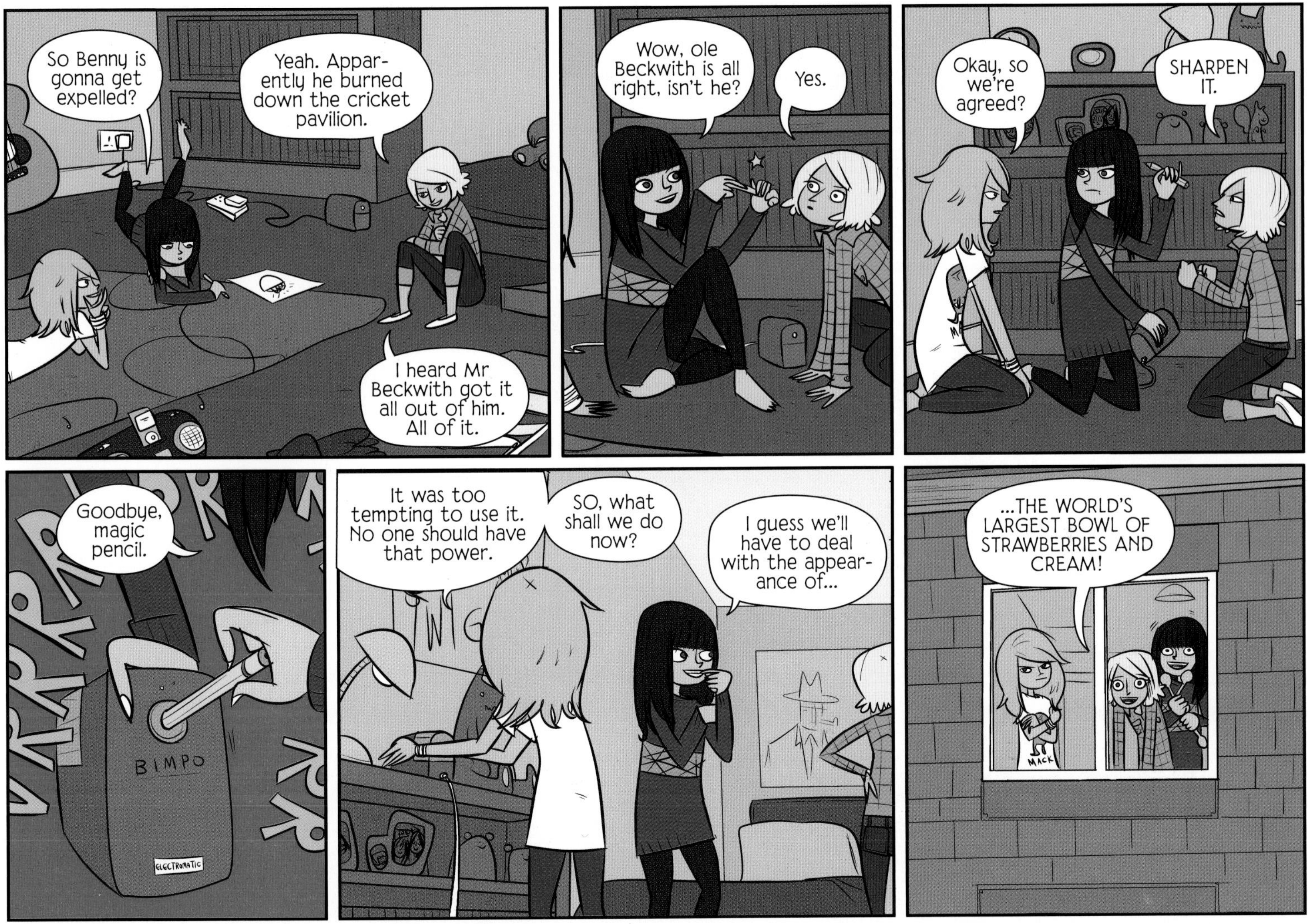
So Benny is gonna get expelled?
Yeah. Apparently he burned down the cricket pavilion.
I heard Mr Beckwith got it all out of him. All of it.
Wow, ole Beckwith is all right, isn't he?
Yes.
Okay, so we're agreed?
SHARPEN IT.
Goodbye, magic pencil.
BIMPO
ELECTROMATIC
It was too tempting to use it. No one should have that power.
SO, what shall we do now?
I guess we'll have to deal with the appearance of...
...THE WORLD'S LARGEST BOWL OF STRAWBERRIES AND CREAM!
MACK

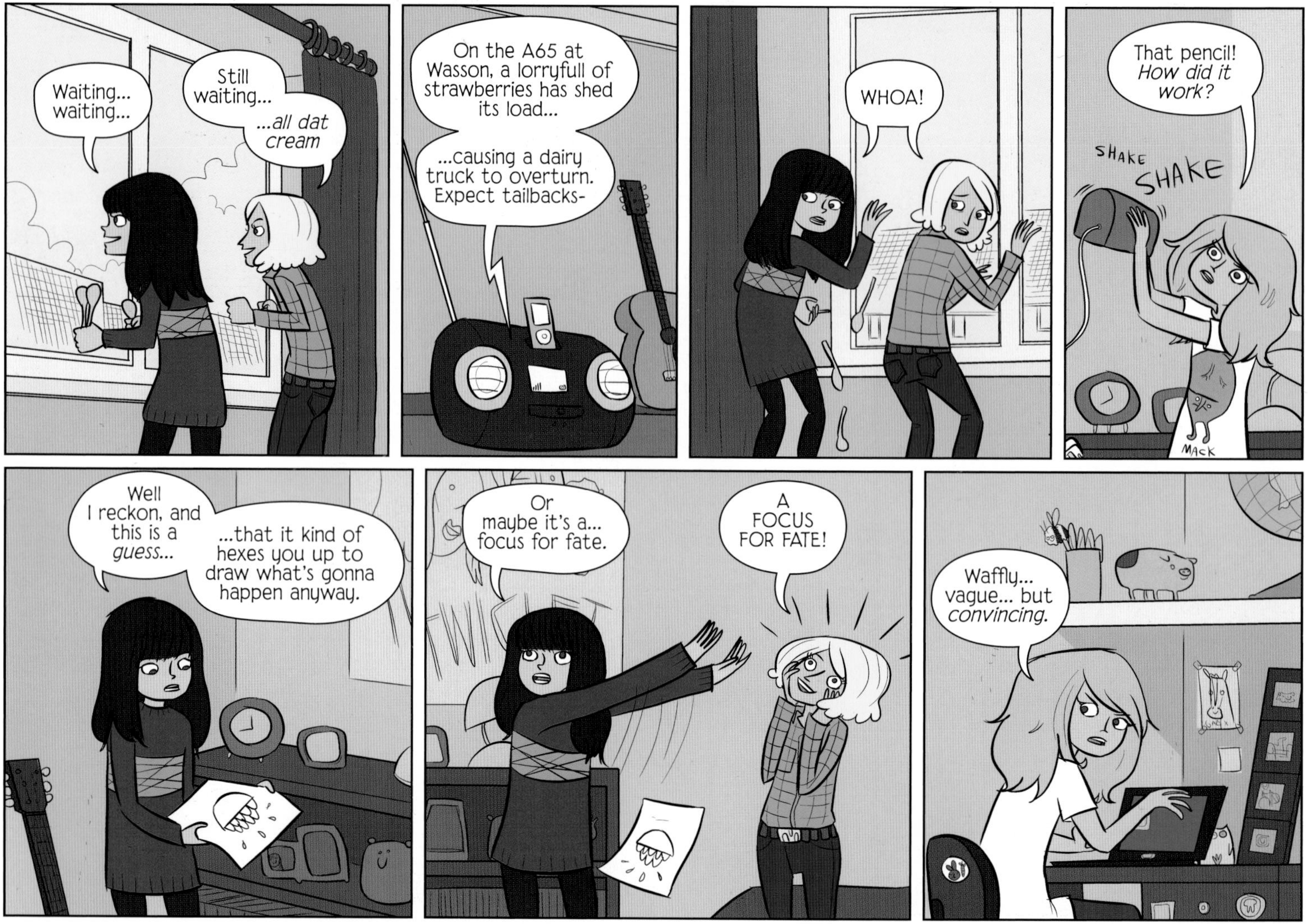
Waiting... waiting...
Still waiting...
...all dat cream
On the A65 at Wasson, a lorryfull of strawberries has shed its load...
...causing a dairy truck to overturn. Expect tailbacks-
WHOA!
That pencil! How did it work?
SHAKE SHAKE
MACK
Well I reckon, and this is a guess...
...that it kind of hexes you up to draw what's gonna happen anyway.
Or maybe it's a... focus for fate.
A FOCUS FOR FATE!
Waffly... vague... but convincing.

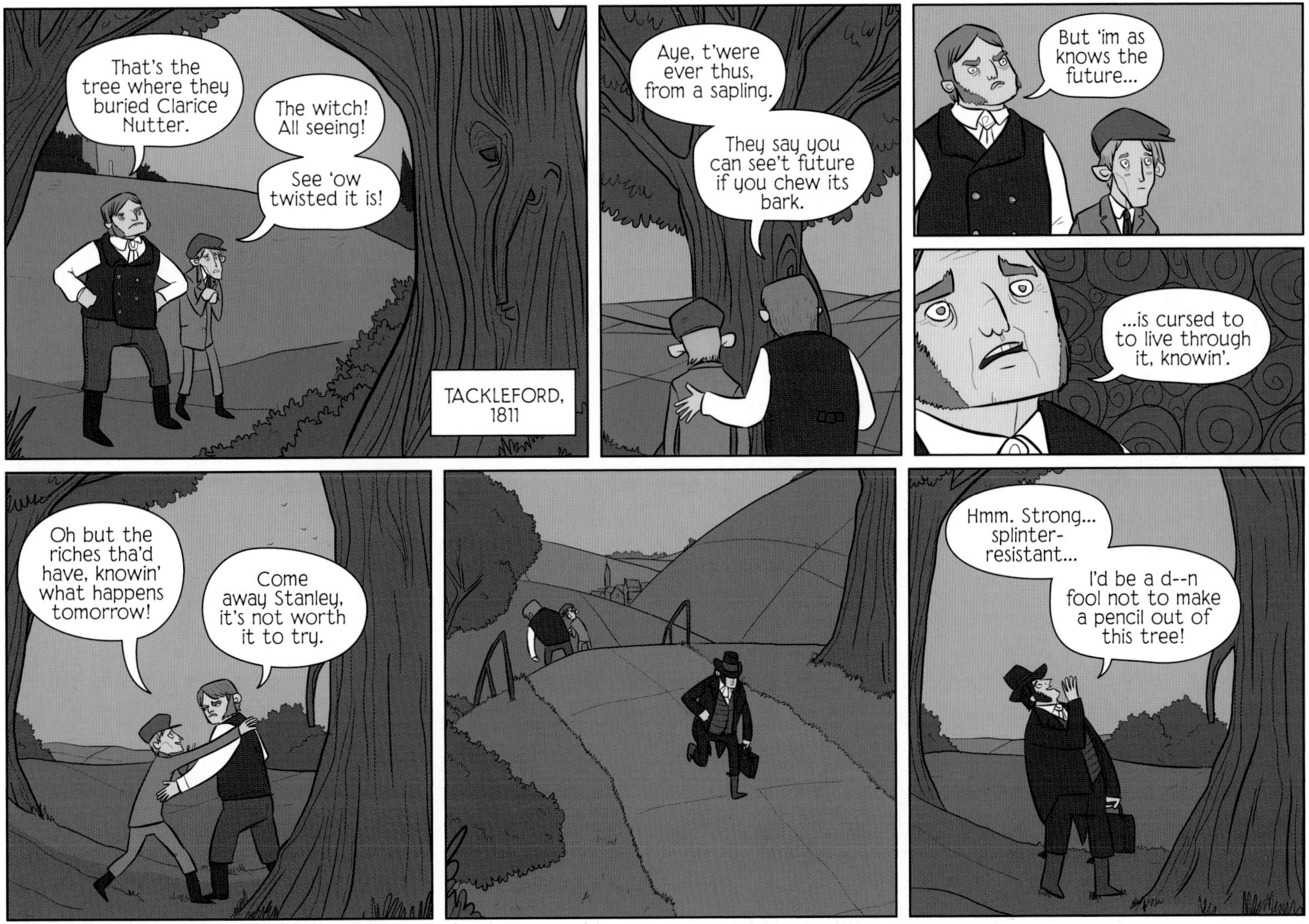
That's the tree where they buried Clarice Nutter.
The witch! All seeing!
See 'ow twisted it is!
TACKLEFORD, 1811
Aye, t'were ever thus, from a sapling.
They say you can see't future if you chew its bark.
But 'im as knows the future...
...is cursed to to live through it, knowin'.
Oh but the riches tha'd have, knowin' what happens tomorrow!
Come away Stanley, it's not worth it to try.
Hmm. Strong... splinter-resistant...
I'd be a d--n fool not to make a pencil out of this tree!

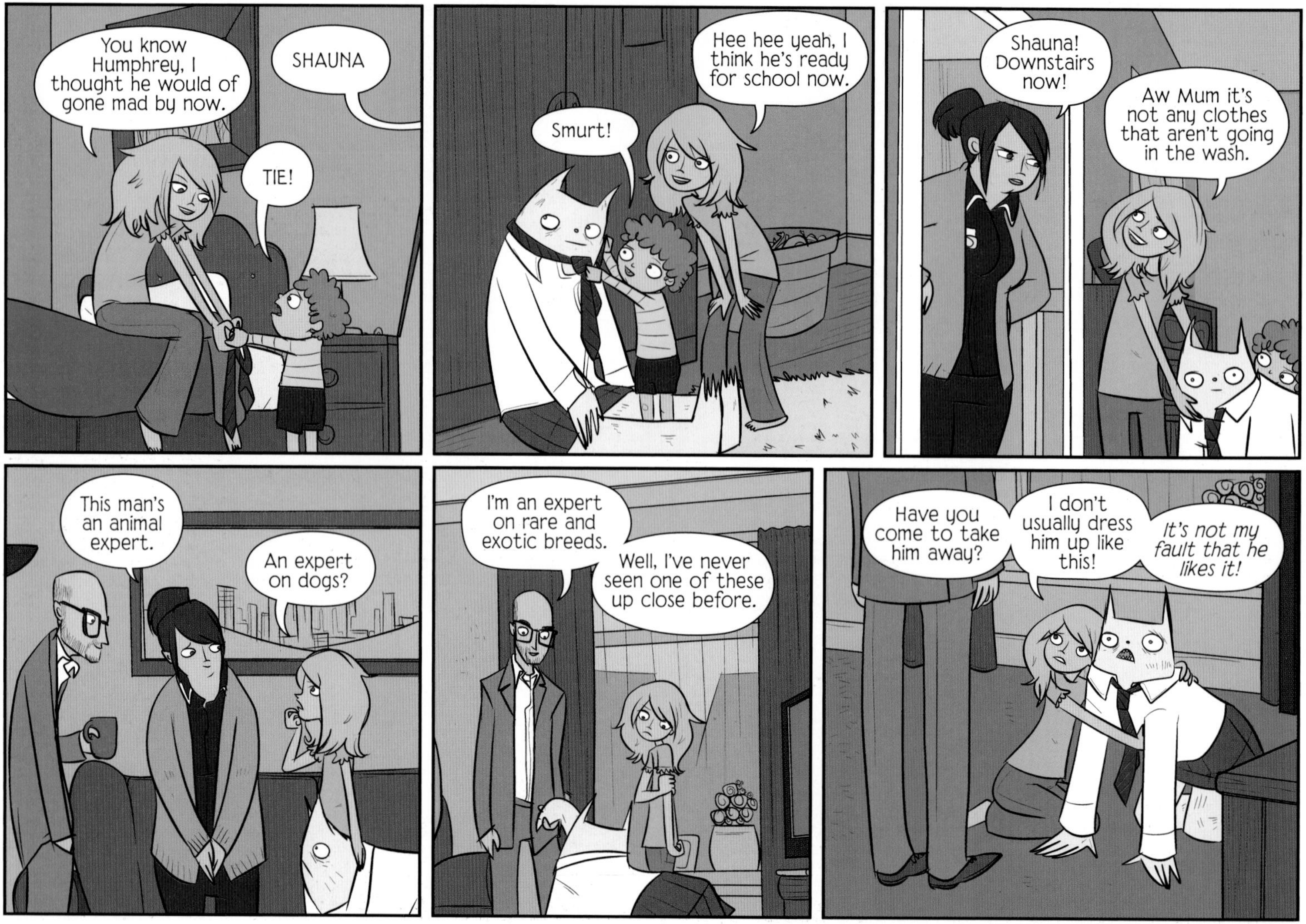
You know Humphrey, I thought he would of gone mad by now.
SHAUNA
TIE!
Smurt!
Hee hee yeah, I think he's ready for school now.
Shauna! Downstairs now!
Aw Mum it's not any clothes that aren't going in the wash.
This man's an animal expert.
An expert on dogs?
I'm an expert on rare and exotic breeds.
Well, I've never seen one of these up close before.
Have you come to take him away?
I don't usually dress him up like this!
It's not my fault that he likes it!

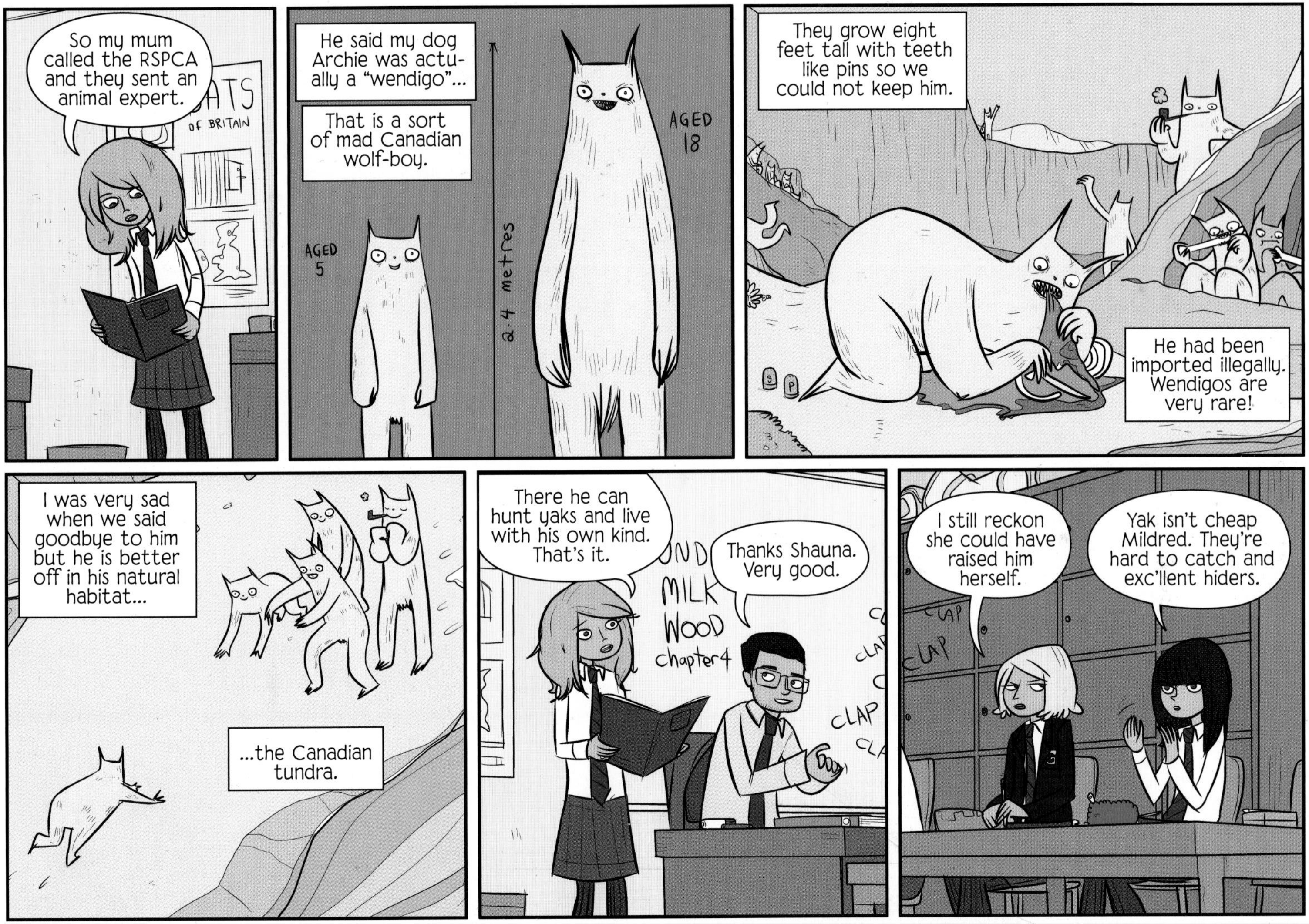
So my mum called the RSPCA and they sent an animal expert.
OF BRITAIN
He said my dog Archie was actually a "wendigo"...
That is a sort of mad Canadian wolf-boy.
AGED 5
2.4 metres
AGED 18
They grow eight feet tall with teeth like pins so we could not keep him.
He had been imported illegally. Wendigos are very rare!
I was very sad when we said goodbye to him but he is better off in his natural habitat...
...the Canadian tundra.
There he can hunt yaks and live with his own kind. That's it.
MILK WOOD
chapter 4
Thanks Shauna. Very good.
CLAP
CLAP
I still reckon she could have raised him herself.
Yak isn't cheap Mildred. They're hard to catch and exc'llent hiders.
CLAP
CLAP

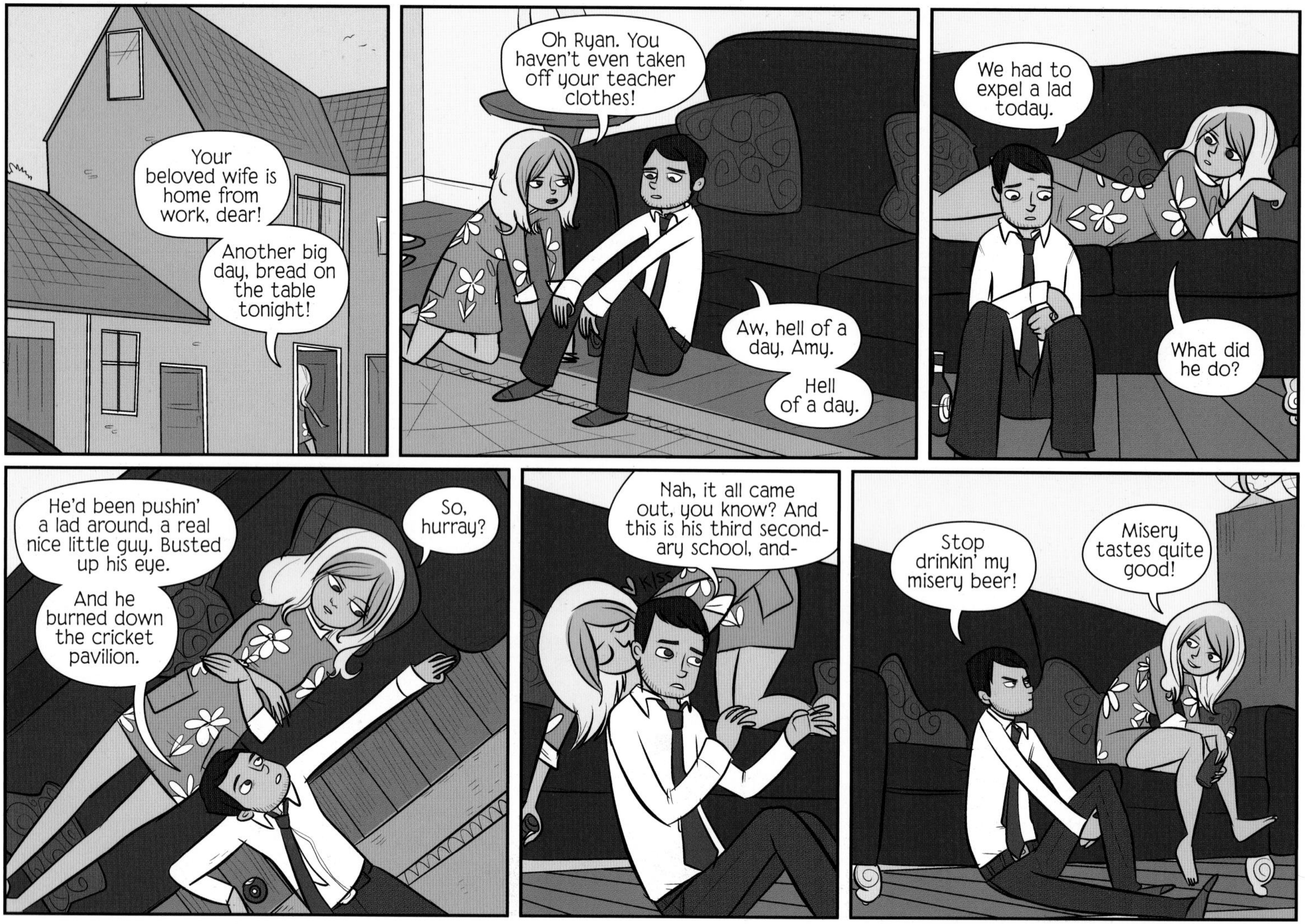
Your beloved wife is home from work, dear!
Another big day, bread on the table tonight!
Oh Ryan. You haven't even taken off your teacher clothes!
Aw, hell of a day, Amy.
Hell of a day.
We had to expel a lad today.
What did he do?
He'd been pushin' a lad around, a real nice little guy. Busted up his eye.
And he burned down the cricket pavilion.
So, hurray?
Nah, it all came out, you know? And this is his third second-ary school, and-
kiss
Stop drinkin' my misery beer!
Misery tastes quite good!

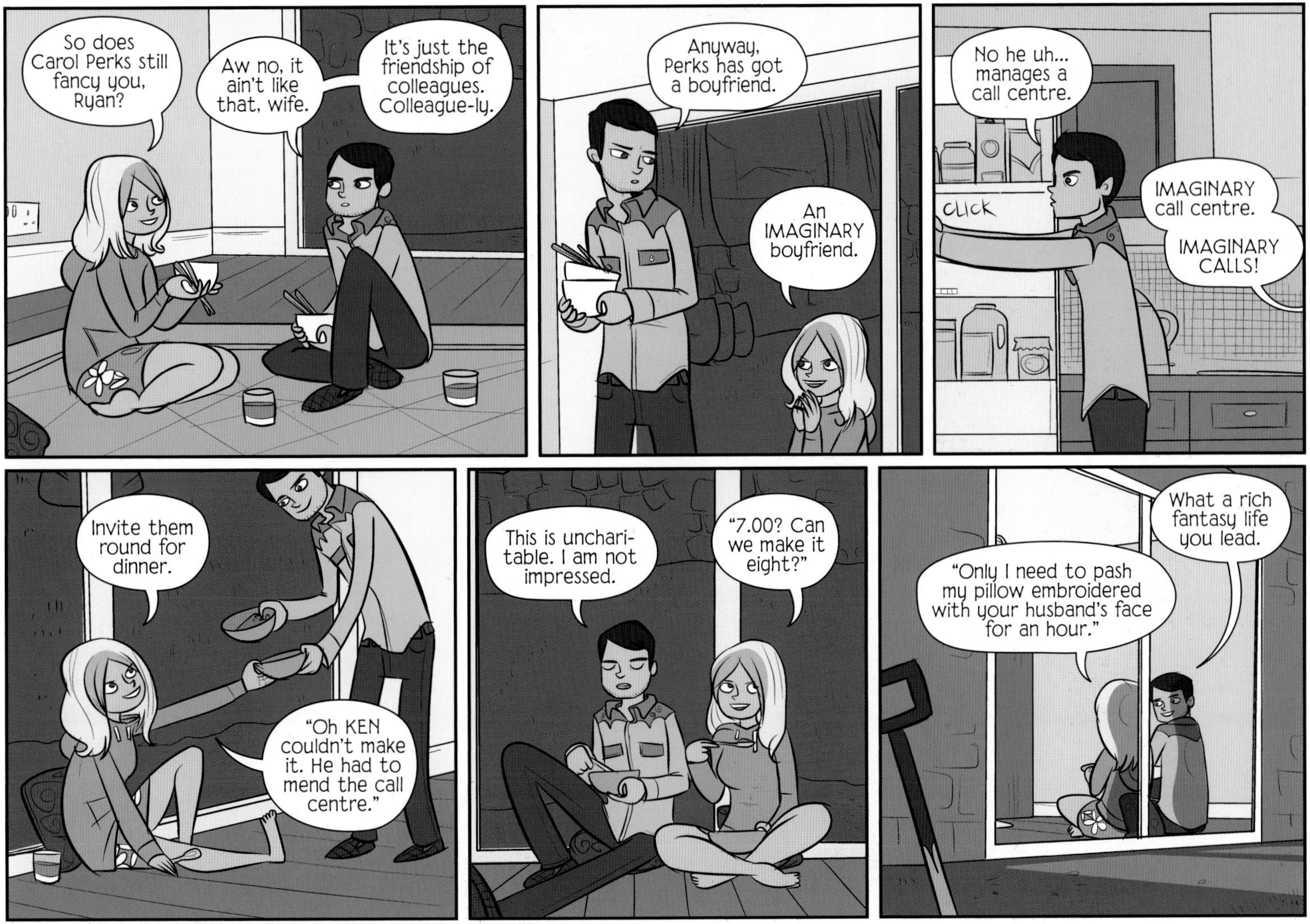
So does Carol Perks still fancy you, Ryan?
Aw no, it ain't like that, wife.
It's just the friendship of colleagues. Colleague-ly.
Anyway, Perks has got a boyfriend.
An IMAGINARY boyfriend.
No he uh... manages a call centre.
CLICK
IMAGINARY call centre.
IMAGINARY CALLS!
Invite them round for dinner.
"Oh KEN couldn't make it. He had to mend the call centre."
This is unchari-table. I am not impressed.
"7.00? Can we make it eight?"
"Only I need to pash my pillow embroidered with your husband's face for an hour."
What a rich fantasy life you lead.

Bad Machinery, Volume Two

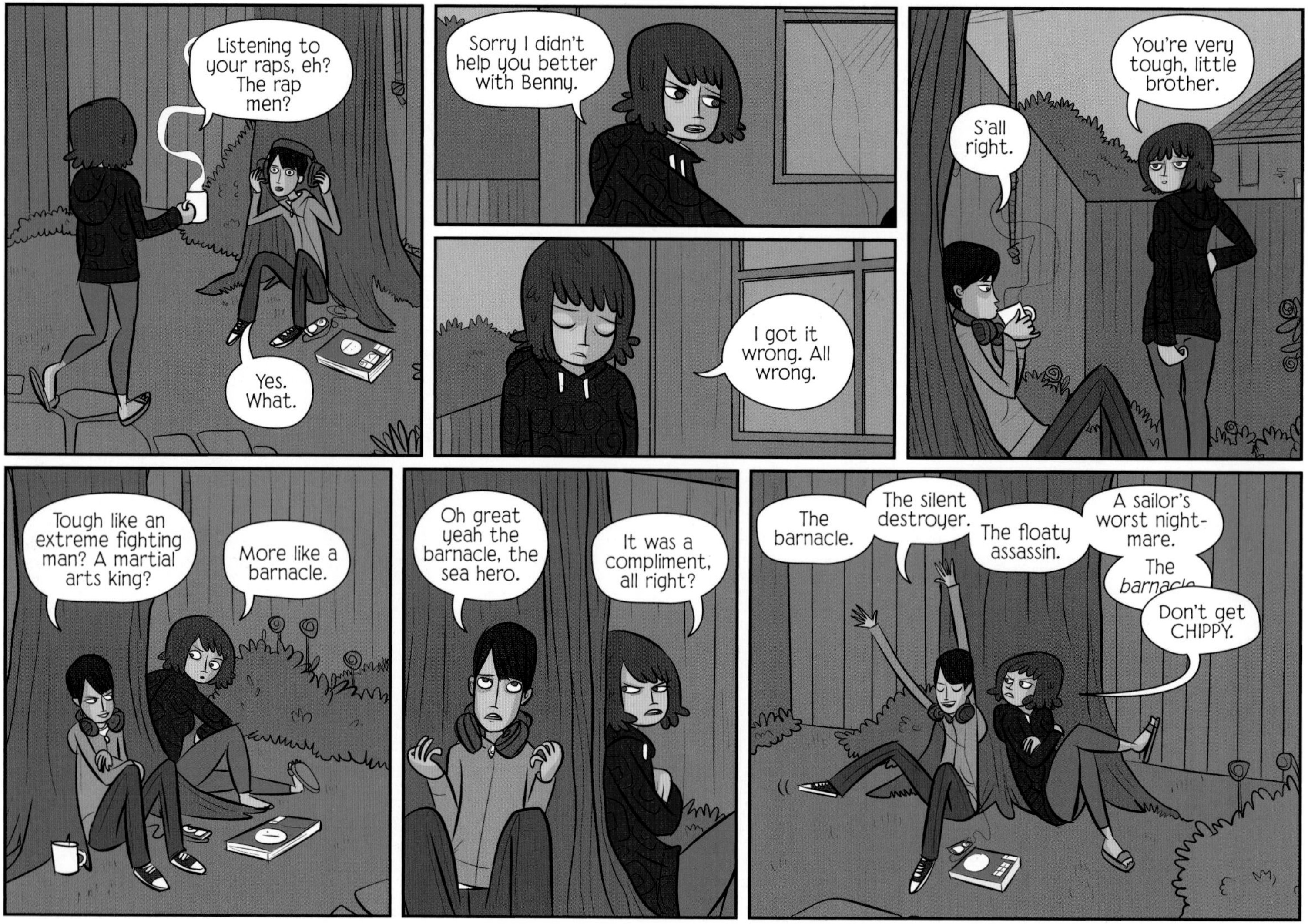
Listening to your raps, eh? The rap men?
Yes. What.
Sorry I didn't help you better with Benny.
I got it wrong. All wrong.
S'all right.
You're very tough, little brother.
Tough like an extreme fighting man? A martial arts king?
More like a barnacle.
Oh great yeah the barnacle, the sea hero.
It was a compliment, all right?
The barnacle.
The silent destroyer.
The floaty assassin.
A sailor's worst night-mare.
The *barnac*
Don't get CHIPPY.

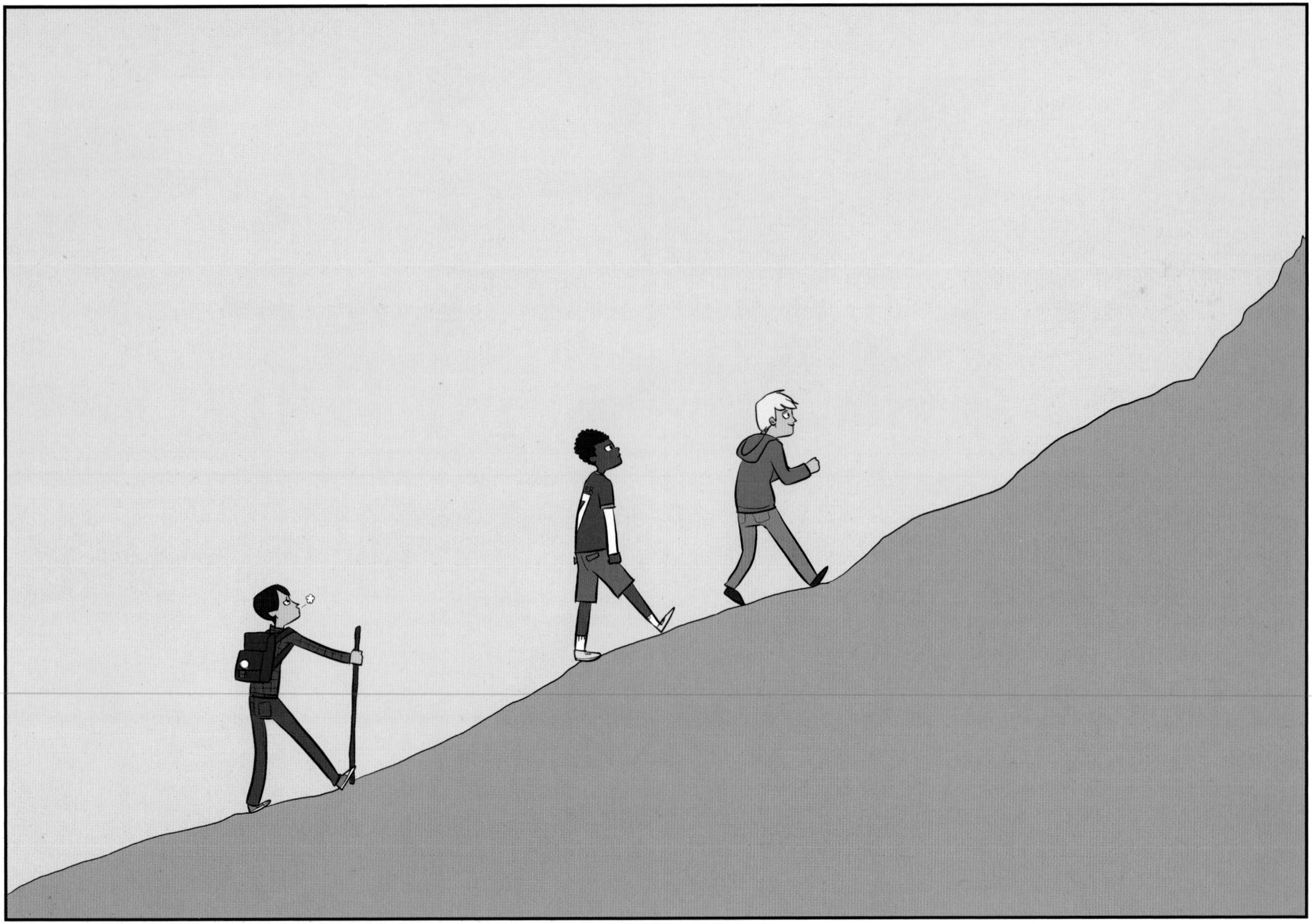

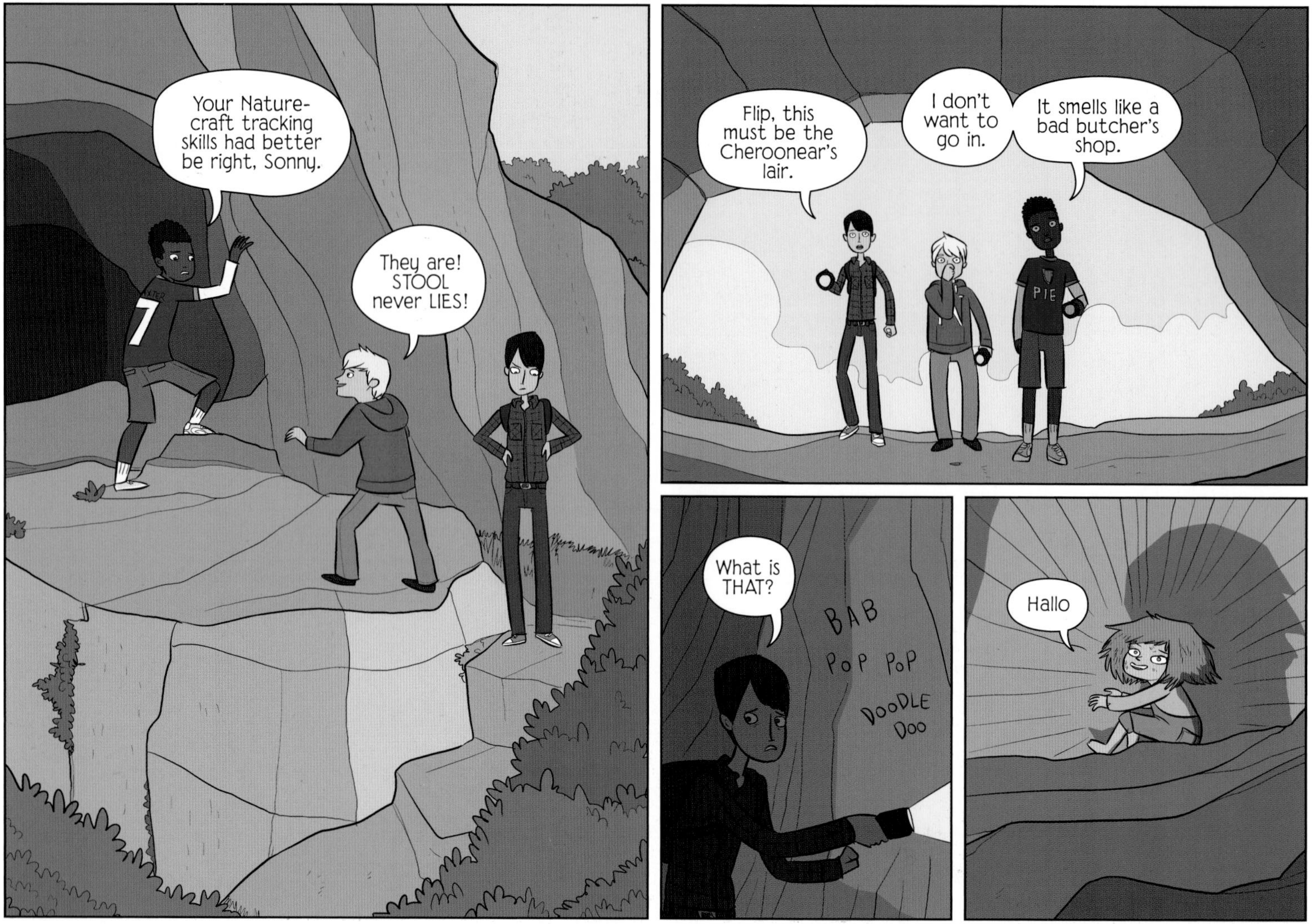
Your Nature-craft tracking skills had better be right, Sonny.
They are! STOOL never LIES!
Flip, this must be the Cheroonear's lair.
I don't want to go in.
It smells like a bad butcher's shop.
What is THAT?
BAB
POP POP
DOODLE DOO
Hallo

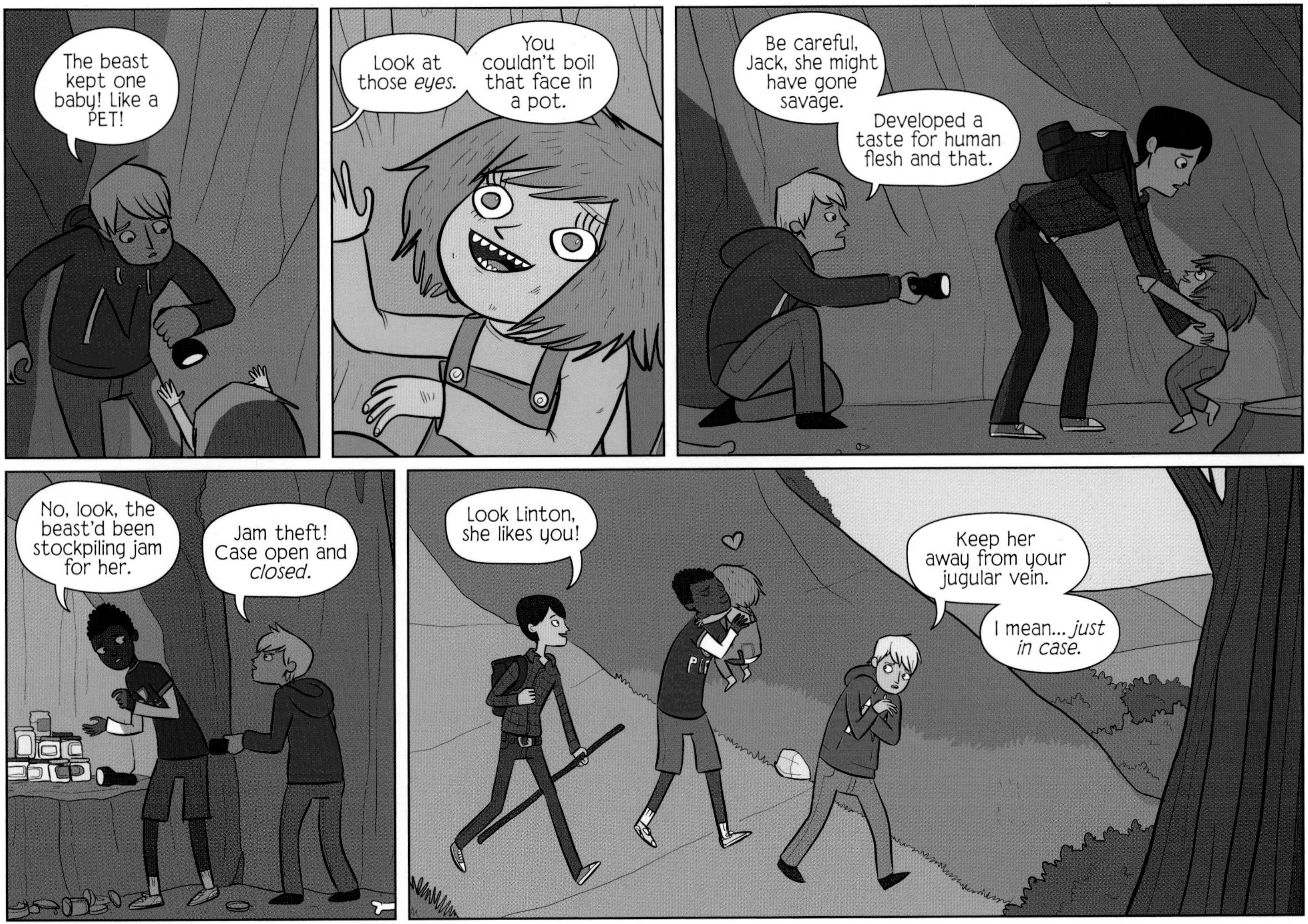
The beast kept one baby! Like a PET!
Look at those *eyes.*
You couldn't boil that face in a pot.
Be careful, Jack, she might have gone savage.
Developed a taste for human flesh and that.
No, look, the beast'd been stockpiling jam for her.
Jam theft! Case open and *closed.*
Look Linton, she likes you!
Keep her away from your jugular vein.
I mean... *just in case.*

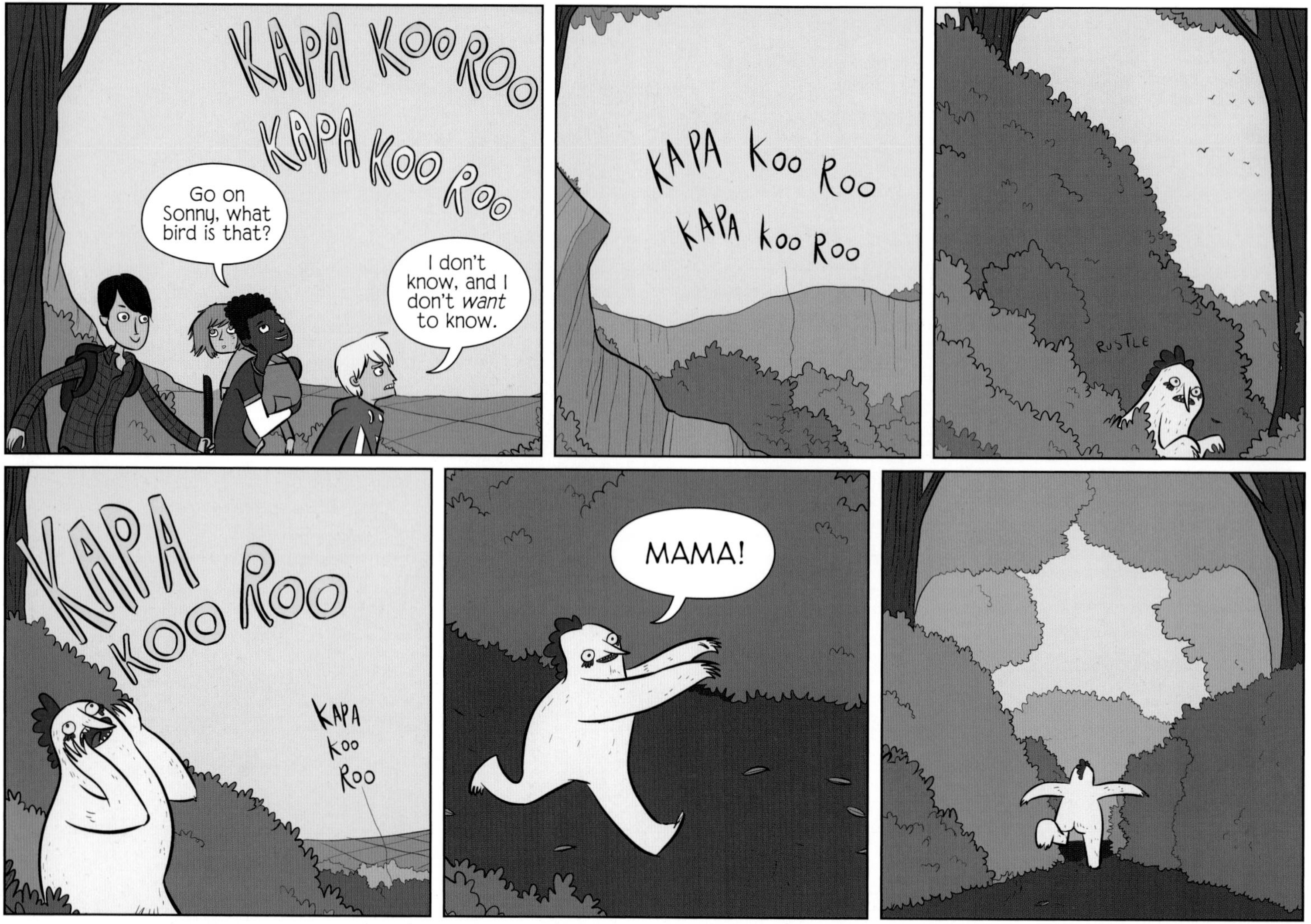
KAPA KOOROO
KAPA KOO ROO
Go on Sonny, what bird is that?
I don't know, and I don't *want* to know.
KAPA KOO ROO
KAPA KOO ROO
RUSTLE
KAPA KOO ROO
KAPA KOO ROO
MAMA!

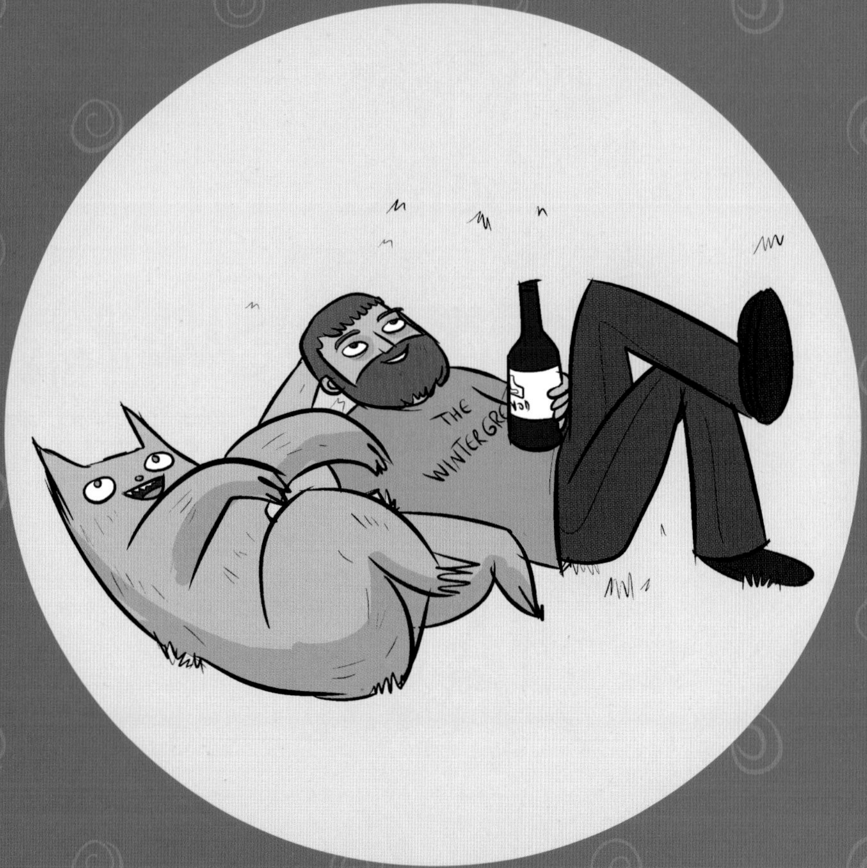
THE
WINTERGR

Dear Jack
would you like to see
Hero Man 2 on Saturday?
If so meet ME outside

✰SHAUNA✰

Charlotte Grote

*"Well the good news is, I've gone
mad with fear now too."*

Sonny Craven

*"Well, there are going to be risks
on a man's adventure."*

Jack Finch

*"The babies of today are idiots, but
tomorrow they could be scientists."*

Shauna Wickle

*"Being in a zoo means getting fed. That's the compensation
for getting gawked at while you're doing your business."*

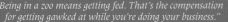

Linton Baxter

*"I wonder how my dad's going to
embarrass me tonight."*

Mildred Haversham

*"WE'RE PLAYING UNICORN FRENZY
AND WE'RE PLAYING IT NOW."*

GRISWALDS GRAMMAR SCHOOL

ESTABLISHED 1701

GRISWALDS
EX VENTO SCIENTIA
EST. 1701

GLOSSARY

Great Britain is an island and we have our own ways. Yes we are a simple people, but we are sophisticated enough to have made up our own versions of words and phrases just for us. I will take you through them and if you complain after this, it is your problem as far as I am concerned. We're not IDIOTS, they're just IDIOMS.

LOVE,
Charlotte
XXX

Making the place look untidy: This is when you have arranged yourself very neatly on the floor and then your mum trips over you and stubs her toe because she was not paying attention jeez louise.

Nits: Headlice. Now I have never had nits but if you do get them they put this shampoo on your head that smells like the curtains at an old folks' home. Bad news. Or they use the electric comb on you which, to be honest, sounds quite good. See also: "nit nurse". The nit nurse is a woman who comes to school and checks your head for nits, she probably hates her life a great deal.

Sick: Vomit. It is a versatile word: "I felt sick, I sicked up on Grandma and now there is sick all over my Christmas presents."

Mongrel: What the Americans call a "mutt". That is, a dog what does not cost two grand while having weak lungs and then gets stolen by dog criminals. A mongrel is a better sort of dog.

Skint: Not having any UK pounds sterling.

Test icicles: Moth balls.

Pram face: A very unkind term used to describe a young mother who has not had the best of education and life opportunities etc.

Cricket pavilion: The house that cricketers go to to put their special outfits on. It is a rarefied zone with a special cupboard for the "boxes" they use to protect their test icicles. It is not beyond imagination to think that maybe while in the pavilion they go for a tinkle before the game. But as I have never been in a cricket pavilion, I do not know.

Little tyke: A young scamp. An annoying child who is probably also quite dirty and won't leave you alone.

Chip off the old block: An apple that has not fallen far from the tree.

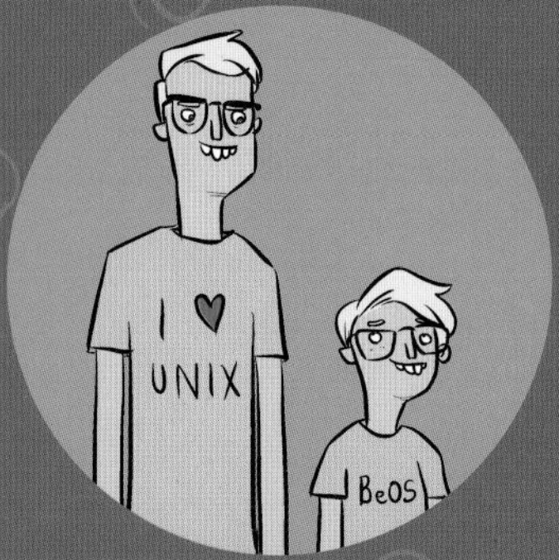

I ♥ UNIX
BeOS

The Velvet Underground: Music band from the past who caused all sorts of trouble. The sound of the Velvet Underground is like a set of bagpipes going through a mangle while a German exchange student lists all the reasons you should take up living homeless as a hobby. Bad news for people who like sounds.

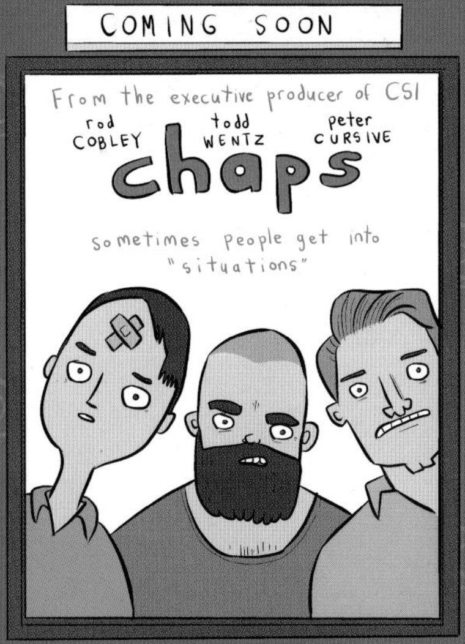

COMING SOON
From the executive producer of CSI
rod COBLEY
todd WENTZ
peter CURSIVE
chaps
sometimes people get into "situations"

Cinema: The movie theatre, where one goes to be richly entertained while enjoying food and drinks at prices that even a king would think was well out of order. Is popcorn actually food? No one has ever proved it.

Pash: Ferocious kissing. Spit everywhere.

"You make a better door than a window": Imagine that you are watching an improving and educational television programme such as *Keeping Up With Kim Kardashian's Lifestyle Choices* and then a family member stands in front of the screen and stops to have a think. This is what you say to them when this happens. It is a simple statement of fact and no one is offended.

Fancy: When you fancy someone, you want to pash 'em up. Fancying develops into various forms of relationship, such as love relationship, or hiding from someone relationship. You can also fancy a cup of tea but I think that is international.

Lorryfull: Metric version of a "trucksworth".

Chippy: Belligerent. "Don't get chippy with me, sunshine," is the sort of thing an imaginary Cockney taxi driver might say if you tell him he has gone the long way round and should have driven through the industrial estate thereby saving you £5.50.

A load of old toss: The kind of items one might discard without second thought.

Quid: One pound sterling. Basic human money for the United Kingdom.

Badger: Like a low-slung bear, but smaller.

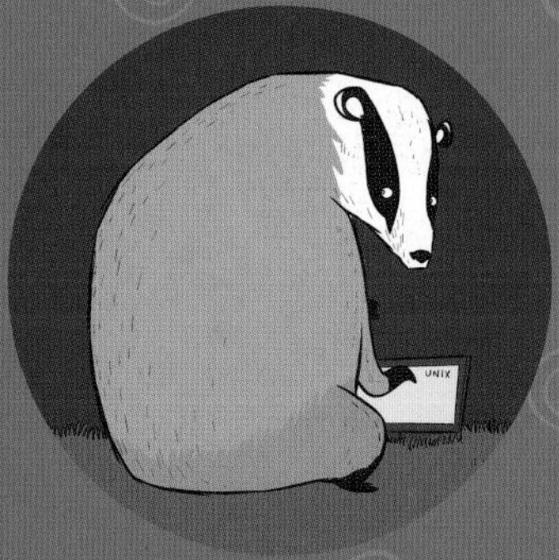

UNIX

JESPER BLOEM
(Master Hunter and Raconteur)
– RECALLS –
THE ONES THAT GOT AWAY

Beasts, critters, animals and natural miscellanea who avoided capture against all odds.

I was born a baby in South Africa in the difficult years between the Great Struggle and the Big Push. Though my hands were small and weak, my father quickly pushed a crossbow into them and told me what to do. Before my first birthday, our humble mantlepiece featured a delicately stuffed bee. Sadly, that infant trophy burned, as so many things did, in the Huge Situation, but its memory will live as long as its life was short. Every Ahab has his whale, and here are mine. Eleven creatures who bested Bloem, and may yet best him again. Animals of wit, primitive intelligence, or luck. The ones that got away.

COULOMB'S BOAR *(Bombus Bombus)*

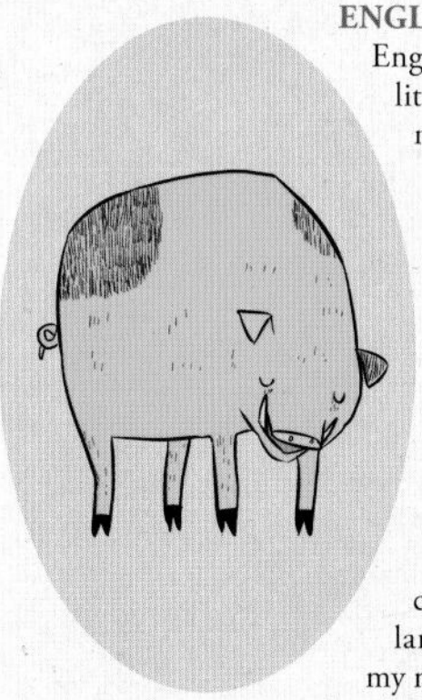

ENGLAND—Having made my home in England, I expected that there would be little to hunt besides rabbit, grouse and maybe a pheasant for the pot. But during a heathland ramble on my estate I came across the unfamiliar form of Coulomb's Boar. Packing only a shotgun, I was overcome by the thought of bacon, when a second boar butted me from behind, knocking me onto the ground where I stunned myself on a protruding stone. When I awoke, my shirt had been completely eaten away by the little wretches. Bare-chested, I returned to the house for a larger and more vindictive weapon, but my manservant had prepared a delicious broth for lunch, so I nursed my sore head and cold breast by the fireside instead.

SILVER TOM *(Bombus Bombus)*

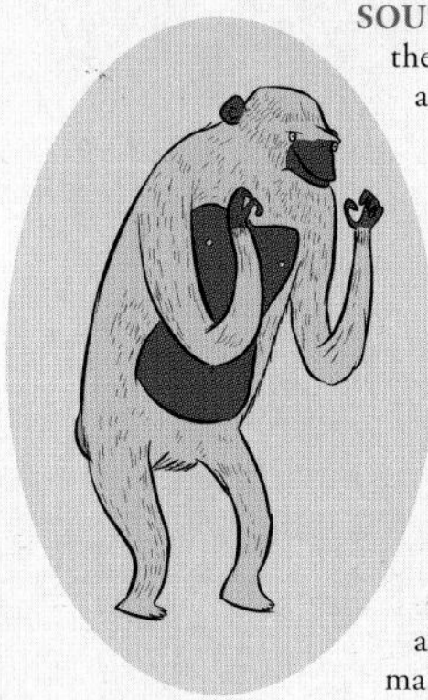

SOUTH AFRICA—Some say th the Silver Tom is the cleverest ape, others that he is simply a man covered head to toe in fur, with a violently pink bottom. All I know is tha for two years, Silver Tom was employed as my driv and valet. I have no idea how he hoodwinked me, but his erratic driving an abysmal ironing were off by his wicked sense of fur have no wish to shoot Silv Tom, I simply wish to see h his furry face again, and sha a banana with him as I did on many a pleasant evening years a

KRAKEN *(Bombus Bombus)*

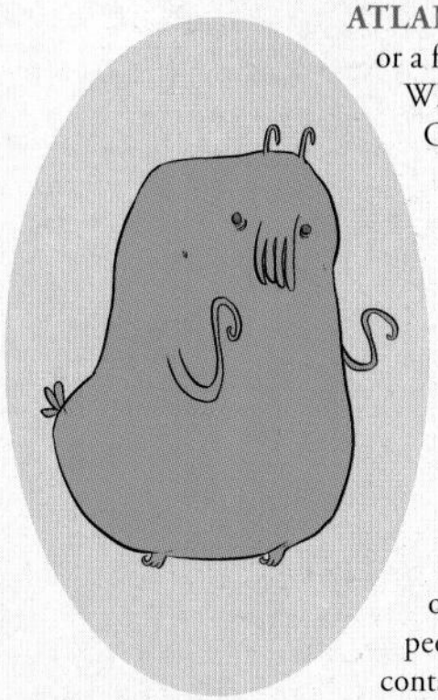

ATLANTIC OCEAN—It is a brave man, or a fool, who does not respect the ocean. While hunting sharks off the coast of Cuba, the men aboard the ship began a great hullabaloo. I expected a beast of some variety, but could not have anticipated a Kraken making its appearance. A hundred feet in girth, if not more, it lashed the boat with its tentacles, easily snapping it in two. As I drifted in open waters, waiting for rescue or the infinite, I was sustained by the thought of catching that sea monster, stuffing it, mounting it on a handsome plinth, and charging people to see it. I imagined a gift shop containing stuffed Kraken, sold at a handsome profit. Fortunately I was borne to safety by a man passing by in a coracle.

GIRAFFE SNAKE *(Bombus Bombus)*

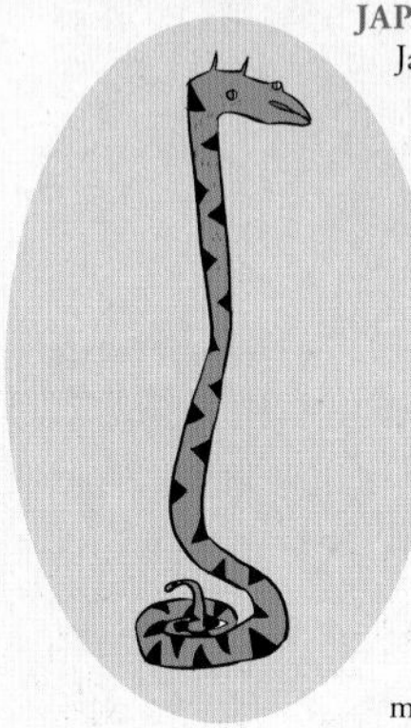

JAPAN—I have a powerful love for the Japanese people, with their culture founded on respect, politeness, efficiency, organisation, technology, and vicious feudal weaponry. During a spiritual retreat in Nagoya, I took time out from my meditation to walk in a glorious flower garden. Resting beneath the wisteria, I felt a sudden slithering around my ankles, and saw a Giraffe Snake curling around my feet. Knowing it to be both venomous and quick to strike, I gently reached inside my kimono for a ceremonial dagger. Heart quickening at its silvery hiss, I positioned myself for the kill. It was to my great disappointment when the snake was suddenly vacuumed up by an elderly gentleman on a futuristic hovercraft.

JENNY HEN *(Bombus Bombus)*

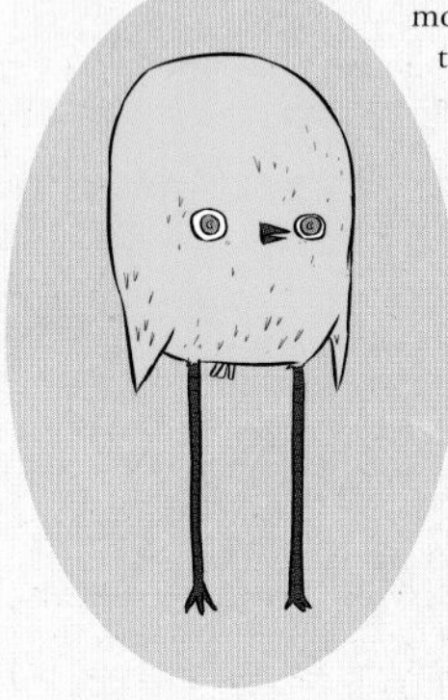

TEXAS, USA—Seldom have I fe more at home away from home than among the big hats and big guns of Texas. Strolling amid the oil derricks, I caught sight of the Jenny Hen, a grossly elongated, flightless bird bred for its meat in the 1950s but ultimately deemed too weird and dangerous to l cooked for dinner. I took couple of pot shots at it b managed only to explode a pile of oil barrels, to my hosts' evident delight.

TOOKEY'S POSSUM *(Bombus Bombus)*

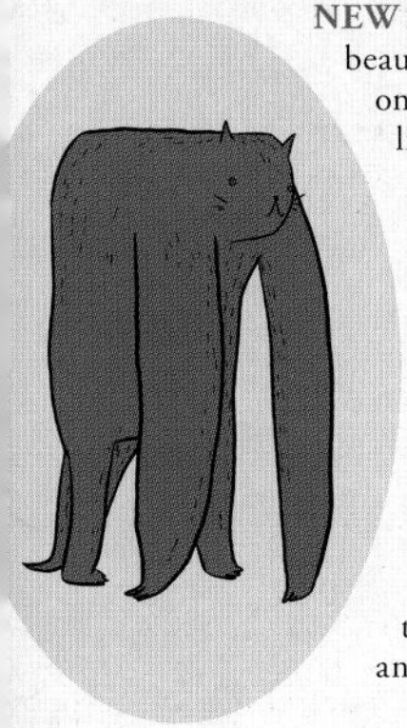

NEW ZEALAND—Glimpsed this beauty from my bathroom while on a weekend jaunt to Wellington. He was gnawing on chicken bones. By the time I'd got downstairs with my gun, he'd gone. In my disappointment, I failed to notice that I was completely naked, until a passer-by pointed out my embarrassment.

Tookey's Possum is renowned for its smell, which is described by locals as "a mixture of lavender, honeysuckle, and an open sewer."

SHORT-CRESTED OTTO *(Bombus Bombus)*

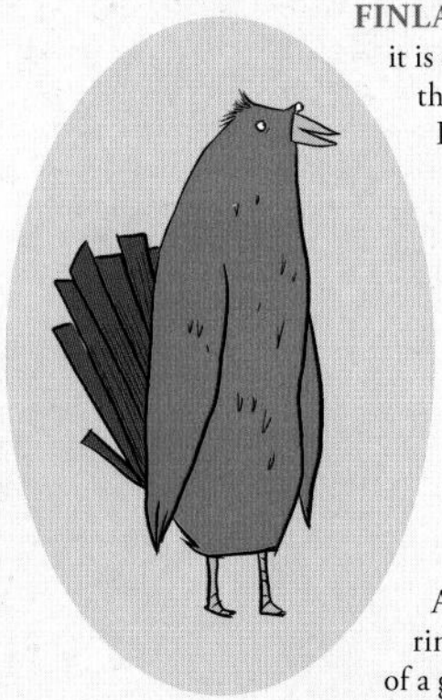

FINLAND—Finland has many lakes, but it is only on the banks of Lake Saimaa that one finds the Short-crested Otto. It was during an off-the-books hunt for the Ringed Seal at Imatra that I spotted the Otto, his magenta plumage clearly visible on the shore. Armed only with four or five of my favourite clubs, I was unable to pick off the bird.

Once riled, it pursued me without mercy until I was forced to undertake the "wasp defence", submerging myself in the lake waters. At this point I was set upon by several ringed seals, and only the intervention of a gentleman in a coracle prevented my demise at their hands. Short crest, short temper, as I told the boys back at the lodge.

CUBIC SALAMANDER *(Bombus Bombus)*

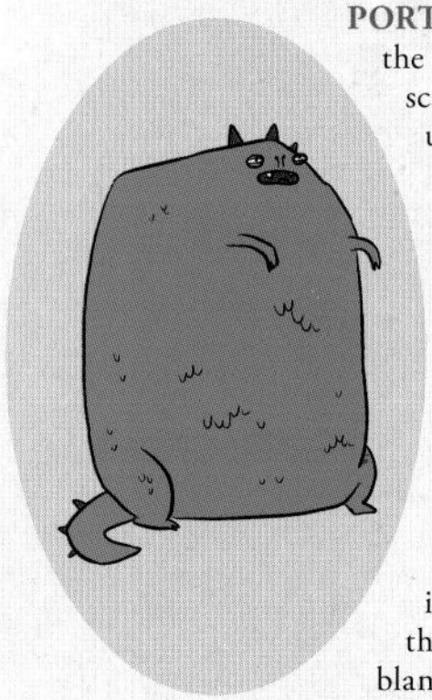

PORTUGAL—Hot climate favours the lizard, with his cold blood and scaly skin. While sunbathing upon a rock, not unlike a lizard, I caught sight of this square specimen darting behind a boulder. I reached for my dart gun and pursued him down the beach for a mile, all the while keeping pace and lining up my shot. Just as he paused, I was apprehended by the authorities, as I had strayed from the nude beach to the conventional, clothed bathing area. As I was bundled into the police car, wrapped in a dirty blanket, I could see the Cubic Salamander laughing from a promontory. With luck on my side, I hope one day to craft a pair of bathing trunks from this species.

SCOTCH KITTY *(Bombus Bombus)*

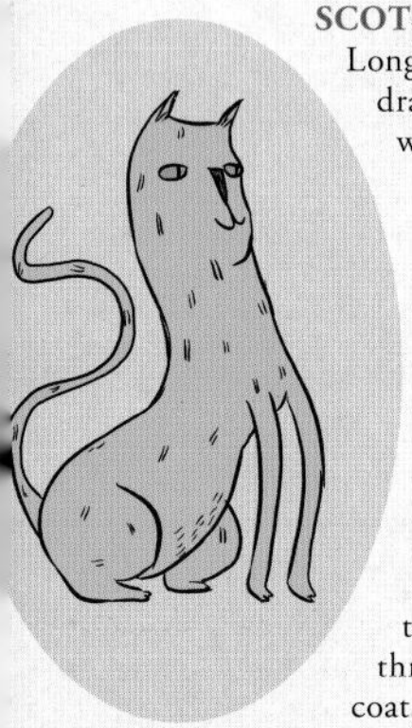

SCOTLAND (HIGHLANDS)—Long-fabled but seldom seen, drawings of the Scotch Kitty were dismissed as mere doodles by respected naturalists including Herman Weißgarten and Hennig Plum. And in many ways it does resemble the kind of cat one might draw while on the telephone waiting for an appointment to have cable internet installed. However, I spied one on Ben Nevis, but did not have a weapon to hand. The beef sandwich I threw at it glanced off its glossy coat with little effect.

BEAVER WASP *(Bombus Bombus)*

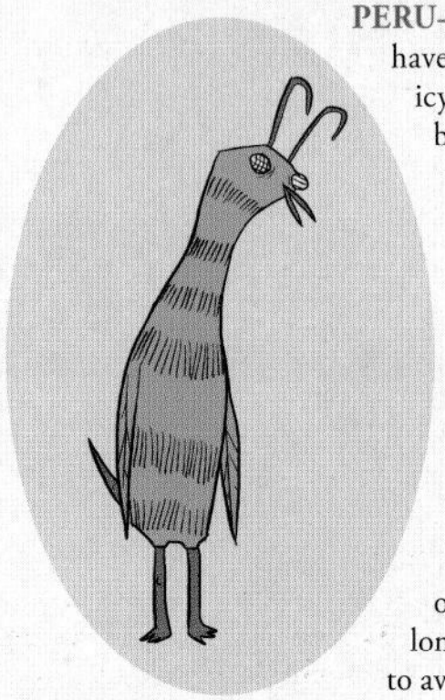

PERU—The mysteries of darkest Peru have confounded many a hunter. From icy mountain to torrid rainforest, it boasts a biodiversity that sends even the most jaded hunter to the gun cupboard with a spring in his step. I will not, however, return to Peru. My encounter with the Beaver Wasp in the province of Madre de Dios, took place not in the boundless kingdom of nature, but rather in my own bedroom. I awoke with a powerful thirst in the night and reached for a glass of water in the dark. But instead of a tumbler of Adam's ale, I grasped a two-foot long insect with duck legs. I managed to avoid its vicious sting only by hiding under the covers, where I remained until my discovery by the hotel maid the next day.

HERBERT *(Herbertus)*

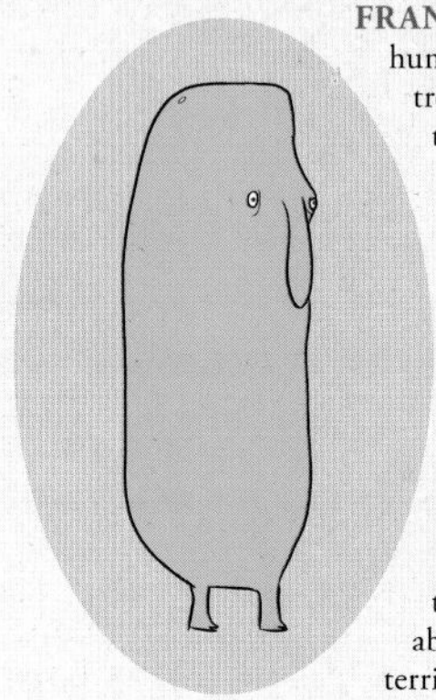

FRANCE—At the end of a long hunting season, with many trophies gained, I retired to the south of France for a little light relaxation. I anticipated a few weeks of wine, boules, bread, and beef.

It was after an evening of all four that I encountered a creature the Provence folk call "Herbert". The less said about this repulsive animal the better, suffice it to say that my meeting with this savage and unpredictable beast left me semi-nude, terrified, and eager to learn more. I cannot say exactly what Herbert is, but I have a healthy respect for it.

JOHN ALLISON

Born in a hidden village deep within the British Alps, John Allison came into this world a respectable baby with style and taste. Having been exposed to American comics at an early age, he spent decades honing his keen mind and his massive body in order to burn out this colonial cultural infection.

One of the longest continuously publishing independent web-based cartoonists, John has plied his trade since the late nineties moving from *Bobbins* to *Scary Go Round* to *Bad Machinery*, developing the deeply weird world of Tackleford long after many of his fellow artists were ground into dust and bones by Time Itself.

He has only once shed a single tear, but you only meet Sergio Aragonés for the first time once.

John resides in Letchworth Garden City, England and is known to his fellow villagers only as He Who Has Conquered.

—Contributed by Richard Stevens III

"THE TREASURE OF BRITANNIA"

BAD MACHINERY, VOLUME 1:
THE CASE OF THE TEAM SPIRIT
By John Allison
ISBN 978-1-62010-387-6
Pocket Edition In Stores Now!

BAD MACHINERY, VOLUME 3:
THE CASE OF THE SIMPLE SOUL
By John Allison
ISBN 978-1-62010-443-9
Pocket Edition Coming November 2017!

BAD MACHINERY, VOLUME 4:
THE CASE OF THE LONELY ONE
By John Allison
ISBN 978-1-62010-212-1
Pocket Edition Coming March 2018!

BAD MACHINERY, VOLUME 5:
THE CASE OF THE FIRE INSIDE
By John Allison
ISBN 978-1-62010-297-8
Pocket Edition Coming June 2018!

BAD MACHINERY, VOLUME 6:
THE CASE OF THE UNWELCOME VISITOR
By John Allison
ISBN 978-1-62010-351-7
Pocket Edition Coming September 2018!

BAD MACHINERY, VOL. 7:
THE CASE OF THE FORKED ROAD
By John Allison
ISBN 978-1-62010-390-6
First edition now available!
Pocket Edition coming December 2018!

ONI PRESS
www.onipress.com

bad machinery
THE CASE OF THE MODERN MEN

Coming Soon!